UBUNTU Contributionism

A Blueprint For Human Prosperity

By

Michael Tellinger

Published by Zulu Planet Publishers
South Africa – 2013

UBUNTU Contributionism

A Blueprint For Human Prosperity

Published by Zulu Planet Publishers
PO Box 204 Waterval Boven 1195 South Africa
Email: publisher@zuluplanet.com
www.michaeltellinger.com

Michael Tellinger can be contacted on:
publisher@zuluplanet.com

Visit his website and subscribe to his newsletters at:
www.michaeltellinger.com

Become a seed of consciousness – join the global UBUNTU
movement and share the philosophy with everyone.
www.ubuntuparty.org.za

USA Edition 2014
ISBN: 978-1-920153-12-0

Our countries are corporations and the world is a business controlled by a small group of untouchable banking families. The laws that control our society have been meticulously structured over thousands of years to protect the corporations, while giving us the illusion that we are free. We, the people, are blissfully ignorant that we are the slaves and the assets of those who control the business. It is time to wake up and free ourselves. Nobody will do this for us. The universe awaits our action, so that it can respond through the law of attraction, and welcome humanity into the universal community of beings of higher consciousness.

Michael of the family Tellinger - 2005

Love, Honour & Gratitude

I would like to begin by honouring the indigenous people of the world, who have endured unimaginable hardship at the hands of invaders, colonisers and slave traders. It is with respect and humility that I recognise their great contribution to humanity for carrying the spirit of Ubuntu for all these years.

For my beloved Louise
This book would not have become a reality without your continued love, support, and infinite source of inspiration. Thank you for taking this journey with me and showing me the way when I was lost.

UBUNTU

I... am what I am because of who we all are.

"It is the essence of being human – you can't exist as a human being in isolation. It speaks about our interconnectedness. You can't be human all by yourself, and when you have this quality – Ubuntu – you are known for your generosity. We think of ourselves far too frequently as just individuals, separated from one another, whereas you are connected and what you do affects the whole world. When you do well, it spreads out; it is for the whole of humanity."

Archbishop Desmond Tutu

CONTENTS

CONTENTS

FOREWORD

The philosophy of Contributionism as a new social structure was born in 2005. It was a consequence of my extensive research into the origins of humankind and the deeply convoluted path of deception that has lead us to this point in time as the human race.

After several years of testing the basic ideas against the many sectors of our current system, I realised many ancient cultures had similar systems by which their communities were guided. Unfortunately much of this knowledge has been suppressed or lost through the colonisation of the world by the so-called explorers who stole the land from indigenous people everywhere.

Some native people, like the Cherokee, have a saying that *"if it's not good for everyone, it's no good at all."* In Africa, we call it UBUNTU. But this philosophy was shared by hundreds if not thousands of ancient cultures all over the world. Although they may have called it by different names, it all seems to be aligned to the principles of UBUNTU.

These united communities of the past have been maliciously destroyed and replaced by capitalism, industrialisation, modernisation and ultimately the absolute control by a handful of powerful and greedy individuals who have ruled the world for a long time and who want to continue ruling it at all cost.

In this book I share with you the simplicity and joy of UBUNTU, where people do not live divided in fear of each other but rather live in united communities that thrive in abundance on all levels.

All my life I have been appalled by the human suffering and misery on our beautiful planet. Suffering that seems to continue as if there were no solution to the plight of humanity. And yet, in our hearts most of us know that there are solutions to our problems, and that these solutions are really simple. But our so-called leaders do not provide solutions. Instead, they sow more confusion and misery.

As a young child I was deeply affected by this suffering, wondering why there are poor people and rich people – why some people are homeless and hungry while others live in luxury. That feeling has never left me and I know that there are millions who feel the same way. And so a life of protest was laid out for me – sometimes subtle resistance and sometimes public activism against the oppressive regime under which I lived. The 1976 Soweto riots in South Africa left deep emotional scars on my conscience and much of what I did in my life after that time was subconsciously moulded by those events.

In 2005, I had what could be described as an 'awakening experience'. Like millions of people around the world I began to realise that there had to be something more to this life than the strife and misery that so many people experience on a daily basis. I was determined to find a solution and I was not going to accept any of the usual feeble answers from a society that has slipped into complacency and accepted its fate as a slave race in blissful ignorance.

It became clear to me that humanity had become a deeply divided species on so many levels. In this divided struggle for survival and our relentless quest for modernisation we have become separated from our sustaining mother Earth. This human division is in direct conflict with the laws of nature and the resonance of unity consciousness that seems to be the foundation for all of creation.

The great prophets and teachers of the past all tried to teach us the same wisdom: to stand united; to love each and honour each other and live in harmony with all of creation. In fact, these are the same values that many of us try to teach our children.

But suddenly at some mysterious moment in our lives, things change. We stop paying attention to those higher consciousness values and we fall into the routine of life and become entangled in the struggle for survival.

At this point we realise that we need to earn this thing called "money" to be able to survive and live on our own planet – the planet that we were born on. And suddenly this simple question began to ring repeatedly in my heart. How is it possible that we should need money to live on a planet that we were born on? Like many others before me I realised that we are born into pure slavery.

This is indeed the great trap that has been set for us by those who control the creation and the supply of money.

We are trapped in a silent, relentless war of economic slavery that has been so cleverly woven around us that most of us are not even aware of it. This onslaught is controlled by the global banking elite that have taken the world hostage and made each and every one of us their slaves.

All our natural resources are being mined and traded by multinational corporations that have more rights than living, breathing, human beings. We have simply become slaves of these corporations all in the name of money, greed and political control. Most of us do not have the foggiest clue how it all works, how money is created and how a small number of banking families completely rule every imaginable aspect of our lives.

They are the masterminds behind the global economic system that rules the world without being questioned or challenged. This system is designed to destroy everything that opposes it, to ensure its own survival. It has developed into a twisted form of consciousness that has confused humanity about our own destiny.

We are repeatedly told that our problems are insurmountable and that it is all very complicated and that only money can solve the world's problems. We now know that this is a lie – because money does nothing. People do everything – people grow the food, build the bridges and solve the mathematical equations and create the most beautiful works of art. People do everything in great spirit and joy when they are allowed to do so. Money is the obstacle that prevents us all from creating and thriving.

Now that we have recognised this we can do the right thing and inform everyone about this injustice. The past several years have seen a dramatic increase in legal action against the activities of the banking elite and the resistance keeps growing exponentially.

Since 2010, I have personally been involved in a number of highly visible legal actions against the banks in South Africa in an attempt to expose their unlawful activities. Our actions against the banks continue as I write this manuscript.

And so, millions of people are waking up to this silent war against humanity and are standing united for change all over the world. People of courage and vision who know there is a better way ahead for humanity.

It is up to us to be happy or miserable. Personally, I choose love and happiness above all. I believe that this is the common thread that binds us all. But many of us do not know how to attain this state of bliss.

The great masters taught us that material possessions and riches will not bring us happiness. History has shown us that during great times of change, empires of the past have crumbled because of the greed of their leaders.

The time for great change is upon us once again. It is up to us, the people of the world to embrace these changes not through violence and confrontation but through love and unity for all of humanity.

So let us actively begin to spread the message of Unity Consciousness, or as I like to call it, "the breath of GOD" to all humanity, that will allow us to heal our division and change the misery into abundance, within a global community filled with love for each other, instead of fear of each other.

In 2005, I called it Contributionism . A global community where money is unnecessary, because the principles of Unity Consciousness triumph. In Africa, we call this UBUNTU.

It is on these fundamental beliefs of absolute equality and working together for a common purpose of abundance, in united communities that thrive on all levels of society, that UBUNTU Contributionism was established.

It follows the natural order of things in total harmony with nature, our planet, and all of creation. It does not mean going back to the dark ages or living in caves devoid of technology as some may think – in fact it means completely the opposite. Abundance in all spheres of life, beyond our wildest imagination.

We can no longer continue on the path we are on. If we are to survive as a species we have to discard all that is in conflict with our own survival and create a beautiful future for ourselves.

Quantum physics and the Universal law of Attraction teaches us that the observer can influence the outcome of an event and that we can manifest our thoughts and the things we visualise. Those who have studied higher levels of consciousness will have a more refined comprehension of these laws of nature.

But the law of attraction also responds to action – so we need to act and do something to realise our vision.

So – let us not only visualise this beautiful utopian world today – let us do something to manifest it with our hearts and the potential for infinite love we all have within us, as part of the infinite creation. The first thing each one of us can do is to share our knowledge and tell others about the bright future for all of humanity. Then join the UBUNTU Movement and do something else to contribute – something that comes from your heart. Our strength lies in unity.

Michael of the family Tellinger   1 August 2012.

www.ubuntuparty.org.za

> *"Justice is indivisible. Injustice anywhere, is a threat to justice everywhere."* Martin Luther King Jr.

BRIGHT LIGHT AT THE END OF A DARK AND GLOOMY TUNNEL

Every morning, billions of people get up to start their daily chores. A large percentage hate their jobs, they hate their boss, they have to travel to their lousy jobs for hours, on the bus, or train, or bicycle, or walk, in the rain, the snow , the heat, or sit in bumper-to-bumper traffic for hours.

Why do all these people repeat this insanity every day? To earn money – so that they can buy bread and milk and clothing; to pay electricity and send their children to school and somehow make it to the end of the month – and then start the madness all over again.

On a planet of seven billion people the majority of us live in poverty and in a state of quiet desperation, waiting for some kind of miracle to deliver us from the harsh economic times. Millions dream of fame and fortune, which can be seen in the endless number of reality television shows offering exactly that. People are searching for any kind of salvation often choosing the wrong kind that only leads to more misery.

We watch the news and see a world filled with injustice, crime and war and we desperately search for relief from our own personal suffering. Most of us realise that there is something dramatically wrong with this situation. It's as if our society is terminally ill. But how can we cure this human disease if we do not know what the cause of our human disease is?

Until we know what lies behind the human struggle and suffering, we will never eliminate the cause, but blindly continue to treat the symptoms – over and over again. Our ignorance will remain our weakness while the simple solutions glaringly stare us in the face with the rising of every sun.

The so-called "American Dream" remains a dream because we are all asleep, cunningly deceived by those who run the world. The same dream is sold to us as lingering and perpetual "hope", and millions of people around this planet "hope" on a daily basis that things will get better. But hoping and waiting will get us nowhere.

UBUNTU Contributionism presents us with the opportunity to embrace a new reality on our planet with unimaginable prosperity for all its inhabitants, in perfect harmony with all of nature and mother Earth. It is truly a bright light at the end of a dark and gloomy tunnel of quiet desperation and misery shared by most of the people on this beautiful planet.

UBUNTU CONTRIBUTION SYSTEM

- Is a blueprint for a new social structure in which everyone is absolutely free and equal.
- A society that functions without the concept of money, any form of barter or trade, or the attachment of value to material things.
- A culture where each individual is encouraged to follow their passion and contribute their natural talents or acquired skills to the greater benefit of all the people in their community.
- Where everyone can choose to live anywhere and nobody is forced to do anything against their will.
- A society with a new set of laws based on the needs of the people where everything is provided to everyone, because they contribute their Labour of Love.
- A world where there are no jobs, careers, corporations, unemployment, homelessness or hunger.
- A society which promotes the highest levels of scientific and technological exploration because there are no financial restrictions.
- A society in which arts and culture flourish allowing people to experience life to the fullest.
- A society in which spiritual growth of its people, through the explosion of arts and culture, will allow the rapid rise of consciousness to fully embrace the concepts of unity.
- A system that provides unimaginable abundance of all things on all levels, almost impossible to imagine by those trapped in the capitalist consumer-driven environment of today.

THIS IS OUR PLANET

This is our planet, mother Earth, our home in the universe. The only reason we are alive and can exist on this beautiful planet is because she has somehow managed to dish up the perfect set of circumstances that has allowed us to exist here.

If you were lost in space and someone asked you –"where are you from..?" You would turn around and point at this spectacular planet and say, "I am from Earth... that planet over there." You would most likely not say "I am from the USA; or Japan; or Australia...!"

From a distance Earth looks so beautiful and peaceful and wholesome and united and yet, as we get closer we begin to see the great divisions that have been forced on the beings that inhabit this planet. From the day we are born we are divided on so many different levels and in so many ways that we don't even recognise our division any more.

We are divided by country, flag, province, religion, city, state, continent, what car we drive, what job we have, what school we go to, what sport we follow, brand of clothing, credit card, what beer we drink, what music we listen to, and how much money we have... the division is endless. Think about it – we live in 'apart'-ments.

It is through this division that we allow ourselves to be manipulated and controlled beyond our wildest imagination. Without most of us realising it, the 'divide & conquer' principle has been successfully implemented on our planet and is being used very effectively to keep us under control and in a perpetual state of conflict.

BORN FREE – BUT IMPRISONED ON OUR OWN PLANET

We are all born free on our planet and yet we cannot move around freely; we cannot live where we choose to; we have to follow rules and laws that we did not agree to; we have to work to earn money and we have to pay taxes to some authority that we know nothing about. All we know is that if we do not abide by these rules we will be at odds with the system and possibly end up in court and quite possibly go to a place called jail. We only realise how enslaved we are when we try to challenge the system or extricate ourselves from it.

None of us agreed to any of these rules and restrictions before we were born or at any stage after we were born, especially not in those first few minutes after we emerged from our mother's womb as free human beings. We entered this world without any commitments to anyone; without agreeing to rules that limit our freedom; without agreements; no contracts; no submission to anyone or anything; we entered this world FREE in every respect.

While we honestly believe that we are born free, we are all in fact born into lifelong slavery and servitude to a system that has been imposed on us for thousands of years.

It is at that critical moment when we are born that our parents sign away all our rights and hand us over as property to our respective governments, by signing what is known as a "birth certificate". By doing so our parents unwittingly and innocently change our status from "free human" to that of "citizen" and property of the state. And so begins a life filled with lies and deception so deep and so severe that most of us have simply chosen not to believe it because the consequences of such allegations being true, are simply too horrific for most people to deal with.

But these are the cold harsh facts we all have to face and decide what we are going to do about it. And just as children that were born into slavery in the southern USA or ancient Egypt, had to face the facts at some stage of their lives, we, as humanity, have to face these facts as we realise that the entire planet is a giant slave camp – not just some people or countries of the past.

LESSONS FROM HISTORY

Every socio-political system we have ever had as the human race has failed us dramatically. Humans everywhere live in misery – there seems to be no happy outcome to the political and economic mess on our planet; every year, every month, every week it gets worse. We have to wake up earlier, work longer and work harder to survive. There is more poverty, more hunger, more homelessness, more despair than ever before. Life has become too unbearable for too many to make any sense of any more. Millions are drowning in debt, suffer marital problems and often look to anti-depressants or other addictive substances just to get through the day. The fact is that exploitation does not discriminate.

The daily reports of financial doom and gloom are clear signs that the system cannot continue like this for much longer. The whole world is on the verge of a devastating economic meltdown with catastrophic results.

The global economy and natural resources have been plundered by reckless and ignorant politicians with no accountability to the people they are supposed to serve, but somehow this thing called 'an economy' keeps going and keeps us growing against all odds and against the predictions of many experts – how is this possible? Who or what is propping up the global economy and preventing it from imploding?

HUNGER ON A PLANET OF ABUNDANCE

On a planet with over 7 billion people, more than half of us live below the breadline, surviving from day to day. According to the Guardian newspaper, 12 May 2011, the United Nations announced that one third of the world's food goes to waste every year. Over 1.3 billion tonnes of food is discarded, not because there is no one to eat it, but because people do not have money to buy the food. And so, thousands of people die of starvation every day and billions more go hungry for lack of money or any other means to care for themselves.

If ever there was an example of deep division between the 'haves' and the 'have-nots' this is it. If we think that the 'authorities' are going to do something about it, we are grossly mistaken. It is the 'authorities' that are squarely behind this manipulation of people's lives. This is where it starts to get complicated for the average person who believes that the government is doing what it can to help us. Nothing could be further from the truth, so let me be very clear on this – the government is not your friend.

Our governments have allowed giant agricultural corporations like Monsanto, DuPont and others to slowly take control of the global food supply. These giant multi-billion dollar corporations have thousands of patents on genetically modified seeds and they are rapidly replacing all our natural seeds with their genetically modified organisms. Many of their seeds are sterile and cannot regenerate themselves, leaving Monsanto and alike in control of seed and food supply to the world. And those who control the money and the food, control the world.

It is almost impossible to get natural food on any supermarket shelf any more. Most of the products are genetically modified with uncertain effects on the human population. In some countries and states it is now illegal to grow your own food, thanks to new bogus laws and by-laws instigated by these corporations to take more of a stranglehold on people everywhere. Although there are some countries like Brazil that have stood up against Monsanto, this inhumane activity is supported by our governments.

In the USA a large group of around 300,000 organic farmers filed a lawsuit against Monsanto who have in recent years squashed independent organic farms from coast to coast. The global farming community is under full onslaught by these GMO (Genetically Modified Organism) giants who are out to take control of all the farms and global food supply.

DuPont have contracted hundreds of retired law enforcement officers to patrol farms in the US to seek out any potential intellectual property theft. As a result, thousands of farmers in the USA and around the world have lost their farms to the extortion tactics of these giant corporations. Any farmers caught with patented crops growing on their land are prosecuted. In most cases the farmers do not have the funds to defend themselves against the most powerful corporations in the world and lose their farms to the corporation.

And so, the silent war against humanity continues right under our noses, but most of us are simply too ignorant, too gullible, or too busy to see it. The war on our food supply is just one of many endeavours across many sectors to keep humanity under control. We keep falling for the lies and deceptions of our politicians. We believe that the government is our friend and that they would not allow nasty corporations to harm us. But unfortunately for the ignorant humans, nothing could be further from the truth – but something has to give.

WAKING UP TO THE TERRIBLE TRUTH

The system is fundamentally flawed and is not sustainable for very much longer on a planet with a rapidly rising consciousness. It is this rise in global consciousness and rapid awakening taking place among humanity that has become our saving grace.

People everywhere are waking up to the fact that the system is broken – it cannot be fixed – there is no remedy for the current crisis. There is no happy outcome to the money-driven system that we have all been lured into by our leaders and the banking elite.

Imagine a complex mathematical equation in 1000 parts. At the end of it, you realise that the final outcome is incorrect. It is no use fixing step 999 if that is not the root of the problem. Nor can you fix it at step 950, or even at step 500. In the case of our planet, the problem occurs at step 1: the fundamental basics of the global monetary system.

But if we want to find a true and lasting solution, we have to truly comprehend the cause of our demise. We have to be brave enough to face the terrible truth of our past and the road that brought us here. And so, we have to ask - how did it get so bad? How did we get to this point of degradation on a planet that is perfectly balanced with its natural order of things? Why has humanity become the virus that is causing the demise of its own host?

By now many people have heard the term 'illuminati' and some are not quite sure what it means or who these people are. They have been called many names over the years. What we need to realise is that this group of secretive and very powerful people have been at this for a very, very, long time.

The conspiracy to control the world is not something that happened a few decades ago, or a few hundred years ago. This manipulation of the human race goes back thousands of years to the very murky beginnings of what is often called the rise of civilisation. This is where we find the first written evidence of a global elite that took control of our world.

ANCIENT ORIGINS OF ROYAL BLOODLINES AND GLOBAL CONTROL

The Sumerian tablets are the oldest written and deciphered record of human history. Millions of clay tablets have been collected in the Middle East and Near East, mainly in places like Iraq. This used to be the ancient land of milk and honey known as Mesopotamia, that also contained the Babylonian empire. Thousands upon thousands of these clay tablets that are inscribed with what is called cuneiform style of writing, have been deciphered with some startling information about our distant past.

One of the most chilling pieces of information we receive, is from a clay tablet known as the "Kings List". It gives us critical information about our ancient past which includes the names of many kings who ruled the world, where they ruled and how long they ruled. It also tells the story and the relationship between the kings and the gods of the time that were both worshiped and feared.

But the most important revelation it makes is the explanation of how kingdoms and kings were created on Earth. "In the days when kingdom was lowered to Earth from heaven and the gods appointed kings from among the men..." to rule over the humans. *(Zecharia Sitchin – The 12th Planet)*

MS 2855
List of Kings and Cities from before the Flood.
Babylonia, 2000-1800 BC

This Kings List from around 2000 BC in Babylonia, tells us that kings on Earth were appointed by the gods to rule over humanity. It gives us the names of 8 kings, where they ruled, and for how long, and it tells us that a great "flood swept over" everything.

Many have speculated as to the mysterious origins of kingdoms and how some individuals suddenly became kings from among all other humans. This translation provides us with the oldest reference to royal bloodlines and the mysterious origins of priest-kings and their kingdoms in ancient times on planet Earth. It clearly tells us that there was a time when kings were suddenly appointed by entities called the gods. These early priest-kings were given special knowledge, powers and weapons to be able to control their subjects. This is the rise of the royal bloodlines that continue to rule the world today. Most of us never give these matters any thought at all because we think of our royalty going back a few hundred years before it gets all too confusing and we lose interest. Once again, this ignorance among humans is used against us because once we discover this ancient mystery, we uncover the clues to help us free ourselves from thousands of years of servitude.

The worshiping of royalty is alive and well in the 21st century in England where millions of people are obsessed with the queen. They hang on her every word, follow her around, go to all her public appearances, buy memorabilia with the queen's face on it and idolise her for no apparent reason other than it has been bred into the human subconscious, to worship royalty.

ORIGINS OF MONEY

One of the first things these ancient priest-kings did when they took control of the people, was to introduce a thing called 'money'.

Money did not evolve from thousands of years of barter and trade as we are lead to believe. That is mere disinformation aimed at

A Sumerian clay tablet from the city of Ur, Mesopotamia, circa 2046 BC. Exhibited in the British Museum. It records a financial transaction of depositing silver shekels at the palace/temple. It is one of the earliest examples of a "Bill of Exchange" used by modern banks, and tells us that the Temples in antiquity served as the first banks – creating a link between the bankers and royal bloodlines as far back as we can trace. The translation reads as follows: "8 shekels of silver as interest from Lu-Ninshubur, the official (being) Mansi, son of Ur Suen, has entered the Palace. Seal of the governor." Source - British Museum

keeping us in the dark and in servitude to money itself. Because if we believe that money is somehow linked to the evolution of humanity we will believe that money was part of a natural process of evolution accompanying us as a species to where we are today. This is one of the reasons we falsely believe that we simply cannot do without money – because according to our historians money makes the world go round.

That is not true. Money was maliciously introduced to the human race as a tool of enslavement by the earliest kings thousands of years ago. Money appeared suddenly out of the blue, just like the written language of the Sumerians.

In his excellent documentary *The Ascent of Money*, Professor Niall Ferguson of Harvard University tells us that the earliest money found to date was in the form of clay tablets that served as tokens of exchange and payment for goods and services. They had a variety of descriptions inscribed on them to indicate the goods or transaction in question. In essence it was the first known form of money or promissory note, which is exactly what our paper money has become in later years. But today our paper money is mere paper with some logos and numbers on it with no value other than the value that the people ascribe to it. We use what is called "fiat" money, with no intrinsic value whatsoever, completely controlled by the bankers.

But in those ancient times only the royalty and the elite were literate and only the scribes who were appointed by the priest kings could inscribe the tablets. And because all the written tablets were commissioned by the kings, including the money, we can trace the control of the supply of money going back thousands of years, as it continues to be controlled by the elite today.

EMPIRE OF THE ELITE BANKERS

The creation and supply of money lies in the hands of a few families, mainly the Rothschild, Rockefeller, Morgan, Carnegie, Harriman, Schiff, Warburg and a handful of others.

These incredibly powerful families control the entire planet's money supply. They have the right to print and distribute money without restriction. Their rights are protected by the current governments of the world and the military might that upholds the governments. These are further supported by the laws that are made by the governments and the courts that uphold such laws. All of this activity is kept nice and tidy under control of the banking elite who in turn keep the governments in power.

It is a system so skilfully crafted that we have to admire its architects for keeping us in the dark for so long. But now that we have figured out that we are mere pawns in a huge game of global slavery, it is time for change.

Within a few short years after being born free as living breathing human beings on our own planet, each one of us is absorbed into brainwashing camps, which are conveniently called schools, to begin a process of induction into the matrix system by a process they conveniently call education. It has become such a twisted and convoluted system that the average person simply cannot comprehend the sheer scale of the deception. And when they are confronted by it, they simply discard it or deny it because the truth is simply too horrible to face.

Many of us believe that we are 'free', and that we have choice and free will. These are mere illusions we were granted to make us believe that we are free and that we have rights. We are bombarded by the media with slogans like, human rights; bill of rights; liberties; democracy; majority rule; freedom, and so on.

Unfortunately the opposite is true because what we believe to be our 'free will' is just a cleverly disguised set of options which will guarantee a predetermined outcome for those pulling the strings. We don't have choices either, we have selections, which are also predetermined – like a big Mac, or a cheese burger – our selection is limited – choice is infinite.

The choices we are presented with give us the illusion that we are participants in shaping our future and that we can make a difference. Unfortunately this is just an illusion because all the choices we make remain inside the slave system. To make a true difference we have to see the system as a whole and recognise that it has been designed for one thing only – slavery.

We choose democrats or republicans who both operate within the same system – they are no different. It is this misconception that keeps us exactly where we are, because "none are more enslaved than those who believe they are free" as was clearly outlined by German poet and philosopher Johann Wolfgang Goethe.

But the human ego seems to be insatiable. It feeds the arrogance in so many of us to do inhumane things. Such behaviour is commonly boosted by social status and the acquisition of wealth that keeps the hierarchy and separation alive among humanity. The ones who have bought into the deception and the never-ending lies are most often the ones that will fight to protect it.

When we are told about the "American dream" it is exactly that – a dream of freedom that we can never attain under the current system. And so ignites the conflict among friends and brothers, driven by ego and patriotism. It is our duty not to fight those who oppose us, but to rather show them another way. A way of cooperation instead of conflict that will benefit all of humanity and not only a chosen few.

TRAPPED IN THE MATRIX

There have been many movies that try to shine a light on our status as a slave species. It is curious that movies are the vehicles that carry deeply encoded messages to help us escape this slavery. I expand on this in a later chapter when I deal with frequency and sound used as a tool in weapons and advanced technology. Some of the obviously encoded movies are: *Network; Contact; Moon; Frankenstein; Planet of The Apes; Avatar, Wizard of Oz* and hundreds more.

'The Matrix' was one of the most powerful and memorable of these movies. In a spine chilling scene where Neo meets Morpheus, he learns about the matrix prison for unconscious humans.

Morpheus: *"The Matrix is a system, Neo. That system is our enemy. But when you're inside, you look around, what do you see? Businessmen, teachers, lawyers, carpenters. The very minds of the people we are trying to save. But until we do, these people are still a part of that system and that makes them our enemy. You have to understand, most of these people are not ready to be unplugged. And many of them are so inured, so hopelessly dependent on the system, that they will fight to protect it."*

And so, these powerful elite banking families continue to run the world filled with unconscious people, not only because they seem to own everything and all the large corporations, but they also own and control the three main banking institutions that feed the banks with an infinite supply of money and bail them out when they run into trouble. These are the World Bank, The International Monetary Fund and the Bank of International Settlements in Basel, Switzerland.

Their power and control is immeasurable. They control our governments, the rise and fall of stock markets, the World Trade

Organisation and all the major industries that keep them in control, like oil, energy, pharmaceutics, and especially the media. The unconscious slaves that are firmly plugged into the matrix believe every word they are told by the talking heads on their televisions, continuously promoting the agenda of these organisations.

MEDIA – STRATEGIC TOOL OF INDOCTRINATION

The entire global media empire is owned by a handful of people and a handful of individuals. Media corporations have bigger budgets than some nations and they carry so much influence over humanity that it simply boggles the mind. Very few people truly understand the sheer impact and influence of this critical sector. To successfully compete, some media companies establish partnerships with financial investors, which in some cases have garnered considerable influence. This is the list of the 50 largest media companies in the world during 2012 according to the Institute of Media and Communications Policy.

Top 50 - International Media Corporations

1.	Comcast/NBCUniversal, LLC (Philadelphia / USA)	€ 40.116 billion
2.	The Walt Disney Company (Burbank / USA)	€ 29.377 billion
3.	Google Inc. (Mountain View/ USA)	€ 27.231 billion
4.	News Corp. Ltd. (New York/ USA)	€ 23.998 billion
5.	Viacom Inc./CBS Corp. (New York / USA)	€ 20.948 billion
6.	Time Warner Inc. (New York / USA)	€ 20.815 billion
7.	Sony Entertainment (Tokyo / JP)	€ 16.750 billion
8.	Bertelsmann SE & Co. KGaA (Gütersloh/GER)	€ 15.253 billion
9.	Vivendi S.A. (Paris/ Frankreich)	€ 12.486 billion
10.	Cox Enterprises Inc. (Atlanta / USA)	€ 10.560 billion
11.	Dish Network Corporation (Englewood, CO / USA)	€ 10.092 billion
12.	Thomson Reuters Corporation (New York/ USA)	€ 9.919 billion
13.	Liberty Media Corp./Liberty Interactive (Englewood, CO / USA)	€ 9.080 billion
14.	Rogers Comm. (Toronto / CA)	€ 9.031 billion
15.	Lagardère Media (Paris/ Frankreich)	€ 7.657 billion

16. Reed Elsevier PLC (London/ GB)   € 6.902 billion
17. Pearson plc (London / UK)   € 6.754 billion
18. Nippon Hoso Kyokai (Tokyo / Japan)   € 6.405 billion
19. ARD (Berlin, München/GER)   € 6.221 billion
20. BBC (London / UK)   € 5.893 billion
21. Fuji Media Holdings, Inc. (Tokyo / JP)   € 5.490 billion
22. Bloomberg L.P. (New York / USA)   € 5.460 billion
23. Charter Comm. Inc. (St. Louis/ USA)   € 5.175 billion
24. Cablevision Systems Corp. (Bethpage, NY/ USA)   € 4.814 billion
25. Globo Communicação e Participações S.A.   € 4.728 billion
(Rio de Janeiro/ BRA)
26. Advance Publications   € 4.705 billion
(Staten Island, New York / USA)
27. The McGraw-Hill Comp. Inc. (New York/USA)   € 4.487 billion
28. Clear Channel Comm. (San Antonio / USA)   € 4.426 billion
29. Mediaset SpA (Mailand / IT)   € 4.250 billion
30. The Nielsen Company (Haarlem/ NL)   € 3.974 billion
31. The Naspers Group (Kapstadt / ZA)   € 3.856 billion
32. Gannett Co. Inc. (McLean, Virginia / USA)   € 3.764 billion
33. Grupo Televisa (Mexico City / MX)   € 3.620 billion
34. Yahoo! Inc. (Sunnyvale/ USA)   € 3.580 billion
35. Shaw Communications (Calgary /CA)   € 3.445 billion
36. Wolters Kluwer nv (Amsterdam / NL)   € 3.354 billion
37. Bonnier AB (Stockholm / SWE)   € 3.302 billion
38. Tokyo Broadcasting System Holdings, Inc.   € 3.205 billion
(Tokyo / Japan)
39. Axel Springer AG (Berlin /GER)   € 3.185 billion
40. Quebecor Inc. (Montreal/ CA)   € 3.057 billion
41. Discovery Communications (Silver Spring/ USA)   € 3.042 billion
42. The Washington Post Company   € 3.028 billion
(Washington D.C. / USA)
43. France Télévisions S.A. (Paris/ FRA)   € 3.004 billion
44. RAI Radiotelevisione Italiana Holding S.p.A.   € 2.974 billion
(Rom / IT)
45. ITV plc (London / GB)   € 2.802 billion
46. ProSiebenSat.1 (Unterföhring/ GER)   € 2.756 billion
47. Sanoma Group (Helsinki / FI)   € 2.746 billion
48. The Hearst Corporation (New York/ USA)   € 2.730 billion
49. Grupo PRISA (Madrid / ES)   € 2.724 billion
50. TF1 S.A. (Boulogne, Cedex / FRA)   € 2.620 billion

These companies pretty much control everything we consume in the form of movies, television, music, newspapers, magazines, internet, telecommunication; and more. They are funded and ultimately controlled by the bankers.

Rupert Murdoch is the undisputed king of news media and the controller of what people get to see on the global news channels. There have been many well known reporters and TV anchor hosts who have been vocal about Murdoch's draconian control regarding the content, down to the actual phrases used by the news readers.

The media networks and especially the NEWS channels are the perfect Cinderella medium through which the population is continuously indoctrinated. The majority of people will believe everything they see on the news, for no other reason than because they saw it on TV. We are told exactly what they want us to think and believe. The so-called news channels do not bring us any news. These channels are mere propaganda platforms to tell us who is good, who is bad, promote political and economic agendas of the Illuminati and even suggest which country should be invaded next.

Every bit of information is very cunningly compiled with an agenda attached to its release. The news is used very shrewdly to desensitise us to death by repeatedly showing us images of war, violence, riots, crimes, terrorism, war on drugs, war on terror (which is also a construct of the Illuminati) and so-called combat situations. The media go into war "embedded" in the military vehicles of the instigator. To any peace-loving human being, this kind of activity is simply unimaginable and yet this is precisely what our current generation has grown up with – violence, death and destruction under the guise of freedom and liberty.

Those that have tamed and mastered the media monster have been using this propaganda tool with surgical precision against their own people since the printing press was invented and newspapers could be distributed on a regular basis. The introduction of the transistor radio and broadcasting, speeded up this process of mind control, which continues today with unimaginable success, using the latest satellite technology.

The same techniques that were used by the Nazis in Germany before and during the war, were used by the USA and English leadership before and after the war, with equal success. Neither the Germans nor the Americans, or even the British, had any clue that their leaders were lying to them and manipulating them into a false sense of unbridled patriotism – for which millions were prepared to die. This is what Hermann Goering had to say about war and the manipulation of the masses.

"Naturally the common people don't want war. Neither in Russia, nor in England, nor for that matter in Germany. That is understood. But, after all, it is the leaders of the country who determine the policy and it is always a simple matter to drag the people along, whether it is a democracy, or a fascist dictatorship, or a parliament, or a communist dictatorship. Voice or no voice, the people can always be brought to the bidding of the leaders. That is easy. All you have to do is tell them they are being attacked, and denounce the peacemakers for lack of patriotism and exposing the country to danger. It works the same in any country."

Hermann Goering – Adolf Hitler's deputy.

This was exactly the same philosophy applied by George W. Bush, after the 9/11 false flag event in New York City in 2001. America was under attack and anyone who did not agree with going to war, was unpatriotic, un-American, and on the side of the vile and evil terrorists.

WHO IS BAILING OUT THE BANKS?

The past decade has seen an unprecedented number of banks being "bailed out" from bankruptcy. This was further extended to entire countries being bailed out. We watch the news in amazement, shaking our heads in disbelief, to witness corrupt bankers being bailed out from foreclosure, while our homes are being repossessed and auctioned by the same banksters, without remorse.

Some independent reports claim that by the end of 2012 the Federal Reserve in the USA spent $26 trillion (that is 26 thousand billion US$) on bailing out US banks.

It is fascinating that out of thousands of reports on these billion dollar bail outs, where intelligent reporters speak volumes about these events, not a single reporter has asked the most important question that needs answering in detail. "Who is doing the bailing out?"

Who is this invisible entity that has an infinite supply of money that they can keep on bailing out banks and even countries at the drop of a hat? They are the banking elite families – those that have somehow given themselves the right to print money and control the supply of all the currency in the world; the ones that own all the major banks in the world. This includes most of the central banks of all the countries, most of which are private companies under their control. This is why they are called the banking elite or more commonly referred to as the "banksters".

The simple fact is that the reporters on the mainstream news channels are not allowed to ask such potentially damaging questions because all the main media corporations in the world are also owned by these banking families.

There is constant talk of "debt" and "injecting more money into the economy" and every country in the world owes some other country money. The banks keep getting bailed out by some magical wave of the government's wand, as the Central Banks/Reserve Banks "inject more funds" or they "release more money" to the various banks and into economies to bail them out. With every new "injection of money" the people become more indebted and more enslaved. The burden of these bailouts is passed onto the people.

Jamaica is a very good example. Of every dollar in its budget, 55 cents go towards paying its debt, 20 cents to service government, and the remaining 25 cents to pay for services required by the population. http://blogs.ft.com/beyond-brics/2013/02/12/jamaicas-crisis-debt-swap/#axzz2RQOQBdhZ

How do we stop this deepening crisis – is there a way out of this mess for the people of the world?

A LEGACY OF CONTROL BY THE BANKING ELITE

When I talk about the banking elite it includes the royal families and the royal bloodlines that have been in control of our world for thousands of years. Keep in mind that it was the ancient Priest-Kings who first introduced the concept of money, which means that this control of the supply of money has been handed down by these royals to their descendants and by extension the bankers must be a branch of the royal bloodlines. This is why many claim that the Queen of England is the wealthiest person on Earth. The Crown is by far the largest single owner of land in the world, but do not be fooled. The Crown is NOT the queen, the Crown is the corporation that operates using the Queen's name and goodwill.

In the last 300 years the world has seen a spectacular display of manipulation of global affairs by the bankers. Influencing the governments of major countries, creating revolutions and wars, introducing new laws into legislation, eliminating presidents who stood in their way, setting up secret organisations of and ensuring that they stay in control whatever it takes.

The most horrific discovery is that the bankers manipulate the global conflicts and wars for their own benefit and continued control. Using humans as their willing and loyal pawns every step of the way – filled with pride, honour and bursting with patriotism as they march to their death.

"Theirs not to reason why, theirs but to do and die." (Alfred Tennyson - The Charge of the Light Brigade – 1854)

WARS ARE CONTROLLED BY THE BANKERS

Wars are started by kings, queens, politicians and religious leaders backing a corporate agenda, not people. People have been the cause of many uprisings and revolutions but those are generally against the oppressive regimes where the intent never seems to be war, but freedom – the freedom that the politicians keep promising the people, yet never deliver.

And so we come face to face with some of the pivotal historic events of the past few centuries only to face the sobering realisation that the bankers have been manipulating all of it for their own benefit.

One of the founding fathers of the USA, Benjamin Franklin stated that "The refusal of King George 3rd, to allow the colonies to operate an honest money system, which freed the ordinary man from the clutches of the money manipulators, was probably the prime cause of the revolution."

And so the American Revolution exploded primarily over the Currency Act of King George 3rd, which forced the colonies to conduct their business by using printed bank notes borrowed from the privately owned Bank of England, at interest. After the revolution, the new United States adopted a very different economic system in which the government issued its own money, so that private banks like the Bank of England were not siphoning off the wealth of the people through interest-bearing bank notes.

Both the French and Russian revolutions were a response by the people against the oppression by royalty, the state of poverty and the control of money.

The First Bank of the United States was set up in 1791 as the first private central bank in the USA by the Rothschild banking family. It was at this time that we start reading the spine-chilling statements by the bankers and other industrialists regarding their global perspective.

The patriarch of the Rothschild empire at the time, Mayer Amschel Rothschild made his intentions clear with his infamous, "Let me issue and control a nation's money and I care not who makes the laws".

Twenty years after the launch of the first private central bank, the US Congress refused to renew the charter and voiced their intention to go back to a state issued value-based currency on which the people paid no interest to any banker.

Once again we see the level of influence by the bankers on global political affairs when Nathan Mayer Rothschild issued a blatant threat against the US Government. "Either the application for renewal of the charter is granted, or the United States will find itself involved in a most disastrous war."

After a resolute US Congress still refused to renew the charter for the First Bank of the United States, Nathan Mayer Rothschild blurted, "Teach those impudent Americans a lesson. Bring them back to colonial status."

Shortly after this inflammatory statement Britain launched the war of 1812, financed by the Rothschild controlled Bank of England to re-colonise the United States and force them back into slavery under the Bank of England. The plan was to plunge the United States into so much debt through the war that they would be forced to accept a new private central bank - and the plan worked.

The United States Congress was forced to grant a new charter for yet another private bank that supplied the currency and provided the public with loans at interest, the Second Bank of the United States. Once again, private bankers were in control of the nation's money supply and did not care who made the laws or how many British and American soldiers had to die for it.

In 1832, US President Andrew Jackson successfully campaigned for his second term as President under the slogan, "Jackson And No Bank".

"Gentlemen! I too have been a close observer of the doings of the Bank of the United States. I have had men watching you for a long time, and am convinced that you have used the funds of the bank to speculate in the breadstuffs of the country. When you won, you divided the profits amongst you, and when you lost, you charged it to the bank. You tell me that if I take the deposits from the bank and annul its charter I shall ruin ten thousand families. That may be true, gentlemen, but that is your sin! Should I let you go on, you will ruin fifty thousand families, and that would be my sin! You are a den of vipers and thieves. I have determined to rout you out, and by the Eternal, (bringing his fist down on the table) I will rout you out!"

President Andrew Jackson, February 1834.

Jackson succeeds in blocking the renewal of the charter for the Second Bank of the United States and went on to become the only president to actually pay off the national debt created by the bankers.

BANKERS TURN TO CRIME AND ASSASSINATION

Three prominent US presidents had assassination attempts, two of them successful, when they became too vocal about the bankers and secret societies. Jackson, Lincoln and Kennedy all stood up to the unlawful activities of these bankster families, but they knew exactly how to deal with the troublesome presidents and hide their crimes successfully.

Shortly after President Jackson ended the Second Bank of the United States, there was an attempted assassination that failed when both pistols used by the assassin, Richard Lawrence, failed to fire.

When the Confederacy seceded from the United States, the bankers once again saw the opportunity for a rich harvest of debt. They offered to fund Lincoln's efforts to bring the south back into the union, but President Lincoln refused and instead issued a new government currency that became known as the "greenback". This was a direct threat to the wealth and power of the central bankers, who quickly responded.

"If this mischievous financial policy, which has its origin in North America, shall become indurated down to a fixture, then that Government will furnish its own money without cost. It will pay off debts and be without debt. It will have all the money necessary to carry on its commerce. It will become prosperous without precedent in the history of the world. The brains, and wealth of all countries will go to North America. That country must be destroyed or it will destroy every monarchy on the globe." This was an article in The London Times responding to Lincoln's decision to issue government Greenbacks to finance the Civil War, rather than agree to private banker's loans at 30% interest.

It is quite obvious from this article as to who was in control of The London Times. It also provides clear evidence that "monarchy" or royalty, is directly linked to the elite banking families.

But the bankers' greed and desire to control the people is insatiable. In 1872, New York bankers sent a letter to every bank in the United States, urging them to fund newspapers that opposed government-issued money such as Lincoln's greenbacks.

"Dear Sir: It is advisable to do all in your power to sustain such prominent daily and weekly newspapers... as will oppose the issuing of greenback paper money, and that you also withhold patronage or favors from all applicants who are not willing to oppose the Government issue of money... To restore to circulation the Government issue of money, will be to provide the people with money, and will therefore seriously affect your individual profit as bankers and lenders."

The banksters continued to manipulate control with statements like this, "It will not do to allow the greenback, as it is called, to circulate as money any length of time, as we cannot control that." Extracted from: *Triumphant Plutocracy – The Story of American Public Life From 1870 to 1920*, by Lynn Wheeler.

The bankers understood very clearly that money is the perfect tool of control and enslavement, infinitely more clinical than the physical form of slavery whereby the owners had to house and feed their slaves. Money could be applied far more effectively as a cunning tool to propagate slavery among humanity without the masses ever realising it. They will be so blinded by their perception of freedom and democracy that they will not realise they are utterly enslaved by those who control the money.

Lynn Wheeler gives us another startling example of the banker's malicious intent in her book *Triumphant Plutocracy*. "Slavery is likely to be abolished by the war power, and chattel slavery destroyed. This, I and my European friends are in favor of, for slavery is but the owning of labor and carries with it the care for the laborer, while the European plan, led on by England, is for capital to control labor by controlling the wages. This can be done by controlling the money."

There is hardly a more sobering statement in recent times to make the ordinary people of the world realise how they are viewed by the banking elite – chattel and slaves. Chattel is defined by Encarta Dictionary as follows:

"movable property - an item of personal property that is not freehold land and is not intangible. Chattels are typically movable property chattels personal, e.g. furniture or cars, but may also be interests in property chattels real, e.g. leases"

The modern banking industry and the families that control it, is the largest organised crime syndicate in the world. What makes them infinitely more dangerous than any other cartel, is that they perform all their unlawful activity while protected by the laws of our countries that were written to protect them, and the courts and judges that uphold such laws.

BANKS ARE ABOVE THE LAW

Since 1913, the currency of the United States has been owned and managed by a private corporation of international bankers known as the "Federal Reserve System". This group prints "Federal Reserve Notes" and loans them out to the United States Treasury. The American people, blissfully ignorant of this great deception, pay interest to the Federal Reserve banking families for the rights to use their money – or fancy pieces of paper. This formula is applied in almost all countries by the privately owned central banks.

The Federal Reserve banking families can therefore print as much money as they want, creating it out of thin air, giving it to whomever they want, secretly, with no oversight or input from the United States government.

In a television interview with Jim Lehrer, former Federal Reserve chairman Alan Greenspan, outlines that the Federal Reserve is an independent agency whose decisions cannot be overruled by any agency or elements of the legitimate United States government. And that because of this, the relationship between the FED and the president of the USA has no effect on the decisions or activities of the FED.

This is a most spine-chilling realisation that the FED is not answerable to anyone. Neither the government nor any of its organs have jurisdiction or control over the FED. In other words, the FED can do as it pleases without any repercussions or possibility of arrests for its fraudulent actions. And this is what central banks have been doing for centuries. Here is an extract from the interview, which can be seen on this link: http://www.youtube.com/watch?v=ol3mEe8TH7w

"JIM LEHRER: What is the proper relationship... what should be the proper relationship between a chairman of the Fed and a president of the United States?

GREENSPAN: Well, first of all, the Federal Reserve is an independent agency. And that means basically that, uh... there is no other agency of government which can overrule actions that we take. So long as that is in place, and there is no evidence that the administration, the Congress or anybody else is requesting that we do things other than what we think is the appropriate thing, then, what the relationships are, don't frankly matter... and I've had very good relationships with presidents."

FUNDING THE WARS

The banking families have huge investments in the many industries they own around the world. None are more profitable than those who feed the war machine. We can say with comfortable certainty that all the wars in human history have been manipulated by those who control the flow of money. The Rothschild, Rockefeller, Morgan, Harriman and Warburg families were some of the primary funders of the Bolshevik Revolution, World War 1 and World War 2.

Hitler's popular rise to power in Germany sent shockwaves through the banking elite. Not because of his military power, but because of his economic policies. Hitler's first financial move was to issue his own state currency which was not borrowed from private central bankers and which could be used by the people without paying interest to the bankers. Germany blossomed and quickly began to rebuild its industry. The media called it "The German Miracle" and Hitler was made TIME Magazine's Man Of The Year in 1938 for the amazing improvement to the life of the German people and the explosion of German industry.

The royal banking families did not like this at all and they used the British Prime Minister, Winston Churchill, as the messenger of things to come.

"Should Germany merchandise (do business) again in the next 50 years we have led this war (WW1) in vain." **Winston Churchill in The Times (1919)**

"Germany becomes too powerful. We have to crush it." **Winston Churchill** (November 1936 speaking to US - General Robert E. Wood)

"We will force this war upon Hitler, if he wants it or not." **Winston Churchill (1936 broadcast)**

"This war is an English war and its goal is the destruction of Germany." - **Winston Churchill (Autumn 1939 broadcast)**

Churchill makes it clear that WW2 could have been avoided but it made financial sense to engage in a war to conquer "sales markets".

"The war wasn't only about abolishing fascism, but to conquer sales markets. We could have, if we had intended so, prevented this war from breaking out without doing one shot, but we didn't want to." **Winston Churchill to Truman (Fultun, USA March 1946)**

In the following statement Churchill admits exactly what the war was about but at the same time makes a sinister remark that suggests he realised that the bankers were the real culprit who had taken over the control from Hitler.

"Germany's unforgivable crime before WW2 was its attempt to loosen its economy out of the world trade system and to build up an independent exchange system from which the world-finance couldn't profit anymore. ...We butchered the wrong pig." **Winston Churchill (The Second World War - Bern, 1960)**

From 1933, Wall Street bankers had bankrolled the successful coups by both Hitler and Mussolini. Brown Brothers Harriman in New York continued to finance Hitler right up to the day war was declared with Germany, and probably continued the funding in clandestine ways during the war. Although reports claim that there was a fallout between the parties, I cannot imagine any banker shying away from such a lucrative opportunity, as funding a war machine.

The bankers decided that a fascist dictatorship in the United States based on the one in Italy would be far better for their business interests than Roosevelt's "New Deal", which threatened massive wealth redistribution to recapitalize the working and middle class of America.

A sinister plot to overthrow the US Government was devised by Wall Street tycoons who recruited General Butler to lead the way by installing a "Secretary of General Affairs" who would be answerable to Wall Street and not the people. General Butler pretended to go along with the scheme but unexpectedly exposed the plot to Congress. Unfortunately the congress was then, as it is now, in the pocket of the Wall Street bankers, who refused to act.

HITLER AND THE BUSH FAMILY EMPIRE

A report in The Guardian, on Saturday 25 September 2004, gives us an insight into how the Bush family profited and created an empire off the back of Hitler's war machine. Here is an edited version of the article.

"George Bush's grandfather, the late US senator Prescott Bush, was a director and shareholder of companies that profited from their involvement with the financial backers of Nazi Germany.

The Guardian has obtained confirmation from newly discovered files in the US National Archives that a firm of which Prescott Bush was a director was involved with the financial architects of Nazism.

The debate over Prescott Bush's behaviour has been bubbling under the surface for some time. But the new documents, many of which were only declassified last year, show that even after America had entered the war and when there was already significant information about the Nazis' plans and policies, he worked for and profited from companies closely involved with the very German businesses that financed Hitler's rise to power.

While there is no suggestion that Prescott Bush was sympathetic to the Nazi cause, the documents reveal that the firm he worked for, Brown Brothers Harriman (BBH), acted as a US base for the German industrialist, Fritz Thyssen, who helped finance Hitler in the 1930s before falling out with him at the end of the decade. The Guardian has seen evidence that shows Bush was the director of the New York-based Union Banking Corporation (UBC) that represented Thyssen's US interests and he continued to work for the bank after America entered the war.

Prescott Bush was also on the board of at least one of the companies that formed part of a multinational network of front companies to allow Thyssen to move assets around the world.

Thyssen owned the largest steel and coal company in Germany and grew rich from Hitler's efforts to re-arm between the two world wars. One of the pillars in Thyssen's international corporate web, UBC, worked exclusively for, and was owned by, a Thyssen-controlled bank in the Netherlands.

Three sets of archives spell out Prescott Bush's involvement. The first set of files, the Harriman papers in the Library of Congress, show that Prescott Bush was a director and shareholder of a number of companies involved with Thyssen."

BANKSTERS ASSASSINATE JFK

When President John F. Kennedy wrote and signed Executive Order 11110 on the 4th of June 1963, which ordered the US Treasury to issue a new public currency, the United States Note, he essentially signed his own death warrant.

Kennedy's United States Notes were not borrowed from the Federal Reserve private bankers but were created by the US Government and backed by the silver stockpiles held by the US Government.

Some four and one half billion dollars went into public circulation, reducing the interest payments to the Federal Reserve and loosening its control over the nation. Five months later JFK was assassinated in Dallas, Texas, and his United States Notes were pulled from circulation almost immediately and destroyed.

John J. McCloy, who was then the president of Chase Manhattan Bank, and president of the World Bank, was appointed to the Warren Commission, to make certain that the banking connection behind the assassination was well concealed from the public. The truth is that the US government, as do many other governments, still has the power under its constitution to issue debt-free money but the control of the banksters is so severe that our servants, our governments, are not doing what is best for the people.

An example of this, hit mainstream media for weeks in the US during January 2013, when it was discovered that a "loophole" could allow the entire US debt to be paid off with a single platinum coin. This coin, dubbed *"The trillion dollar coin"* proved beyond any doubt that the US government had the means and opportunity to settle the country's debt. This was the first time that mainstream media offered their viewers a glimpse of the enormity of the fiat currency deception. This is only a small taste of what the banksters are capable of and how they have manipulated our world for a very long time. It seems that it is up to us, the people, to do something about it.

Ref: All Wars are Banker's Wars - Michael Rivero

MONEY DOES NOT MAKE THE WORLD GO ROUND

On this long and convoluted path of deception about money, we have become well trained soldiers marching to the beat of the invisible drum, of the money makers. We have cleverly been fed statements like "money makes the world go round" and "if you work hard, you will make it to the top", and "the money buys the whiskey"... without ever questioning it for too long.

The truth is that the world goes around all by itself; and when you get to the top, it's never quite enough; and while at present it may be the money that buys the whiskey, it is people who make the whiskey, and therefore it should be the people, and not the money, who decide how and by whom the whiskey is consumed.

Through subtle indoctrination, money has become the life-blood of the human psyche. But in fact it is more like a drug and humanity is addicted to it because most of us believe that we cannot survive without money. Well, nothing could be further from the truth. Just open your eyes and look at the world around you. Everything around us exists in abundance and functions without money. We are the only species known to us, that has adopted this thing called money.

Millions of people around the world create millions of things every day that fill the shelves of supermarkets, warehouses and showrooms. Millions of farmers around the world produce millions of tons of food every year – our engineers design the most spectacular structures that take our breath away – our musicians reduce us to tears of emotion with their performances that move us at the very core of our souls – and our children fill our hearts with joy and the hope for a better life with their innocence. Money does not make the world go around – people do.

But for now, there is repeated talk about stimulating the economy; capital injection; job creation; stabilising business growth; increasing international trade and other such failed actions of the past that have landed us in this mess in the first place. None of what the governments and bankers are proposing are solutions for the people.

Their solutions are just further acts of enrichment for the banks and their owners. It is a well orchestrated and devious manoeuvre by the banskters that has been called PROBLEM – REACTION – SOLUTION. *(David Icke)*

BANKS GET BAILED OUT – PEOPLE PAY THE DEBT

The sad thing is that every time the banks get bailed out by the central banks, the people have to pay it back – not the banks. Let me make this very simple for you – there is no magical vault full of money hidden in a secret place. The banking elite have given themselves the right to print money – that is, to create money out of thin air.

Just picture this scene. You walk into a printing factory and next to a very expensive printing machine lies a pile of paper that is worth one hundred dollars. A man comes along and starts feeding the pieces of paper into the printer which emerge on the other side covered in fancy designs, a logo, a name and some numbers printed in the corners of the pieces of paper, now worth 100 billion dollars. These papers then get cut and trimmed to look really neat and tidy, wrapped in more fancy paper in bundles of 100 and shipped off to the banks.

What you have just witnessed is the creation of money out of "thin air" by the central banks. These pieces of paper are then loaned out to people for which they have to pay back interest, which amounts to more pieces of paper of a similar nature being obtained by the people to do so. But the people cannot print their own pieces of paper because if they did, they would go to jail for a very long time. Only the bankers have the right to create these fancy papers without getting into trouble with the law – because they caused the laws to be written as such to give them these privileges.

This is how quickly and simply a global scam can be created if you have the power to write the laws that will enforce the scam. Then you need to be able to control the armies and police through the governments to enforce the laws and pretty soon you will be untouchable, playing God with everyone around you.

There will be those that fiercely defend these acts arguing that this is how things work and that we need order and structure to be able to function as a civilised society – they will say that it has taken us a long time to get to the pinnacle of civilisation where we can all benefit from the luxuries provided by advanced technology. There will be those in the financial sector who will try to explain to you how complicated all of this is and that it's not as simple as that. They have a global army of well trained accountants and traders who are completely brainwashed into believing they are doing very important work that keeps the world going around.

Those are all just lies and deceptions for the banks to hide behind. Do not believe anything they say other than this simple version of the facts. The central banks create money out of thin air; they give it to the government to bail out the banks, and we, the people, have to work longer and harder to pay them back – not with 'thin air' but with our sweat and blood. This is the immaculate deception of humanity. We are the slaves that keep the banksters in power.

Let me not mince my words and repeat what I have already stated. The banking industry is the biggest organised crime syndicate that has ever been exposed. But somehow they have managed to make themselves appear to be legitimate and their activities legalised and accepted by the very people they are extorting from. I will expand on the laws that were maliciously created to enslave us in later chapters. Laws that we believe are there to protect us, are actually created to protect the interests of multinational corporations.

THE MUSCLE BEHIND THE BANKERS – CROWN TEMPLE

How do the banking elite control this huge financial monster that seems to be infinitely complex and out of control? How and when did they organise themselves to be so powerful? Where is their head office? Who keeps the wheels turning every minute of every day without any rest?

It is known as the "Crown". While many assume that the Queen of England is behind this power and that the Royal Family of Britain own the USA, this is a different "Crown", established by the infamous Knights Templar, when they built the Temple Church in the City of London in 1185. The "Crown" is also known as the "Crown Temple" or "Crown Templar".

Both the governmental and judicial systems within the United States of America, at both federal and local state levels, are owned by the "Crown", a private foreign power, whose head office is in the centre of London, England, in a sovereign state know as the City of London. The control of the banking elite and their lawmakers is strategically located inside three independent and sovereign states that exist within other countries and cities, namely, Vatican City in Rome; Washington DC, and the City of London. The City is also referred to as the Square Mile, and holds city status in its own right. It is a sovereign and separate ceremonial county.

The Temple Church is located between Fleet Street, the financial head office of the City of London, and the Victoria Embankment by the River Thames. Its grounds also house the Crown Offices at Crown Office Row. This Temple "Church" is outside any canonical jurisdiction. This means that no government or other so-called authority has any control or power over it – Just like the FED in the USA. The Master of the Temple is appointed and takes his place by sealed (non-public) patent, without induction or institution.

The international Bar Association is located at the Inns of Court at Crown Temple, which are physically located at Chancery Lane behind Fleet Street. This is where all Bar attorneys find their origins while all Bar Associations throughout the world are signatories and franchises to the Crown at this site.

The local authority for the City, the City of London Corporation, is unique in the United Kingdom, and has some unusual responsibilities for a local authority in Britain, such as being the police authority for the City. It also has responsibilities and ownerships beyond the City's boundaries. The Corporation is headed by the Lord Mayor of the City of London, an office that is separate from, and much older than, the Mayor of London.

This is where and how the current global banking and legal systems have laid the foundations for the control and tyranny imposed on humanity today. More than 800 years in the making – meticulously planned and executed, conning and fooling the ignorant people every step of the way. From here they dictate the legal and financial policy for most of the world, which includes the launching of wars and invasions of countries, as a strategic tool of control and the never ending creation of debt for countries and their people .

The USA is not a free and sovereign nation as proclaimed by the federal government. If this were true, the USA, just like virtually all other countries, would not be dictated to by the Crown Temple through its bankers and attorneys. The USA is controlled and manipulated by this private foreign power and its unlawful Federal Government is their pawnbroker.

The banks or banking elite, Rule the Temple Church and the Attorneys carry out their Orders by controlling their victim's judiciary. It's a perfect plan for a perfect crime that has been executed meticulously since the building of the Temple in 1185, without too many questions being asked – until now.

The private Federal Reserve System, which issues fiat U.S. Federal

Reserve Notes, is financially owned and controlled by the Crown from Switzerland, which is the home and legal origin for the charters of the United Nations, the International Monetary Fund, the World Trade Organization, and most importantly, the Bank of International Settlements. Even Hitler respected the Crown bankers by not bombing Switzerland. The Bank of International Settlements in Basel, Switzerland, controls all the central banks of the G7 nations and far beyond. He who controls the gold, rules the world.

Important definition to comprehend:

ATTORN [e-'tern] Anglo-French aturner, to transfer (allegiance of a tenant to another lord), from Old French atorner to turn (to), arrange, from a- to + torner to turn: to agree to be the tenant of a new landlord or owner of the same property. Merriam-Webster's Dictionary of Law ©1996.

ATTORN, v.i. [L. ad and torno.] In the feudal law, to turn, or transfer homage and service from one lord to another. This is the act of feudatories, vassals or tenants, upon the alienation of the estate.- Webster's 1828 Dictionary.

All the legalistic scams promoted globally by the exclusive monopoly of the Temple Bar and their Bar Association franchises come from four Inns or Temples of Court: the Inner Temple, the Middle Temple, Lincoln's Inn, and Gray's Inn. These Inns are exclusive and private country clubs, that are in fact secret societies of world power in commerce. They are well established, some having been founded in the early 1200s.

Just like all USA based franchise Bar Associations, none of the Four Inns of the Temple are incorporated or registered as corporations, for a simple reason: You can't make a claim against a non-entity and a non-being. They are private societies without charters or statutes, and their so-called constitutions are based solely on custom and self-regulation. In other words, they exist as secret societies without a public "front door".

More important definitions:
FEALTY, n. [L. fidelis.] Fidelity to a lord; faithful adherence of a tenant or vassal to the superior of whom he holds his lands; loyalty.

Under the feudal system of tenures, every vassal or tenant was bound to be true and faithful to his lord, and to defend him against all his enemies. This obligation was called his fidelity or fealty, and an oath of fealty was required to be taken by all tenants to their landlords. The tenant was called a liege man; the land, a liege fee; and the superior, liege lord.

By swearing to the 1213 Charter in fealty, King John declared that the British-English Crown and its possessions at that time, including all future possessions, estates, trusts, charters, letters patent, and land, were forever bound to the Pope and the Roman Church, as the landlord. Some five hundred years later, the New England Colonies in America became a part of the Crown as a possession and trust named the "United States."

Alexander Hamilton was one of the many Crown Templars who was called to their Bar. He entered King's College, now named Columbia University in New York City, in 1774, which was funded by members of the London King's Inns. In 1777, he became a personal aide and private secretary to George Washington during the American Revolution.

In May of 1782, Hamilton began studying law in Albany, New York. This was a three-year course, which he miraculously completed in only six months and was admitted to the New York Bar. The New York Bar Association, was and is, a franchise of the Crown Temple through the Middle Inn. After a year's service in Congress during the 1782-1783 session, he settled down to legal practice in New York City as Alexander Hamilton, Esqr. In February 1784, he wrote the charter for, and became a founding member of, the Bank of New York, the State's first bank.

On the 18th of June 1787, at the Federal Convention in Philadelphia, Hamilton delivered a five-hour speech in which he stated, "an Executive for life will be an elective Monarch". When all his anti-Federalist, New York colleagues withdrew from the Convention in protest, he alone signed the Constitution for the United States of America, representing New York State, one of the legal Crown States or Colonies.

We need to pay attention to the play on words here and notice that a lawful state is made up of the people, but a State is a legal entity of the Crown - a Crown Colony. This is an example of the deceptive ways by which the Crown Temple, through the Middle Templars - have taken control of America and many other parts of our world.

But the trickery continued when Hamilton laid the foundation of the first Federal U.S. Central Bank, as the Secretary of the U.S. Treasury under President Washington. He secured credit loans through Crown banks in France and the Netherlands, and increased the power of the Federal Government over the hoodwinked nation-states of the Union.

Americans were fooled into believing that the legal Crown Colonies comprising New England were independent nation states. They were, and still are, Colonies of the Crown Temple, through letters patent and charters, who have no legal authority to be independent from the Rule and Order of the Crown Temple. A legal State is a Crown Temple Colony.

Neither the American people nor the Queen of England own America. The Crown Temple owns America through the deception of those who have sworn their allegiance by oath to the Middle Templar Bar. The Crown Bankers and their Middle Templar Attorneys rule America through unlawful contracts, unlawful taxes, and contract documents of false equity through debt deceit. This is all strictly enforced by their entirely unlawful, but "legal" Orders, Rules and Codes of the Crown Temple Courts, which is the so-called judiciary in the USA. This is because the Crown Temple holds the land titles and estate deeds to all of North America.

But the convoluted control continues further down the rabbit hole. The Pope and his Roman Church control the Crown Temple because his Knights established it under his Orders.

Ref: Michael Edward – Ecclesiastic Commonwealth Community (ECC)

HE WHO OWNS THE GOLD CONTROLS THE WORLD

The Vatican is often said to be the largest owner of gold in the world. And he who controls the gold controls the world. This is why South Africa and Zimbabwe did not escape the attention of the Crown. It is after all where most of the world's gold has come from; and why Paul Kruger became so famous; and why Cecil John Rhodes was sent to claim it for the Crown; and the reason why Great Britain launched the most expensive war it has ever been engaged in, to date, in South Africa.

From 1899 to 1902 there were around 470,000 (four hundred and seventy thousand), British troops securing the land for the Crown during the South African War, against some 60,000 Boers or farmers, and a similar number of indigenous Africans from various Bantu tribes. This is nearly twice the number of British and US troops that were involved in the Gulf War during 2012. The British had to secure the control of the gold fields for the Crown, no matter what the cost was. And so they did.

To achieve this, the British had to go to drastic measures and adopted the "scorched earth" policy, burning down homes, villages and farms, killing or confiscating livestock and putting thousands of women and children from the Boer farms and Bantu tribes into concentration camps scattered across South Africa. It is estimated that at least 34,000 people died in these camps but the number is most likely much higher. This was the model that was improved upon by Adolf Hitler in his own version of concentration camps some 40 years later.

Eight years after the end of the war, in 1910, The Union of South Africa was established by King George V, and came to an end on the 31st of May 1961, when it became the REPUBLIC OF SOUTH AFRICA, a corporation. And so the control continues – a different time; a different name; a different leader, slowly rolling from one form of control to the next, all under the ownership of the Crown.

What is quite confusing and greatly disturbing is a letter written on the 16th December 1918, by the early leaders of the ANC (African National Congress), to King George V, pledging their allegiance and loyalty. This is an extract of the first part of a lengthy letter.

Petition to King George V, from the South African Native National Congress

16 December 1918

Memorial

To His Most Gracious Majesty King George V of Great Britain and Ireland including the Dominions and Colonies, and Emperor of India.

May It Please Your Majesty-

1. We, the Chiefs and delegates assembled at Johannesburg, this 16th day of December, 1918, in the Special Session of the South African

Native National Congress, a political body representing the various tribes of the Bantu people in South Africa, record the expression of our satisfaction and thankfulness in the triumph of righteousness in this great war by the victory of the forces of Great Britain, her noble Allies, and the United States of America.

2. We beg to convey to Your Majesty our affectionate loyalty and devotion to Your Majesty's person and Throne and the sincerity of our desire that Divine Blessing and prosperity may attend Your Majesty and all Your Majesty's Dominions in the dawn of a better age.

3. We further express the hope and wish that during Your Majesty's Reign all races and Nations will be treated fairly and with justice, and that there will be no discrimination on account of colour or creed; and will enjoy the right of citizenship, freedom and liberty under your flag.

This kind of declaration of allegiance flies in the face of the principles of a liberation movement that should  represent the absolute liberation of the people. Liberation from all forms of oppression and control. Especially financial and economic control of the people, which is more accurately defined as slavery.

The Crown Templars have many names and many symbols to signify their private Temple. One of the best examples hidden in plain sight is the one dollar bill of the private Federal Reserve System in the USA, which is nothing more than a Crown banking franchise debt note.

The base of the pyramid clearly shows the Roman date for the year 1776, written in Roman numerals MDCCLXXVI. The Roman Latin words ANNUIT COEPTIS NOVUS ORDO SECLORUM are proudly displayed for all to see. It means ANNOUNCING THE BIRTH OF THE NEW ORDER OF THE WORLD. The year 1776 signifies the birth of the New World Order under the Crown Temple. That is when their American Crown Colonies became a chartered government called the United States.

THE WORLD IN PROTEST

There has never been a time like the present, when the entire world is rapidly rising up in protest against the banksters and the political regimes that increasingly curtail the freedom of their people.

By the end of 2012 there were massive protests in virtually every country and thousands of cities all over the world sparked mainly by the Occupy Wall Street (OWS) initiative. This caused many more protests around the world to flare up against a wide range of burning issues, that were effecting people's lives. It is an indication that in truth, there is very little being done by the many governments of the world to serve the people who elected them. Based on the extent of these actions it is estimated that more than 10 million people around the world were involved in protests between 2010 and the end of 2012.

As expected, the mainstream media did not report on most of these protests, but rather did their best to play it all down and treat the protestors with the usual ridicule we have become accustomed to.

The Occupy Wall Street protest started on 17 September 2011 in Zuccotti Park, New York. By the end of 2011 there had been more than 1000 Occupy protests around the world. The main issues raised by OWS were social and economic inequality, greed, corruption and the perceived undue influence of corporations on government, particularly from the financial services sector. It was becoming evident to millions, that corporations were the enemies of the people, spearheaded and supported by the banks and the unlawful legal system.

The OWS slogan claims that *We are the 99%*. The UBUNTU movement agrees with this wholeheartedly and reminds people to take this to heart and not be confused, baffled or intimidated by the 1% that has assumed control of our planet. The only constant in this universe is change, and so will the draconian regime that has enslaved the 99%.

Many believe that the so-called "upper class" is part of the 1%. It should be stressed that the "upper class" is not the highest class of earners. Because, even if people are perceived to be extremely wealthy, they mostly do not fall into the 1%, and in most cases should not be demonised. The 1% is a very exclusive club, that remains invisible and untouchable to the global population.

Protesters were forced out of Zuccotti Park on November 15, 2011. After several unsuccessful attempts to re-occupy the original location, protesters turned their focus to occupying banks, corporate headquarters, board meetings, college and university campuses.

The secret government agencies will stop at nothing to spy on its people and use whatever measures to eliminate troublemakers. If they could eliminate Lincoln and JFK, they can do it to anyone. But this only causes more trouble for them in the long run. And so the government made sure that it gathered as much information about the leaders of OWS in the event they had a potential case of treason or terrorism on which to arrest people who stand up for their rights and the rights of others.

Proof of this was delivered on 29 December 2012 by Naomi Wolf of The Guardian newspaper who provided US Government with documents which revealed that the FBI and DHS (Department of Homeland Security) had monitored Occupy Wall Street through their joint terrorism task force despite labelling it a peaceful movement.

While we may see it as our right to protest, they see it as a potential threat to the system. A system designed to destroy anything that threatens its own survival. By the time 2012 came to a close, senior stock brokers, bank executives like Greg Smith, and senior World Bank insiders like Karen Hudes had spilt the beans on the countless criminal activities by the global banking elite. Here is a video clip from Russia Today exposing just some of these atrocities. https://www.youtube.com/watch?v=c7E9SUwlooE&feature=player_embedded

The world in protest: Here is a taste of what escaped most of the mainstream media.

This list is only the tip of the iceberg but it does give us a glimpse of the state of unhappiness of the global population. It does not include actions like the Occupy activity in South Africa and many other protests against various governments of the world.

USA:
More than 150 protests across the USA by students against the education system. http://teacherunderconstruction.com/2012/11/22/list-of-2012-student-protests-regarding-education-in-the-u-s/

Afghanistan:
Afghans protest recent public killing of woman
http://www.sfgate.com/news/article/Afghans-protest-recent-public-killing-of-woman-3698266.php

Australia:
Indigenous leaders urge protest vote against Labor
http://www.radioaustralia.net.au/international/2012-07-13/indigenous-leaders-urge-protest-vote-against-labor/979840
Protesters 'will be waiting' for G20
http://www.brisbanetimes.com.au/queensland/protesters-will-be-waiting-for-g20-20120711-21w0w.html

Bahrain:
Protests hit Bahrain after opposition restrictions
http://www.huffingtonpost.com/huff-wires/20120714/ml-bahrain/

Belgium:
EU farmers deliver moo-ving "milk lake" protest
http://www.reuters.com/article/2012/07/10/eu-dairy-lake-idUSL6E8IA7CT20120710

Bolivia:
Bolivia to revoke mine licence after protests
http://mwcnews.net/news/americas/20104-mine-licence.html

Burma:
Burmese Protest Thai Takeover of Monastery
http://www.irrawaddy.org/archives/8897

Canada:

Reserve in 'turmoil' over Keeyask dam: Protesters
http://www.winnipegsun.com/2012/07/13/reserve-in-turmoil-over-keeyask-dam-protesters
Rally to Save Kitpu – July 12, 2012
http://halifax.mediacoop.ca/photo/rally-save-kitpu-july-12th2012/11685
Hundreds rally for missing, murdered women inquiry
http://www.winnipegsun.com/2012/07/11/hundreds-rally-for-missing-murdered-women-inquiry

China:

China pollution protest ends, but suspicion of government high
http://articles.chicagotribune.com/2012-07-08/business/sns-rt-us-china-pollutionbre8670hp-20120708_1_protests-shanghai-stock-exchange-china
Chinese city halts copper smelter after protest over pollution fears
http://world.time.com/2012/07/04/chinese-city-halts-copper-smelter-after-protest-over-pollution-fears/

Egypt:

No longer off limits: Presidential palace becomes a new space of protest
http://www.egyptindependent.com/news/no-longer-limits-presidential-palace-becomes-new-space-protest

France:

Hundreds protest anti-prostitution plans in Paris
http://articles.chicagotribune.com/2012-07-07/news/sns-rt-us-france-prostitutionbre8660hs-20120707_1_prostitution-paris-human-trafficking

Germany:

Activists Protest H&M Clothing Production Labor Conditions
http://www.google.com/hostednews/getty/article/ALeqM5jod0NmdFFVpQWz3J2Lhg8fVeqATA?docId=148321096

Greece:

Greek seniors protest pension cuts
http://photoblog.msnbc.msn.com/_news/2012/07/12/12700405-greek-seniors-protest-pension-cuts?lite

Guyana:

OP faces protest over 'divide and rule' Linden power hike
http://www.stabroeknews.com/2012/news/stories/07/13/op-faces-protest-over-divide-and-rule-linden-power-hike/

Haiti:

About 100 protest planned eviction in Haiti
http://www.charlotteobserver.com/2012/07/12/3378930/about-100-protest-planned-eviction.html

Hong Kong:

Protesters Fill Hong Kong As New Leader Sworn In
http://blogs.wsj.com/chinarealtime/2012/07/01/protesters-fill-hong-kong-as-new-leader-sworn-in/

India:

Jharkhand parties join tribals protest against land for IIT, IIM
http://www.deccanherald.com/content/263384/jharkhand-parties-join-tribals-protest.html

Protest at Delhi
http://www.e-pao.net/GP.asp?src=7..140712.jul12

Vokkaligas protest Gowda's removal in Karnataka
http://india.nydailynews.com/politicsarticle/0c357453a962d9417f7cf0dc12ca01ca/vokkaligas-protest-gowda-s-removal-in-karnataka

Indonesia:

Thousands of Indonesian workers take to streets in protest against outsourcing, low wages
http://www.brandonsun.com/business/breaking-news/thousands-of-indonesian-workers-take-to-streets-in-protest-against-outsourcing-low-wages-162180325.html?thx=y

Ireland:

Parade Protesters Clash with Police
http://www.crewechronicle.co.uk/crewe-news/uk-world-news/2012/07/12/parade-protesters-clash-with-police-96135-31379180/

Israel:

Israelis protest military draft exemptions for ultra-Orthodox

http://seattletimes.nwsource.com/html/nationworld/2018631765israele
xempt08.html

Israeli man sets himself on fire during Tel Aviv social protest
http://www.haaretz.com/news/national/israeli-man-sets-himself-on-
fire-during-tel-aviv-social-protest-1.451041

Kenya:
**Kenya: Ijara Women Protest Domination By Male Politicians
During Elections**
http://allafrica.com/stories/201207121228.html

Kuwait:
**Kuwait must respect freedom of expression and assembly for
Bidun**
http://www.amnesty.org/en/news/kuwait-must-respect-freedom-
expression-and-assembly-bidun-2012-07-13

Maldives:
Violence in the Maldives as Protests Continue
http://india.blogs.nytimes.com/2012/07/13/violence-in-the-maldives-
as-protests-continue/
Manilla:
Defective passports trigger protest
http://manilastandardtoday.com/www2/2012/07/14/defective-
passports-trigger-protest/

Mexico:
"The Largest Protest the World has ever Seen" in Mexico
http://the2012scenario.com/2012/07/the-largest-protest-the-world-has-
ever-seen-in-mexico/

New Zealand:
Protest Called By Aotearoa Is Not For Sale
http://www.google.com/hostednews/getty/article/ALeqM5h7wptHBd
QDON3Kg4vsgjZgwlLreg?docId=148316185

Oman:
Oman protests suggest jobs, reform pledges fall short
http://in.reuters.com/article/2012/07/04/oman-crackdown-
idINL5E8HLB2620120704

Pakistan:
Activists of Jamiat-e-Ulema Islam, commonly called JUI, chant slogans against the reopening of NATO supply routes, during a protest demonstration in Lahore.
http://www.demotix.com/news/1332039/pakistanis-protest-lahore-against-reopening-nato-supply-route

Peru:
Peru's Repression of Mining Protesters Condemned
http://www.ens-newswire.com/ens/jul2012/2012-07-11-01.html

Phillipines:
Police to set up barriers against SONA protesters
http://www.philstar.com/Article.aspx?articleId=826214&publicationSubCategoryId=63

Portugal:
Portugal faces health sector shutdown in cuts protest
http://www.thejakartaglobe.com/afp/portugal-faces-health-sector-shutdown-in-cuts-protest/529915

Russia:
Opposition Gearing Up for 'Hot July' Protest
http://www.themoscowtimes.com/news/article/opposition-gearing-up-for-hot-july-protest/462037.html

Saudi Arabia:
Angry Throngs at a Funeral in Saudi Arabia
http://www.nytimes.com/2012/07/11/world/middleeast/in-saudi-arabia-thousands-at-funeral-of-protester.html

Spain:
Spain Protests: Civil Servants Protest Wage Cuts
http://www.huffingtonpost.com/2012/07/13/spain-protests_n_1671028.html?utm_hp_ref=world

Sudan:
Sudan clamps down on the "Kandaka" protest of Friday
http://www.sudantribune.com/Sudan-clamps-down-on-the-Kandaka,43261

Swaziland:
Swaziland police fire rubber bullets to stop march
http://www.lasvegassun.com/news/2012/jul/11/af-swaziland-protests/

Syria:
Demonstrators protest against Syria's President Bashar al-Assad after Friday Prayers in Houla
http://www.trust.org/alertnet/multimedia/pictures/detail.dot?medialnode=8e3a54c8-9c65-4625-a398-06ea091aae48

Ukraine:
Ukraine activists protest Russia language bill
http://articles.boston.com/2012-07-05/news/32553689_1_opposition-activists-riot-police-protest-legislation

United States:
Some arrests as LA police break up protest
http://www.huffingtonpost.com/huff-wires/20120713/us-police-protesters-clash/
Opening of Bohemian Grove encampment draws small protest
http://www.pressdemocrat.com/article/20120713/ARTICLES/120719784/1010/sports?Title=Opening-of-Bohemian-Grove-encampment-draws-small-protest
Displaced families at center of fracking protests
http://www.timesonline.com/news/local_news/displaced-families-at-center-of-fracking-protests/article_6dc8f7da-8121-5873-a73f-3550cc1b4d9e.html
When The Chalk Dust Settled, Opinons of Occupy LA's Latest Demonstration Varied
http://www.nbclosangeles.com/news/local/Downtown-LA-Art-Walk-Protest-Arrest-DTLA-162338316.html
Environmental groups organize walk along oil pipeline, tar sands protest
http://vtdigger.org/2012/07/15/environmental-groups-organize-walk-along-oil-pipeline-tar-sands-protest/

Angola:
Angolan police arrest 12 at anti-government rally
http://in.reuters.com/article/2012/07/14/angola-protest-idINL6E8IE30O20120714

Israel:

Netanyahu orders probe into case of demonstrator who set himself alight

http://www.jta.org/news/article/2012/07/15/3100756/demonstrator-who-set-himself-alight-a-great-personal-tragedy-netanyahu-says

England:

The English Defence League (EDL) protest peacefully in Bristol

http://www.digitaljournal.com/article/328635

Jordan:

Jordan police disperse protesting Libyans

http://thegardenisland.com/news/world/jordan-police-disperse-protesting-libyans/article_7019779f-a052-5f8c-ad17-e857df73529b.html

Jordan's Islamists say they will boycott elections

http://www.statesman.com/news/nation/jordans-islamists-say-they-will-boycott-elections-2415896.html

Mali:

Islamists in Mali Detain Protesters

http://www.nytimes.com/2012/07/15/world/africa/mali-islamists-briefly-detain-protesters.html

Vietnam:

Vietnam: mass protests after government crackdown on Catholic Church

http://www.indcatholicnews.com/news.php?viewStory=20803

South Africa: 6 December 2012

One of the most important protests in South Africa during 2012 was the blocking of toll-gates on several major highways, by COSATU, the largest labour union in SA, which is affiliated to the ANC ruling party. They sent a strong message to the government to stop privatising the roads in South Africa by allowing private consortiums to erect toll-gates, preventing the people from travelling freely, extorting money from people unlawfully. This is not the will of the people and the message was very clear that the actions will not stop until all toll-gates are dismantled. Only time will tell how long COSATU will hold out against the ANC government and the influence of the banksters on them.

In 1922 Henry Ford made a statement that is beginning to unfold with the awakening of the people and the rise of global consciousness.

"It's well enough that the people of the nation and the world do not understand our banking and monetary system, for if they did, I believe there would be a revolution before tomorrow morning." **Henry Ford 1922**

THE CORPORATIONS THAT OWN THE WORLD

Between the 19th and 24th October 2011, while the Occupy Wall Street action was in full swing, *New Scientist* and *Forbes* magazines ran similar articles under the following headlines:

Revealed – the capitalist network that runs the world
http://www.newscientist.com/article/mg21228354.500-revealed--the-capitalist-network-that-runs-the-world.html#.UkqrtX-o0_w

The 147 Companies that control everything.
http://www.forbes.com/sites/bruceupbin/2011/10/22/the-147-companies-that-control-everything/

The articles outline the research of three systems theorists at the Swiss Federal Institute of Technology in Zurich, who took a database listing of 37 million companies and investors worldwide, and found that a staggering 43,060 of these were transnational corporations who share ownerships. They built a model of who owns who, and what their revenues are and mapped out the whole structure of economic power.

The research revealed a core of 1318 companies with interlocking ownerships. Each of these had ties to two or more other companies, and on average they were connected to 20 corporations. Although they represented 20% of global operating revenues, the 1318 appeared to collectively own through their shares, the majority of the world's large blue chip and manufacturing corporations, representing a further 60% of global revenues.

When the Zurich team untangled the web of ownership even further, they discovered 147 companies at the core of global corporate control. Each of these 147 companies own interlocking stakes of one another and together they control 40% of the wealth of the global network. Further analysis exposed that a total of 737 control 80% of it all. It should not be surprising that most are financial institutions that include Barclays Bank, Bank of America, JPMorgan Chase, Deutsche Bank, Goldman Sachs, Credit Suisse, and other lesser known brands to the man on the street. Interesting to note that the South African based insurance group, Old Mutual, is number 30 on this list. Its wealth cannot come from insuring South African households and vehicles. So who and what are they involved in?

Previous studies have found that a few transnational corporations own large chunks of the world's economy, but they included only a limited number of companies and omitted indirect ownerships. This was the first real scientific exposure that goes beyond ideology, to accurately identify such a network of power. It combines the mathematics used to model natural systems with comprehensive corporate data, to map ownership among the world's transnational corporations.

"Reality is so complex, we must move away from dogma, whether it's conspiracy theories or free-market," said James Glattfelder, of the research team. "Our analysis is reality-based."

The top 50 of the 147 companies that run the world.

1. Barclays plc
2. Capital Group Companies Inc
3. FMR Corporation
4. AXA
5. State Street Corporation
6. JP Morgan Chase & Co
7. Legal & General Group plc
8. Vanguard Group Inc
9. UBS AG
10. Merrill Lynch & Co Inc
11. Wellington Management Co LLP
12. Deutsche Bank AG
13. Franklin Resources Inc
14. Credit Suisse Group
15. Walton Enterprises LLC
16. Bank of New York Mellon Corp
17. Natixis
18. Goldman Sachs Group Inc
19. T Rowe Price Group Inc

20. Legg Mason Inc
21. Morgan Stanley
22. Mitsubishi UFJ Financial Group Inc
23. Northern Trust Corporation
24. Société Générale
25. Bank of America Corporation
26. Lloyds TSB Group plc
27. Invesco plc
28. Allianz SE 29. TIAA
30. Old Mutual Public Limited Company
31. Aviva plc
32. Schroders plc
33. Dodge & Cox
34. Lehman Brothers Holdings Inc*
35. Sun Life Financial Inc
36. Standard Life plc
37. CNCE
38. Nomura Holdings Inc
39. The Depository Trust Company
40. Massachusetts Mutual Life Insurance
41. ING Groep NV
42. Brandes Investment Partners LP
43. Unicredito Italiano SPA
44. Deposit Insurance Corporation of Japan
45. Vereniging Aegon
46. BNP Paribas
47. Affiliated Managers Group Inc
48. Resona Holdings Inc
49. Capital Group International Inc
50. China Petrochemical Group Company

GLOBAL ECONOMIC COLLAPSE IS IMMINENT

By the end of 2012 the world had been bombarded by negative
sentiments regarding the global economy for well over a decade and it
has not stopped. And as time marches on, daily news headlines are a
constant reminder that we are all in deep financial trouble. All we hear
about is doom and gloom in the financial sectors of the world and how
everybody will have to tighten their belts and work harder.

And suddenly, it wasn't only banks that were bailed out, but countries too. Greece, Ireland, Italy, Portugal, Spain and Cyprus have been bailed out while other countries have not called it 'bailouts' but received huge loans that really mean the same thing.

The more bailouts we see, the more the banking families smile because they have the right to print an unlimited amount of money. And every time they create more money out of thin air to solve our problems, they take more of our land, our passions, and the people become more enslaved to the bankers.

How is it possible that the global economy continues to grind along? Why has it not imploded in a spectacular display of financial carnage? By now everyone should be able to recite the answer automatically – the banksters can continue printing money out of thin air for as long as they are alive. They don't seem to mind what the consequences are as long as they keep control of the governments and the masses. To achieve this they use the police, the army, intelligence agencies, and all the other government bodies at their disposal.

NEGATIVE GROWTH – A FICTIONAL CONCEPT

How is it possible that a world with seven billion people who all work like slaves every day and create something every day, can amount to a negative outcome?

Remember that negative numbers are imaginary or theoretical numbers. They don't really exist. In mathematical terms any number that does not have a square root cannot exist and is purely theoretical. For example the square root of 9 is 3. But -9 does not have a square root.

This simply means that living breathing human beings cannot create something negative. You can't have negative sex, or eat a negative carrot, or give a negative present to someone. The word 'create' is an expression of the Divine Creation that is directly connected to our humanness and our ability to create infinitely as a species – as expressions of the Divine Creator of all.

Humans are not capable of creating "negative growth" – only fictional entities or corporations can do that using simulated models. This is why we are treated as such by our governments – we are not seen as human beings – we are "juristic persons" or fictional entities; pieces of paper and "straw men" represented by our birth certificates and ID numbers, which are instruments and assets of the government corporations – and that is how negative growth is achieved. The fictional entities are creating the negative growth – not human beings.

How long do these bankers think that they can fool the people? It is up to us to share this knowledge with everyone. Sooner or later we will reach a critical mass of consciously awake humans and the tipping point, where no amount of money will be enough to solve the financial problems. Once the critical mass of people wake up to the great deception, there will be no turning back. We will face a massive economic meltdown and the collapse of the entire global financial systems.

The question we need to ask is – what are we going to do when this happens?

The Occupy movement played a key role in igniting the awareness of banker fraud, causing millions of people to start asking questions about the banks. They waved banners like "jail the bankers"; "eat the bankers"; "bail out the people not the banksters"; "too big to fail, too big to jail" and many more. They made millions of people around the world aware that something was dramatically wrong with the banking industry as they called for the closing down of Wall Street. But unfortunately, all that focused occupy activity only highlighted the problem, it did not present a workable alternative or any realistic solutions.

AFTER THE FALL OF WALL STREET – A NEW PATH OF ABUNDANCE

The question we need to ask is; what are we going to do when it all collapses? What are we going to do if the banks close their doors and the money runs out? Because if we do not have a clear plan for the future, the human race will be in big trouble.

Albert Einstein defined insanity as doing the same experiment over and over, expecting different results. This means that we must be insane because we have been going around in circles for more than 6,000 years using the same financial system of money – a system that does not work and has led to continuous conflict and misery among the people.

So as the old "age" drew to a close in 2012 and the "new age" of consciousness approached, it became clear that the people of the world had had enough of the abuse. This massive global outcry by millions of people sent a strong message to everyone alive today that the time has come to find a brand new system – a new social structure that is different from anything we have ever used as a so-called civilised species.

Such a new system will require great vision, great courage and great determination to free ourselves from those who choose to control us. It will require a paradigm shift in our thinking to achieve what many believe is unachievable – a utopian world of unity and abundance for all.

But more than anything else, it will require a new level of unity consciousness by a critical mass of the people of the world. Because we cannot solve our problems if we continue to approach them from the same level of consciousness we currently embrace. So, let us become the seeds of consciousness and create that utopia that we yearn for and that we are born to experience. In Africa, we call it UBUNTU.

UBUNTU Contributionism

A new social structure for a new world.

A blueprint for human prosperity.

Where everyone contributes their natural talents or acquired skills for the greater benefit of all in their community.

The beauty of Contributionism lies in its simplicity. But because the system is so simple, every bone in our indoctrinated bodies instantly rebels against it, and we tell ourselves that it cannot be so simple – otherwise it would have already been done.

Six thousand years of enslavement by money is tough to erase in a flash. So keep your mind completely open – not just half open – and be prepared to entertain new ideas that are completely alien to a sick capitalist society, filled with poisoned minds and poisoned bodies that desperately need to find a cure.

OUR INALIENABLE RIGHTS – HUMAN RIGHTS

We, the people, have appointed the politicians as our servants to do the best they can for us, the people. But the moment that they are elected they seem to forget this and start doing as they please, not delivering to the people what the people want. There are always a million excuses. The net result is that the government is not serving the people. The politicians and the government have failed us dramatically on every level. They have betrayed the dreams of millions who include elders of integrity like Ghandi, Nelson Mandela, Martin Luther King, William Wallace, John Lennon and many others, who dedicated their lives to our freedom.

We are all born free on this planet, as living breathing human beings, with inalienable rights that nobody may take from us. And yet, through a great deception, this is not the case. All our rights are desecrated from the moment our umbilical cord is cut and we take our very first breath. I have to draw a distinction between rights of human beings, and the rights of fictional entities that are created by birth certificates, and represented by identity documents and other official papers that lead people to believe they are a name on a piece of paper or an ID number. Such entities are known as Juristic Persons in legal terms and represent pieces of paper – not flesh and blood human beings.

This is a very important concept to understand. Look at your birth certificate and ask yourself these questions:

1. Were you old enough to consent to the document?
2. Did you sign the document?
3. Whose company name appears on the document?
4. Which company official signed the document?
5. Who gave the company permission to create a certificate of ownership over you at your birth? (Remember that a certificate indicates ownership and somebody now claims to have ownership over you through your birth certificate.)

So let me remind you of our most important inalienable rights – your god-given rights.

- **We are all born free as living breathing human beings of flesh and blood and infinite soul with inalienable rights**
- **Freedom is not our right, it is a gift from the Divine Creator to each and every one of us, which nobody may violate or challenge in any way.**
- **No one, no government, and no corporation may restrict our individual freedom in any way.**

Within these rights there is a set of three common law principles that have stood the test of time and continue to present a foundation of integrity and honour among humanity. These are simply called Common Law.

1) **Do not kill or harm others**
2) **Do not steal or take what is not yours**
3) **Conduct yourself honourably in all that you do and say**

These common law principles are the foundation for all other laws and guidelines we choose to create for our society. If we abide by these, the following rights become enshrined in our culture and allow every human being to live freely or as a part of a community of their choice. The planet and its riches are there to be used by everyone, not for personal gain or the exploitation of others, but for the benefit of everyone in every community and the benefit of all of humanity.

1. The country is there for its people
2. The land is there for its people
3. The water is there for the people
4. The forests are there for the people
5. The rivers and lakes are there for the people
6. The gold, the platinum, diamonds, chrome, copper, iron, uranium, tin, aluminium, and all other minerals in the ground are there for the people
7. The air and the airwaves are there for the people
8. Everything that grows on the land is there for the people
9. The beaches, the mountains and the skies above are there for the people
10. The animals do not belong to us or anyone else, they belong to the planet and we are their custodians and protectors
11. Knowledge and wisdom is to be shared by those who attain it with everyone – so that everyone can benefit from the collective wisdom.

These things do not belong to the politicians, the governments, or any corporation that has unlawfully laid claim to it.

THE GOVERNMENT HAS STOLEN THE COUNTRY FROM ITS PEOPLE

The governments and corporations have laid claim to our countries, our lands, our water, our minerals, our plants and animals, the airwaves, the coastlines and oceans, and they continue to make new laws, almost every day, that grant them more and more control over everything imaginable.

The only conclusion we can reach from the current situation is that the government and the large corporations have stolen the country (land) from its people. All done quietly through lies and deception, feeding on the ignorance and good nature of the people. It is up to us, the people, to take it back.

It is up to us to stop the rapid destruction of our beautiful planet.

The Earth is our MOTHER – we are only here because of her presence against the infinite backdrop of creation. The soil is sacred, the water is sacred and the air is sacred. And therefore we must honour her and protect her against all harm and in so doing, we honour the creator and creation itself.

Here is a more detailed breakdown of our rights that have been stolen. Remember that we have appointed the politicians and the government as our servants – to do the best they can for us, the people – not to take the role of a slave master to enrich themselves and the corporations that keep them in power.

The country belongs to its people.

If this is the case, why is the government making new laws every week that are not for the benefit of the people, without consulting the people? Why is it that the people seem to have no recourse against the abuse of the government and the powerful multinational corporations that have taken our country as their own? Why do the laws of the country not benefit the people but the corporations? Why are the courts actually just instruments to enforce the agenda of the government and corporations? Why did a Johannesburg High Court Judge tell me, "This is not a people's court."

The land belongs to its people.

If this is the case, why is there so much poverty and homelessness? Why are people being evicted from their homes by instruments of the government like the sheriffs and police, who should be protecting and serving the people? How can the government allow the land of the people to be sold to foreign or multinational corporations with no interest to benefit the people but instead use the people as cheap labour for their continued enrichment? Why does the government own so much land, yet denies the people access to land that belongs to the people?

The water belongs to the people.

Why are people paying for water? How can the government claim the rights to the water of our land and force us to pay for it? How can the government sell our water rights to multinational corporations? Why is the government allowing mining corporations to poison our water? Why are all our dams and rivers not producing electricity? There is enough energy in our dams and rivers to provide all of us with FREE electricity. The government and suppliers of electricity like ESKOM, have been lying to the people to keep us enslaved and dependent on them for the supply of electricity. Just so they can keep charging us exorbitant fees for something that belongs to the people.

The forests belongs to the people.
How can the government sell or rent our land to SAPPI and MONDI and other corporations who use the people as slave labour to grow trees and develop other industries on OUR land – without the people getting any reward from any of these activities? While SA is one of the largest forestry areas in the world, we cannot afford wood for housing and wooden furniture. We cannot afford the paper for our children in school – while we have some of the largest paper mills in the world. There is enough wood in SA for everyone to have a beautiful home. The government has failed us dramatically and continues to do so more and more as the years roll by.

The rivers, lakes and the oceans belong to the people.
Why have fishermen been denied the right to fish for their families or communities, while large foreign fishing trawlers are given all the rights they need to deplete our coastlines of fish? All rights must immediately revert to all coastal communities to fish for themselves and provide for themselves and other communities with food from the sea. This must be accompanied by breeding, farming and repopulating efforts to re-energise the oceans around our country to keep them healthy and in harmony with us. All rivers must be monitored and used for the benefit of the communities to also breed fish and other produce attainable by correctly managing our water resources. We will use the oceans and rivers for travelling and transporting whatever we need to serve the people.

The gold, the platinum, chrome, copper, iron, uranium, tin, aluminium, and all other minerals in the ground belong to the people.
If this is the case, why is there so much poverty in our land? For several hundred years the mineral wealth of South Africa has been stolen by our government. They have granted large multinational corporations the rights to the minerals in our ground. They use the people of the land as their slaves and as cheap labour, rewarding us with worthless fiat paper money. The people have been displaced,

used, abused, and exploited for as long as they are needed and then discarded like worthless rubbish, once the needs of the mining companies have been met. This goes on today more than ever before. The greedy multinational corporations are mining and destroying our beautiful land more than ever before. None of this immense wealth is seen by the people – it all goes into the coffers of the corporations to strengthen their grip on controlling the mining operations. This cannot be allowed to continue.

The coal belongs to the people.
If the coal belongs to the people, why are we paying for electricity and why are we paying for petrol created by SASOL? South Africa is the fifth largest coal exporter on this planet – what do the people get in return? The rights to our coal have been given to multinational corporations to export for their own gain and profit, while most ordinary South Africans can hardly afford the price of electricity and petrol.

The diamonds belong to the people
Why have large parts of the country been closed off to us, the people? We are denied access to these restricted ZONES because of the sheer abundance of diamonds on the ground. Why is this so, if the diamonds belong to the people? People who are desperate to survive are being killed in illegal diamond trade because all the rights to mine and trade in diamonds are fiercely guarded by a few families. It is a well kept secret that diamonds are superconductors that are used in advanced technology and the generation of free energy. Our scientists must be given all the support they need from the people and the wealth of the country to develop these energies, using the diamonds that belong to the people, and also in many other applications that have been kept secret from the people.

Everything that grows on the land belongs to the people.
Why are certain plants that are part of the divine creation being banned by our governments, while others that are deadly and poisonous are of no concern to them? How dare they suggest that GOD makes mistakes. Why are traditional healers being marginalised and many of the plants they have used for thousands of years are being banned? It is clear that the government has a hidden agenda beyond common logic and contrary to the will of the people. Why are

*natural herbs and treatments being prohibited in favour of dangerous
drugs created in laboratories by international pharmaceutical
corporations?*

The skies above and the airwaves belong to the people.
*Why are people prevented from starting their own radio and TV
stations? Why has the government claimed the right to restrict
the use of radio waves and given these rights to a handful of
powerful multinational corporations that use them predominantly
to disseminate disinformation with no intention to benefit the
people? These things do not belong to the government and are not
the exclusive property of a few corporations. Broadcasting and
telecommunication frequencies are part of mother nature, like air, and
should be free for all to use for the benefit of the people.*

**The wildlife, animals and plants do not belong to us or anyone
else, they belong to the planet and we are their custodians and
protectors.**
*Why have wild animals been hunted into oblivion from our lands?
Why have we been denied access to the lands where wild animals
roam? Why have large parts of the land been turned into national
parks where people may not enter without paying or a permit? Why
are many of these pristine parts being sold to mining corporations,
to create dams and other activities that only benefit the governments
and their corporations? The land belongs to the people. The ordinary
people who struggle to survive cannot afford to visit the game parks
and are in essence restricted from interacting with the indigenous
animals of our land. The management of our animals and nature parks
needs to be returned to the people who care about the land and the
animals that live on it.*

Let me repeat this statement again because it really needs to sink in.
"The government has stolen the country (land) from its people."
How can we prove this?

OUR COUNTRIES ARE REGISTERED AS CORPORATIONS

All of this only begins to truly sink in and make sense once we see that our countries are registered as corporations. A quick search on the US Securities & Exchange website provides the evidence. And what do listed corporations do? They trade their assets, including their citizens, on the global stock markets. But it does not stop there. The registrations of companies extend into states, provinces, cities, government departments, and even the governments themselves that are registered as corporations. The whole world around us and everything we hold dear, has been tuned into corporate assets, owned and controlled by some corporation somewhere – ultimately controlled by the elite banking families whose royal bloodlines go back thousands of years.

Below is an extract from the U.S. Securities & Exchange website showing South Africa listed among some of the other large corporations that are well known to the people. Nobody would have expected to find their country listed as a company next to Old Mutual, Anglo American or Standard Bank. Yet there it is.

Home | Latest Filings | Previous Page

Search the Next-Generation EDGAR System
EDGAR Search Results

Companies with names matching "SOUTH AFRICA"

Click on CIK to view company filings
Items 1 - 12

CIK	**Company**	**State/Country**

0000801973	ANGLO AMERICAN PLC /FI	T3
	formerly: ANGLO AMERICAN CORP OF	
	SOUTH AFRICA LTD /FI (filings through	
	2004-03-22)	
0001254425	GOVERNMENT OF THE REPUBLIC OF	
	SOUTH AFRICA	
0001076855	LARSON JUHL SOUTH AFRICA LLC	GA
0000919230	LEHMAN BROTHERS SOUTH AFRICA	NY
	GROWTH FUND INC	
0000917715	NEW SOUTH AFRICA FUND INC	NJ
0001003161	OLD MUTUAL EQUITY GROWTH	D0
	ASSETS SOUTH AFRICA FUND	
0001003162	OLD MUTUAL SOUTH AFRICA	D0
	EQUITY TRUST	
0000932419	REPUBLIC OF SOUTH AFRICA	DC
	SIC: 8888 - FOREIGN GOVERNMENTS	
	formerly: SOUTH AFRICA REPUBLIC	
	OF (filings through 2002-04-10)	
0001561694	Sibanye Gold Ltd	T3
	SIC: 1040 - GOLD & SILVER ORES	
	formerly: GFI Mining South Africa	
	(Proprietary) Ltd (filings through 2012-11-	
	08)	
0001003390	SILVERSTAR HOLDINGS LTD	FL
	SIC: 7372 - SERVICES-PREPACKAGED	
	SOFTWARE	
	formerly: FIRST SOUTH AFRICA CORP	
	LTD (filings through 1999-05-17)	
	LEISUREPLANET HOLDINGS LTD	
	(filings through 2001-02-15)	
0000928785	STANDARD BANK OF SOUTH AFRICA	T3
	LTD	
0001442850	TCBY OF SOUTH AFRICA, INC.	X1

http://www.sec.gov/cgi-bin/browse-edgar

Home | Search the Next-Generation EDGAR System | Previous Page
Modified 03/14/2012

Take note that the names of the corporations are written in capital
letters. This is also the case on your birth certificate, driver's licence,
passport, ID document and other official documents. All official
correspondence we receive, displays our names in capitals, indicating

that it is addressed to the corporation called MICHAEL TELLINGER. Official tombstones follow the same rules. This is not by accident, but because of what I highlighted before, regarding newborn babies becoming 'juristic persons' and 'legal fictions' the moment a birth certificate is signed. The government and all their corporate subsidiaries that operate under the authority of the government, see people as little corporations or legal fictions, or juristic persons or even natural persons, and specifically property, under the control and the authority of the government.

This notion is highlighted in the British *Cestui Que Vie Trust Act* of 1666. The Act describes the set-up of a trust where people who are lost at sea, would have to prove that they are not dead within seven years. However, it includes the notion that it's not just for those people who are lost at sea, but for *all people*. Therefore, *all people* are declared legally dead until proven otherwise. This is why the system believes we are dead, and does not "see" living people, it only sees administrators (trustees) of a trust. And any administrator (trustee) who receives benefits from a trust, must pay a fee or tax for using such a benefit. This is why we pay taxes, etc. because our "income" does not come to *us*, it comes into the trust which we are administering. That trust is our name in capital letters, represented by a special certificate – our birth certificate.

A good example of this can be seen in the movie *Castaway*, where Tom Hanks plays a guy who is stranded on an island for 5 years. After being rescued and returning to his home town, his friends rally around him with excitement and disbelief that he could have survived for so long on his own. In his absence however, he was declared dead – so that the government could benefit from his estate. In a strange scene that has no real impact on the movie other than exposing our status as fictional entities, one of his friends excitedly turns to Tom saying, *"tomorrow we bring you back to life"*.

Clearly Tom is not dead – he is standing and conversing with his friends, and yet they have to bring his "straw man" or "juristic person" back to life. This is so that Tom could carry on paying taxes and be controlled by the state. If he continued to walk around while being declared dead, the state would have no control over his flesh and blood human being body and could not benefit from him in any way.

When you are asked to confirm your ID number by an official of the government or bank, you unwittingly admit that you are that special piece of paper which is marked by that ID number. You are acting on behalf of the legal fiction, representing your legal entity and not standing your ground as a living breathing human being, which is not the same thing as a piece of paper. More about this under *The Laws That Enslave Us* chapter.

Below is the front page of the annual report for the corporation called REPUBLIC OF SOUTH AFRICA from the same U.S. Securities & Exchange website, dated 9 January 2012.

FORM 18-K/A

For Foreign Governments and Political Subdivisions Thereof
SECURITIES AND EXCHANGE COMMISSION

Washington, D.C. 20549

ANNUAL REPORT OF
REPUBLIC OF SOUTH AFRICA

(Name of Registrant)

Date of end of last fiscal year: March 31, 2011

SECURITIES REGISTERED*

(As of the close of the fiscal year)

Title of Issue	Amounts as to which registration is effective	Names of exchanges on which registered
N/A	N/A	N/A

Name and address of person authorized to receive notices

and communications from the Securities and Exchange Commission:

Jeffrey C. Cohen, Esq.

Linklaters LLP

1345 Avenue of the Americas

New York, NY 10105

*   The Registrant is filing this annual report on a voluntary basis.

SIGNATURE

Pursuant to the requirements of the Securities Exchange Act of 1934, the Registrant, Republic of South Africa, has duly caused this amendment to the annual report to be signed on its behalf by the undersigned, thereunto duly authorized, in Pretoria, South

Africa, on the 9th day of January 2012.

REPUBLIC OF SOUTH AFRICA

By /s/ Monale Ratsoma

Monale Ratsoma

Chief Director: Liability Management
National Treasury
Republic of South Africa

We need to ask who the hell Jeffrey C. Cohen is, and what influence he holds over the people of South Africa. And why does South Africa submit annual reports to a law firm called Linklaters LLP, in New York City? This has profound implications on the rights of the people and their relationship to the 'corporation' called REPUBLIC OF SOUTH AFRICA.

ALMOST ALL COUNTRIES ARE REGISTERED AS CORPORATIONS

Here is a list of some more countries registered as corporations on the US Securities & Exchange Commission. Some are cleverly listed on other stock exchanges and their listings are hidden from easy access. All this has happened without our knowledge or consent and since we appoint our leaders to do the best for us as the people, we must reach the conclusion that there is malicious intent at play.

According to *Black's Law Dictionary*, the definition of a citizen is a person who pledges their allegiance to the state in exchange for benefits and privileges. Do you even know that by declaring yourself "a citizen" you subjugate all your rights to the state (or the corporation) in exchange for a few benefits and privileges disguised as rights? Did you even bother to look up what the legal definition of a citizen actually is?

If our countries are corporations, it makes the people their stock and property. Our birth certificates are the stock certificates that are being traded on the stock markets. I urge you to verify all this information to feel assured of the great deception. It is time to snap out of our hypnotic state of ignorance and share this with everyone. The whole world is enslaved by those who run the corporations – the elite banking families.

How are we going to explain this to our children?

We have ignorantly and willingly sold them into slavery. They are property of the corporations and absolute slaves to the system - just like we are – without any future, unless we do something about it. Only we can stop the continued chain of enslavement.

"No one is more enslaved than those who believe they are free." Goethe

SOME MORE COUNTRIES REGISTERED AS CORPORATIONS

EDGAR Search Results - Company Search »
Companies for SIC 8888 - FOREIGN GOVERNMENTS
Click on CIK to view company filings
Items 1 – 40 (Edited)

CIK	Company	State/Country
0001016472	CITY OF NAPLES	DE
0001109609	DEVELOPMENT BANK OF JAPAN INC. formerly: DEVELOPMENT BANK OF JAPAN (filings through 2008-09-29)	M0
0000033745	EUROPEAN INVESTMENT BANK	N4
0000276328	EXPORT DEVELOPMENT CANADA/CN formerly: EXPORT DEVELOPMENT CORP (filings through 2002-06-07)	DC
0000873463	EXPORT IMPORT BANK OF KOREA	NY
0000205317	FEDERATIVE REPUBLIC OF BRAZIL	D5
0000035946	FINLAND REPUBLIC OF	DC
0001556421	FMS WERTMANAGEMENT	2M
0001179453	GOVERNMENT OF BELIZE	DC
0001163395	GOVERNMENT OF JAMICA	NY
0000931106	HELLENIC REPUBLIC	NY
0000216105	HER MAJESTY THE QUEEN IN RIGHT OF NEW ZEALAND	Q2
0000889414	HUNGARY formerly: REPUBLIC OF HUNGARY (filings through 2011-11-25)	NY
0000052749	ISRAEL STATE OF	NY
0000052782	ITALY REPUBLIC OF	L6

0000053078	JAMAICA GOVERNMENT OF	L8
0000837056	JAPAN	NY
0001551322	Japan Bank for International Cooperation	M0
0000053190	JAPAN DEVELOPMENT BANK	M0
0001109604	Japan Finance Corp	
0000074615	ONTARIO PROVINCE OF	A6
0000076027	PANAMA REPUBLIC OF	DC
0000077694	PERU REPUBLIC OF	NY
0000836136	PROVINCE OF BRITISH COLUMBIA	A1
0000862406	PROVINCE OF NEW BRUNSWICK	A3
0000842639	PROVINCE OF NOVA SCOTIA	NY
0000722803	QUEBEC	A8
0000852555	QUEENSLAND TREASURY CORP	C3
0001191980	REGION OF LOMBARDY	DE
0000914021	REPUBLIC OF ARGENTINA	DC
0000019957	REPUBLIC OF CHILE formerly: CHILE REPUBLIC OF (filings through 2002-11-01)	F3
0000917142	REPUBLIC OF COLOMBIA	NY
0000873465	REPUBLIC OF KOREA	M5
0000911076	REPUBLIC OF PORTUGAL	DC
0000932419	REPUBLIC OF SOUTH AFRICA formerly: SOUTH AFRICA REPUBLIC OF (filings through 2002-04-10)	DC
0001030717	REPUBLIC OF THE PHILIPPINES	NY
0000869687	REPUBLIC OF TURKEY	NY
0000203098	SASKATCHEWAN PROVINCE OF	NY
0000225913	SWEDEN KINGDOM OF	V7
0000898608	TREASURY CORP OF VICTORIA	C3
0000101368	UNITED MEXICAN STATES	NY
0000102385	URUGUAY REPUBLIC OF	

THE WHOLE WORLD IS A GIANT CORPORATION – ENSLAVING THE IGNORANT PEOPLE

Not only are our countries registered as corporations, but so are the governments, parliaments, provinces, states and cities too. Now that the corporate veil of deception has been removed, the pattern of corruption is clearly visible. Here is an example of the *Parliament of South Africa* and *City of Cape Town*, incorporated.

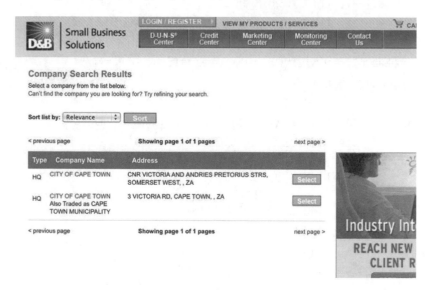

Because the GOVERNMENT OF THE REPUBLIC OF SOUTH AFRICA is also registered as a corporation, it has severe implications on everything the government does and every decision it makes. It changes the relationship between the Government and its people instantly. No longer is the government the servant of the people, but rather the manipulator of the people. It also makes the government untouchable by the people, because the laws of the corporation RSA protect the government and not the people.

So when the government claims to be the sole owner of some industry, like ESKOM, it means that it is owned by a private corporation for the benefit of the shareholders - not for the benefit of the people of the land. And so, we are continuously fooled by a slight twist of words, and we keep paying exorbitant costs for electricity and everything else the government touches – because it has to make a profit for the corporation – not to benefit the people.

All these secret dealings by the government and our president make a mockery of the South African constitution that so many of our people fought for, suffered for, and died for, so that the people could have true freedom. Our constitution declares that it is the highest law in the country and offers everyone equality and freedom and prosperity. But by reading the preamble to the constitution it becomes instantly clear that our rights have been desecrated and we have all been manipulated into subservience without realising it.

CORPORATE TAKEOVER OF THE USA, UNITED NATIONS AND THE WORLD

We have to come to terms with the fact that corporations are enemies of living breathing human beings. Their purpose is to destroy all humanness, reduce people to numbers and keep them dumbed down, happily marching to the orders of their corporate masters.

"I hope we shall crush in its birth the aristocracy of our moneyed corporations which dare already to challenge our government to a trial of strength and bid defiance to the laws of our country."

Thomas Jefferson, 3rd US president 1801-1809

Sort list by: Relevance ▾ | Sort

« Previous Page | Showing page 1 of 10 pages | Next Page »

Company Name	Address	
UNITED STATES GOVERNMENT CONGRESS OF THE UNITED STATES	4007 PARAMOUNT BLVD, LAKEWOOD, CA 907124138	Send DUNS #
UNITED STATES GOVERNMENT UNITED STATES HOLOCAU	425 13TH ST NE, WASHINGTON, DC 200026327	Send DUNS #
UNITED STATES GOVERNMENT UNITED STATES IMMIGRA	46735 US ROUTE 81, ALEXANDRIA BAY, NY 136074155	Send DUNS #
U S GOVERNMENT PLA UNITED STATES GOVERNMENT	110 S CLEVELAND ST, KERSHAW, SC 290671403	Send DUNS #
UNITED STATES GOVERNMENT OFFICES US GOVERNMENT	1015 W 2ND ST, DE WITT, AR 720422300	Send DUNS #

Besides checking the US Securities & Exchange database for registered corporations, there is another source for finding such registrations – Dunn & Bradstreet (D&B).

DUNS code numbers are assigned to corporations to track their credit ratings. It is therefore a great source for finding and tracking registered corporations in the USA and multinational corporations around the world. Below you will find the DUNS numbers for just some of the US government departments, some of the USA states and their major cities, all registered as corporations. And for those who still believe that the United Nations is a good organisation trying its best to bring unity among the nations of the world, think again. The UN is also a corporation with many corporate divisions, under the control of the banking families. These corporate code numbers can be verified by using the following link to the D&B website and typing in the required information: http://mycredit.dnb.com/search-for-duns-number/

When checking DUNS numbers for governments, you will find that they have various subsidiaries and shell corporations scattered all over the place to create confusion. A simple but effective tactic. Some of them are listed in a geographical location other than their actual territorial authority, making their operations even more suspicious. The *City of*

Chicago corporation, for example, is located in Washington, DC; while the *State of Montana* Corporation is located in Chicago, Illinois. The *State of Maine* corporation is listed with a pinch of satire as "State-O-Maine Inc." and is located in New York City. You will also find executive, legislative and judicial offices listed as corporations. The implications of this are staggering. Not only has this corporate subversion of government happened in the USA and the United Nations, but it has occurred in almost all of the nations of the world by utilising similar corporate trickery.

DUNS Numbers of The US Corporate Government And Some of Its Major Agencies

United States Government-052714196
US Department of Defence (DOD)-030421397
US Department of the Treasury-026661067
US Department of Justice (DOJ)-011669674
US Department of State-026276622
US Department of Health & Human Services (HHS)-Office of the Secretary-112463521
US Department of Education-944419592
US Department of Energy-932010320
US Department of Homeland Security-932394187
US Department of the Interior-020949010
US Department of Labor-029536183
Federal Bureau of Investigation (FBI)-878865674 ... the list continues on the D&B website.

DUNS Numbers of Some US Corporate States And Their Largest City

State of Alabama-004027553   City of Birmingham-074239450
State of Alaska-078198983   City of Fairbanks-079261830
State of Arizona-068300170   City of Phoenix-030002236
State of Arkansas-619312569   City of Little Rock-065303794
State of California-071549000   City of Los Angeles-159166271
State of Colorado-076438621   City of Denver-066985480
State of Connecticut-016167285   City of Bridgeport-156280596
State of Delaware-037802962   City of Wilmington-067393900
District of Columbia-949056860   City of Washington-073010550

<u>DUNS Numbers For The United Nations Corporation And Some of Its Major Corporate Agencies</u>
United Nations (UN)-824777304
UN Development Program (UNDP)-793511262
UN Educational, Scientific, & Cultural Organization
(UNESCO)-053317819
UN World Food Program (UNWFP)-054023952
UN International Children's Education Fund (UNICEF)-017698452
UN World Health Organization (WHO)-618736326

Ref: www.removingtheshackles.net

"I see in the near future a crisis approaching that unnerves me and causes me to tremble for the safety of my country...corporations have been enthroned and an era of corruption in high places will follow, and the money of the country will endeavor to prolong its reign by working upon the prejudices of the people until all wealth is aggregated in a few hands and the Republic is destroyed. I feel at this moment more anxiety for the safety of my country than ever before, even in the midst of war."

President Abraham Lincoln

GOVERNMENT AND BIG BUSINESS

If our governments are allowing this to go on behind our backs, they must be involved and they must be implicated in the corruption and crimes against the people. Here is a sobering diagram compiled by Larry Lessig that was published on the www.techdirt.com website, showing the corrupt relationships and revolving doors between big business and USA government. This is one of the best and quickest reference tools you will find that highlights the interference and influence held by large corporations in the USA government. And if governments are voted for, and appointed by the people, as the servants of the people, how can the people allow such interference by corporations in the running of the government?

Corporations are mere pieces of paper controlled by human beings, most of whom are ignorantly devoting their lives for the benefit of the corporation while enslaving their brothers and sisters to a life of servitude and slavery. Only people can undo this great injustice. The corporations cannot, and will not do that.

Federal Government / Big Oil

Federal Government | | **Big Oil**

Federal Government	(name)	Big Oil
Dept. of Energy (Carter)	Andrew Zausner	Dir, Government Relations (Pennzoil)
Staff: US Rep Landrieu (D)	Kevin Avery	Dir, Federal Gov't Affairs (Marathon)
Staff: US Rep Landrieu (D)	Jason Schendle	Washington Rep (API)
Staff: Sen Rockefeller (D) & Biden (D)	William Ichord	VP, Int'l Gov't Affairs (ConocoPhillips)
Staff: Sen Durbin (D) & Biden (D)	James E. Williams	Products Issues Manager (API)
Staff: Sen Lieberman (D)	Matt Gobush	Comm. Manager (ExxonMobil)
Staff: Sen Johnson (D)	Mark Rubin	Upstream Gen. Manager (API)
Staff: Rep Kilpatrick (D) & Boren (D)	Wendy Kirchoff	Dir, Fed Resources (IPAA)
Staff: Sen Feinstein (D)	Rachel Miller	Dir of Federal Affairs (BP America)
Staff: Rep DLipinski (D) & BLipinski (D)	Emily Olson	Lobbyist (BP America)
Dep Staff Dir, HGRC (Clinton)	Judith Blanchard	Fed Gov't Relations (Chevron)
Dir, House Ways & Means (Clinton)	Donna Steele Flynn	Tax Counsel (IPAA)
Dir, SEPWC (Clinton)	Lee Fuller	VP, Gov't Relations (IPAA)
Staff Economist SENRC (Clinton)	Shirley Neff	Economist (Shell Oil)
DA Sec, Dept. of Energy (Clinton)	Theresa Fariello	VP, Gov't Relations (ExxonMobil)
US: Energy for Science, DOE (Obama)	Steven Koonin	Chief Scientist (British Petroleum)

Federal Government / Comcast

Federal Government | | **Comcast**

Federal Government	(name)	Comcast
Staff: FCC Commissioner (Clinton)	James Coltharp	Sr. Director, Public Policy
Legal Counsel, FCC (Clinton)	Jordan Goldstein	Lobbyist
White House OPA (Clinton)	Joseph Trahern	Sr. Director, Fed. Gov't Affairs
Staff: FCC Commissioner (Clinton)	James Casserly	Comcast Attorney
Staff: Sen. Daschle (D)	Melissa Maxfield	Sr. VP, Gov't Affairs
US Representative (D)	William Gray	Lobbyist
US Representative (D)	Ron Klink	Lobbyist
Chief of Staff: Sen. Kohl (D)	Paul Bock	Lobbyist
Chief of Staff: Sen. Reid (D)	David Krone	Sr. VP, Corporate Affairs
Staff: Sen. Rockefeller (D)	Patrick Robertson	Lobbyist
Staff: Sen. Schumer (D)	James Flood	Lobbyist for Comcast-NBC merger
Staff: Rep. Tauzin (D)	Jessica Marventano	Sr. Director, Policy Counsel
Staff: Rep. Schiff (D)	Phil Tahtakran	Lobbyist
FCC Commissioner (Bush, Obama)	Meredith Baker	Sr. VP, Gov't Affairs
FCC Advisory Comm. (Obama)	Rudy Brioche	Sr. Dir, External Affairs/Public Policy
Obama fundraiser	David Cohen*	Executive VP, Gov't Affairs

*Cohen is a prominent, well-connected Democrat, but
has held no official position in the federal government.

Federal & State Government / GE

Federal & State Government | | **GE**

Federal & State Government	(name)	GE
Asst Secretary, HEW (Carter)	Benjamin Heineman	Senior VP, General Counsel
DOJ EES (Carter, Reagan)	Stephen Ramsey	VP, Corporate Envir Programs
DOJ EES (Reagan)	David Buente Jr.	GE Counsel, Sidley Austin
EPA Superfund Attorney	Samuel Gutter	GE Counsel, Sidley Austin
Mass Dept of Envir Protection	Ralph Child	GE Counsel, Mintz Levin
NY Dept of Envir Conservation	Gary Sheffer	GE Spokesman
US Senator (D)	Tom Daschle	Advisor, GE HealthyMagination
Chief of Staff, Max Baucus (D)	Peter Prowitt	Gov't Relations Team Leader
Dir OLA of the SEC (Clinton)	Kathryn Fulton	Mgr, Government Relations
Dep Admin, FRA (Clinton)	Donald Itzkoff	Executive Counsel
Office of Mgmt & Budget (Clinton)	Joshua Raymond	Sr Manager, Government Relations
Dep Secretary of Commerce (Obama)	Dennis Hightower	VP/General Manager
Assistant Attorney General (Obama)	Ignacia Moreno	Atty, Corp Environmental Programs
Chairman, CJC (Obama)	Jeffrey Immelt	CEO

Federal Government / Goldman Sachs

Federal Government		Goldman Sachs
Treasury Sec (Clinton)	Robert Rubin	Co-COO, Co-Chairman
US Senator (D)	John Corzine	CEO
Treasury Sec (Bush)	Henry Paulson	CEO
Chief of Staff (Obama)	Rahm Emanuel	Contract Employee
Under Sec of State (Obama)	Robert Hormats	Vice Chairman, GS Int'l
Chairman, FIAB (Obama)	Stephen Friedman	Co-COO, Chairman
Dep Director, NEC (Obama)	Diana Farrell	Financial Analyst
Ambassador/Germany (Obama)	Philip Murphy	Sr Director (Frankfurt)
Chief of Staff, Treasury (Obama)	Mark Patterson	Goldman Sachs Lobbyist
COO, SEC Enforcement (Obama)	Adam Storch	VP, Business Intelligence
White House staff (Obama)	Alexander Lasry	Analyst, Gov Affairs
White House staff (Obama)	Sonal Shah	VP, Environmental Policy
White House counsel (Obama)	Gregory Craig	Chief Counsel, defending SEC suit
Under Sec of Treasury (Clinton), Chairman, CFTC (Obama)	Gary Gensler	Co-Head of Finance

Federal Government / Media

Federal Government		Media
Staff; US Rep Dingell (D)	John Orlando	Exec VP, Gov't Relations (NAB)
Chief of Staff; US Rep Kennedy (D)	Sean Richardson	Assoc. Producer (CBS News)
Comm. Dir: US Rep Moran (D)	Don Drummond	Reporter (Washington Times)
Staff: Sen Conrad (D)	Chris Thorne	Correspondent (AP)
US Senator (D)	Evan Bayh	Contributor (Fox News)
US Senator (R)	Rick Santorum	Contributor (Fox News)
White House Press Sec (Clinton)	Dee Dee Myers	Contributing Editor (Vanity Fair)
Press Sec, First Lady's Office (Clinton)	Lisa Caputo	VP, Corp. Communications (CBS)
Press Secretary (Clinton)	Joe Lockhart	Dep Assignment Mgr. (CNN)
White House Comm. Dir. (Clinton)	George Stephanopoulos	Anchor, Pol Corres. (ABC News)
Press Sec, VP Gore (D)	Ginny Terzano	News Researcher (CBS News)
Dep Dir OPA, DOJ (Clinton)	Julie Anbender	Chief of Staff (PBS)
Commissioner, FCC (Bush, Obama)	Meredith Baker	Sr VP, Gov't Affairs (Comcast-NBC)
Sr Advisor, Office of President (Obama)	David Axelrod	City Hall Bur Chief (Chicago Tribune)
DAS, Dept of Education (Obama)	Massie Ritsch	Staff Writer (LA Times)
Dep Chief CGAB, FCC (Obama)	Yul Kwon	Corres. (CNN); Host (PBS)

Federal Government / Monsanto

Federal Government		Monsanto
US Congressman (D)	Toby Moffett	Monsanto Consultant
US Senator (D)	Dennis DeConcini	Monsanto Legal Counsel
Dep Dir FDA, HFS (Bush Sr, Clinton)	Margaret Miller	Chemical Lab Supervisor
White House Senior Staff (Clinton)	Marcia Hale	Director, Int'l Government Affairs
Sec of Commerce (Clinton)	Mickey Kantor	Board Member
WH-Appt to CSA, Gore's SDR (Clinton)	Virginia Weldon	VP, Public Policy
White House Communications (Clinton)	Josh King	Director, Int'l Government Affairs
Gore's Chief Dom Policy Adv (Clinton)	David Beier	VP, Government & Public Affairs
WH-Appointed Consumer Adv (Clinton)	Carol Tucker-Foreman	Monsanto Lobbyist
Deputy Admin EPA (Clinton, Bush)	Linda Fisher	VP, Government & Public Affairs
USDA, EPA (Clinton, Bush, Obama)	Lidia Watrud	Manager, New Technologies
Dep Commissioner FDA (Obama)	Michael Taylor	VP, Public Policy
US Sen (D), Sec of State (Obama)	Hillary Clinton	Rose Law Firm, Monsanto Counsel
Dir, USDA NIFA (Obama)	Roger Beachy	Director, Monsanto Danforth Center
Ag Negotiator Trade Rep (Obama)	Islam Siddiqui	Monsanto Lobbyist

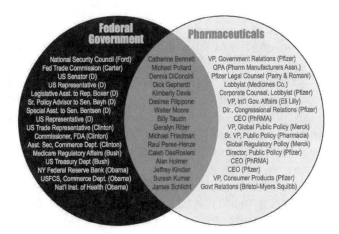

QUESTIONS TO THE PRESIDENTS

In the light of these lies and deceptions, the following questions need urgent answers from the respective governments. I refer to South Africa in this instance because that is where I am located, but it applies to every other country.

1) We, the people, require to view or to obtain a certified copy of the original registration document, founding statement and title deed of this corporation called the REPUBLIC OF SOUTH AFRICA.
2) Who authorised that the REPUBLIC OF SOUTH AFRICA was to be registered as such and why?
3) Who is the CEO of this corporation?
4) Who is the accounting officer and what financial statement does it produce?
5) What are the assets of this corporation?
6) Are these assets traded by this corporation – if so, how and where are they traded?
7) Who is accountable for trading these assets?
8) Who are the shareholders of the corporation and how are they appointed?
9) When and how are dividends distributed to the shareholders?
10) What is the relationship of the people of South Africa to this corporation called the REPUBLIC OF SOUTH AFRICA.
11) Is there any agreement between the people and/or citizens of South Africa and the REPUBLIC OF SOUTH AFRICA? If so, where are those agreements and when were they entered into?

12) Do the people of South Africa have any obligations to this corporation, and if so do they have the right to renounce such obligation?
13) Since our BILL OF RIGHTS and our Constitution, as well as the United Nations Declaration of Human Rights strictly forbid any form of slavery or forced servitude, what rights do the people who live in the land referred to as South Africa have, to cut all their ties and any responsibility to this corporation that they did not even know existed?
14) What is the relationship between this corporation called REPUBLIC OF SOUTH AFRICA and the GOVERNMENT OF THE REPUBLIC OF SOUTH AFRICA, another listed corporation?

THERE IS NO JUSTICE FOR THE PEOPLE

Every week our government makes new laws that are implemented and upheld by the courts and judges of South Africa. We know nothing about these laws, how they are made, why they are made or that they have even been passed. Because the government very conveniently prints the required notices in a paper called "The Government Gazette".

This is an arbitrary government publication that is published every week, but cannot be obtained by the man on the street from a regular news stand. It is only available from the Government Printer that is not easy to find and when you do eventually find them, they may be out of stock of the publication – as was the case on more than one occasion in my experience. This is how the government sneaks in new laws, acts and bills, that the people never really hear about until it is too late.

The word "act" speaks for itself. It is an act, played out on a stage. The stage is the court room where mostly men (and a few women) dress in costumes and robes, bowing and praying to each other for something called "justice," which itself is represented by a statue of a blind woman holding scales that are usually out of balance. When ordinary people inadvertently step onto that stage, they are considered willing volunteers, and the illusion of almighty falseness comes crashing down upon them in an epic tragedy.

Every week thousands of people lose their homes, cars and other property when judgements are granted against them without them ever appearing in court, in front of a judge, to argue their case. In the majority of these cases the people are either unaware of the action against them or they simply cannot afford legal advice. Those among us ordinary people who have had some experience with the courts will know that legal representation is so outrageously expensive that most give up without even trying.

And so, without blinking an eye, the judges and courts destroy the lives of thousands of people every week, in a few seconds without as much as a word in their defence. Those few who are in court to witness their own downfall are required by courtesy to thank the judge and bow to him. Oh how they must be laughing at the ignorant people who do not know how to assert their human rights.

Our youth have been betrayed. Their future and their country has been stolen by multinational corporations and unlawful leaders who have turned our children into their slaves.

THE LAW AND ITS CONNECTION TO MONEY

Now that we know that our country is a corporation it has a profound effect on the laws that are made to govern us. Our laws have nothing to do with HUMAN RIGHTS. The laws that enslave us were created to serve the corporations and our government that serves them. The people have no access to justice. Only those with power and money have access to the courts – including our Constitutional Court. But unfortunately, my own experience has shown me that our *Bill of Rights* is not worth the paper it is written on.

I have had to learn this the hard way and acquired loads of experience in these matters since November 2010, when I launched my first defence against the banks regarding my unlawful home loan. Together with a handful of friends who were sharing information with me, I had to educate myself about the procedures of the High Courts in South Africa to be able to draft the legal papers, serve them and follow the paper trail all the way to representing myself in court. I did this not for myself but for all the millions of people who yearn for justice but never receive it.

It took a lot of time and frustration to follow draconian rules that seem absolutely alien to human beings, coming face to face with lawyers, advocates and judges in black robes that speak a different language and follow rituals that are foreign to ordinary people. If I had used a lawyer or advocate it would have cost me well over one million rand or about US$ 130,000 to date – but the game goes on. Because I did this on my own it only cost my time, petrol, paper, frustration, nerves, public credibility, because the media tends to paint such people as "trying to wangle their way out of debt" and it prevented me from getting on with my own life, because once you get caught up in this legal merry-go-round of deception, it completely consumes your life.

It therefore took me two years longer to finish this book – but, it was all perfectly planned because without all that experience to witness the injustice for myself, I could not have raised the strong sentiments that I do. What this all amounts to is that ordinary people who have 8 to 5 jobs, (that's the normal 9-5 plus interest) who cannot afford the time to do all this, and who are timid or shy and cannot stand up for themselves in such an intimidating environment, could never afford a lawyer to act on their behalf. Because those who work in this system are experts in postponing, extending, avoiding, raising exceptions and creating huge court costs for the people, that most of us eventually fold under the financial pressure.

It is all about the money every step of the way in the courts. If you do not have bottomless pockets like the banks, you cannot get justice.

Everything in the courtroom is about money. You have probably heard that a judge sits on the "bench." The word *bench* is derived from the Italian word *Banka,* because in the market places of Rome, the goldsmiths (who back in Roman times were also the bankers) would work from a bench, as they do to this very day. Ironically this is where the word "bank" comes from, which means that the judge "acts" for "the bank." Interestingly, if a banker / goldsmith was caught cheating, his bench the would be smashed in the market square, and he would be known as *bankrupt* .

Contrary to what people realise, being a bank simply means that your books must be balanced. This is all about debits and credits, which is why, in my court hearing, the judge said very clearly "I am just trying to work out if this guy owes you money or not."

In the US, the Judges are known as "your honour." This has nothing to do with integrity. The word "honour" is used as the antithesis to "dishonour" which is the state when your books are not balanced. Honour simply means that "everything is in balance." Why do you think that the patron goddess holds a scale in her hands – they are scales of justice? Scales are used to balance gold and precious metals formally used as money. So let me repeat this – Everything in the court room is all about money – NOT JUSTICE.

We are told that we have an independent judiciary. This is a blatant lie that has escaped the people because the people just do not know the finer details of the deception. The president appoints the Chief Justice, the Minister of Justice, all the Judge Presidents and the high court Judges. The president has the final word and ultimate control over the judiciary and those appointed to serve on it. The judges and state prosecutors and all other people affiliated to the judiciary are paid by the government. This means that the government can hire and fire them at will if they are unhappy with their performance.

This is what is called an "independent" judiciary.

It should be very clear that the judiciary is far from independent and that the 'corporation' called REPUBLIC OF SOUTH AFRICA and its CEO are in charge of the judiciary. For now we have to assume that the CEO/leader of this corporation is the president, but future investigations may reveal that the president has a board of international directors who are actually in charge of the corporation.

According to Judge David Wynn-Miller, the people that are really pulling the strings are the Postmaster Generals in each nation, and their connection to the *Universal Postal Union.* Historically, two things always happened when new territory was colonised and "settled" by the crown:

1) A flag was planted and 2) A post office was erected. Every military force has a post office and all "cargo" used in commerce must be registered using mail, with a stamp. The connection between law, commerce, banking, courts, government and the "post office" is startling. Co-incidentally, the South African government has just fired their commercial bank, First National Bank, and replaced it with a new bank. Incredibly, their new bank is POSTBANK which is a division of the Post office. Very few South Africans even know the post office has a bank, which is why the deception continues to deepen.

We should not be surprised to see the names of the global banking elite as the chairmen and the executive directors of all the boards that control the corporations that are registered in the names of every country in the world.

CORPORATIONS CANNOT ENFORCE THEIR RULES ON PEOPLE

Because the government is a registered corporation, the laws that they create only really apply to those who work for the corporation or who swear allegiance to the corporation. I trust that this is really clear to you – if not – here is an example.

If you work for KFC you have to follow their code of conduct and abide by their rules. If you do NOT work for KFC they have no right to impose or enforce their laws on you. They have no right to drag you into court and accuse you of not abiding by KFC laws and therefore find you guilty and slap a fine on you or possibly even send you to jail. This would seem completely ludicrous. And yet, this is exactly what happens with the people of the land and the 'corporations' that impose their rules and regulations on the people.

Here is another way to describe how we have been fooled by those who control the supply of money. Imagine that you work for Vodafone. You hear that Vodafone is bankrupt and they can't afford to pay you in real money anymore (real money is defined as gold or silver by the way). So they offer to pay you in *airtime*, which is really their own currency. You agree to this because it's better than nothing. So now you are subject to the same laws of the corporation but you have also agreed to accept the currency of that corporation in exchange for your labour. Because Vodafone print as much airtime as the like, they control your every move. Because your work for a corporation, you are subject to its security features – eye scanners when you walk in the door, fingerprint ID, validation of your past, monitoring of all technology, etc. Imagine the world as one big Vodafone where all money is airtime printed by them, and you begin to realise just how cleverly simple it all is.

Now Imagine that the general staff at Vodafone don't like the way the airtime is being handed out because the guys at the top get most of it. So you all agree to hire an external management consultant like Andersen Consulting to manage the system for you. These guys work like a central bank. Now honestly, do you really think that these management consultants are going to implement a system that isn't weighted in favour of the Vodafone directors?

And so, the laws that are made every week by the government should not apply to the people, unless they work for the government or are the property of the government. Most of us believe that we are

NOT property of the government – we believe that we are free – we believe that the government works for us – well, we may have to reconsider our thinking.

By pledging allegiance to your country or your government, you pledge allegiance to the corporation and the laws they make. This is why they maintain the right to enforce the 'law of the land' on the people.

Each time someone is identified using a legal name and birth date combination or ID Number, they are consenting to the jurisdiction of the corporation called the REPUBLIC OF SOUTH AFRICA – or whatever country they reside in.

In general, the only people who are sworn to oaths and pledges of allegiance to their country are those who join the police force, air force, military or other government agency. The rest of the people are lead to believe that they are citizens of the country they were born in. Well, let me ask you two questions. Firstly, *are you a citizen of your country?* Most people would answer "yes." Now let me ask you a second question: *What is the definition of a citizen?*

Most people have absolutely no idea. If you don't know what the definition of a citizen is, why the hell would you answer yes? According to *Black's Law* dictionary, a citizen is a person who pledges their allegiance to the state in exchange for benefits and privileges. Congratulations, you have just pledged your allegiance to the corporation without even realising it. Like in the military, all your natural "rights" have been stripped away, and replaced with benefits and privileges. These look like rights and sound like rights, but they are not rights. Just like in the army, your privilege of going home for the weekend or driving along the roads for free can be revoked at any time.

By implementing this seemingly harmless process the government deceives all those who serve in the army, police, navy, FBI and other government security agencies, that they are upholding the rights of the people, while in truth they enforce the laws of the corporation that enslave the people, including themselves. It is truly a spectacular deception. Without realising it, the police have been shifted from being peacekeepers, to corporate revenue collectors. Instead of fighting crime, they are now collecting taxes, traffic fines, toll fees and even assist in evicting people from their homes.

On the other hand, if you choose to renounce the corporation and extricate yourself from it, they should have no right to enforce their laws on you. It is this concept that is often referred to as the FREEMAN or SOVEREIGN principle and has been followed by a growing number of people all over the world.

It should be very clear by now that all these laws are created to make things as complex and confusing as possible for ordinary people. It's a deeply convoluted spiral of deception that has prevented the people from seeing the malicious activity of their leaders for such a long time.

QUESTIONS TO THE PRESIDENT ABOUT JUSTICE

In this light we need to ask the following questions of the minister of Justice and the President.

1. Who is the CEO of the corporation called REPUBLIC OF SOUTH AFRICA (or any other)
2. Who is the CEO of the corporation called the GOVERNMENT OF THE REPUBLIC OF SOUTH AFRICA.
3. If the president is the CEO, and the president appoints the Judiciary, it means that the Judiciary can never be called independent – because they answer to the CEO/President of the corporation. YES or NO.
4. Do the laws made by these corporations apply to anyone other than the employees, the property or subjects of the corporations who have pledged allegiance to the corporations?
5. If so, who do the laws apply to and why should they apply to those who do not work for the corporations?
6. What is the relationship of the people of South Africa to these corporations called REPUBLIC OF SOUTH AFRICA and GOVERNMENT OF THE REPUBLIC OF SOUTH AFRICA?
7. Is there any agreement between the people and/or citizens of South Africa and the REPUBLIC OF SOUTH AFRICA or GOVERNMENT OF THE REPUBLIC OF SOUTH AFRICA?
8. If so, where are those agreements and when were they entered into?
9. Do the people of South Africa have any obligations to these corporation mentioned above?
10. If so, do they have the right to resign from the corporations or renounce such obligation?

11. If and when they resign or denounce their obligation or affiliation to the corporations above, will the corporations have any further rights to enforce their laws on them?
12. If so, why, and how will the corporations enforce their laws on people who have resigned from these corporations?
13. Since the BILL OF RIGHTS and the CONSTITUTION, as well as the United Nations Declaration of Human Rights strictly forbids any form of slavery or forced servitude, what rights do the people who live on the land referred to as South Africa have, to cut all their ties and any responsibility to these corporations mentioned above, that they did not even know existed?

WE ARE ALL BORN FREE – SOVEREIGN HUMAN BEINGS – OF FLESH AND BLOOD AND INFINITE SOUL – WITH INALIENABLE RIGHTS FROM THE DIVINE CREATOR – NO ONE MAY TAKE THOSE RIGHTS AWAY OR INFRINGE ON THEM IN ANY WAY.

WHAT IS A CORPORATION?

It is an idea that was written down on paper and a bunch of people run around to enact the idea and the rules set out on that piece of paper. Corporations do not breath, they do not bleed, they do not have emotions and cannot show infinite love – only people can do that.

When the 14th Amendment was passed in the USA during 1868, an era of tyranny was unleashed. This tyranny was subtle, relentless and deadly. It appeared in the form of *The Corporation*. Ironically, the 14th Amendment itself was not intended to cause this tyranny. It was during a connected case shortly after it was signed, that a court reporter incorrectly recorded that a decision had been made regarding the legal status of a Corporation. From that day forth, despite the fact that no such decision had actually been made, a corporation was given the same rights as you and me. This detonated the nightmare that we are stuck with today.

As of 1868, a Corporation was to be treated exactly like a real human being. In fact, the legal term for it is an "artificial person". But because he? she? it? has no morals, it cannot die and has no cells or living tissue, a *Corporation* will continue to expand forever. Human beings, referred to as "consumers" continually feed this monster, nurture it and watch as it sucks the life out of everything it comes into contact with. It devours resources with no accountability and serves one purpose and one purpose only: **to maximise financial profit.**

And yet our laws uphold the rights of corporations – pieces of paper – more than they uphold the rights of living breathing human beings. Corporations are considered "persons" just like we are. The only difference is that we almost always sign contracts with them. They seldom, if ever, sign contracts with us. This places us in the position of having to do the delivering, the working, the paying and repeatedly subjugating our rights in their favour.

The tragedy is that most of these laws are written and enacted by other human beings who have no idea what they are doing. Slaves being enslaved because that is all they know. The words of a wise prophet come to mind at this moment: *"Forgive them for they know not what they do."*

If ever there was a great injustice perpetrated against all of humanity, this is it. And we have no idea that this unlawful activity has been going on for thousands of years.

The brutally inhumane practice of slavery, and the slave trade, especially in the past 500 years, is a sobering reminder of how corporations held infinitely more sway with the law than the human beings who were traded as property or chattel by those slave-trading corporations.

Slave traders were often noblemen of high standing in their societies. Many of them became incredibly wealthy and politically powerful because of their trading in human misery. This is unthinkable to most of us today. And yet, that is exactly what each one of us has become. An ignorant slave to the corporation or so-called country that we are born into – without realising it.

The saddest part of this deception is that many of us slaves are so brainwashed by our slave masters and their system that we are prepared to defend the system and even die for it. So let me remind you of these two historic statements:

"None are more enslaved than those who believe they are free".
Goethe

Morpheus: *"The Matrix is a system, Neo. That system is our enemy. But when you're inside, you look around, what do you see? Businessmen, teachers, lawyers, carpenters. The very minds of the people we are trying to save. But until we do, these people are still a part of that system and that makes them our enemy. You have to* *understand, most of these people are not ready to be unplugged. And many of them are so inured, so hopelessly dependent on the system, that they will fight to protect it." **Matrix – The movie***

- Our laws serve the corporations.
- Our laws do not serve the people.
- Corporations have more rights than living, breathing, human beings.
- We are the 99 percent
- We have appointed the government as our servant
- They are NOT serving us
- What are we going to do about it?

Let us never forget that 'modern' money was created by those with the gold and those with the slaves. They realised that they could give out more paper money than the physical gold they had stored away, and thus they printed money on demand. This money built them a cartel, an empire that continues to flourish to this day. They own the money and so they care not who makes the laws.

We need a brand new legal system that serves the people. Laws that are written by the people, for the people. Laws that put human beings first – above any 'fictional entity' or corporation – we should therefore call it *Human Law*. If we are to have any future, the youth need to be the main authors of the new laws that will guide us into a future of abundance in all areas of human endeavour. Because as it stands now, there is nothing but absolute slavery that awaits our children.

A GREAT SHIFT TOWARDS HIGHER CONSCIOUSNESS

THE NEEDS OF SOCIETY

Let us be really honest and identify the things we truly need as living breathing human beings to live in abundance on this planet. Just follow a basic logic of the most important stuff... food, water, love, friendship, clothing, shelter, fire – those are the obvious things... but let's think more freely about it and look around you where you are at the moment... what else do you see? Tables, chairs, lamps, fridges, paper, pens, books, knives, forks, technology, phones, computers, electricity, shoes, pillows, blankets, reading glasses, cars, lawnmowers, hose-pipes, basins, cupboards, batteries, cups, plates, fans, trees, chickens, cows, goats, plants, seeds, bicycles, prams, mattresses, towels, hairbrushes, book shelves, bottles, carpets, tiles, taps, hammers, nails, screws, timber, bricks, paint... the list is virtually endless.

What is NOT on this list and what we do NOT need in our lives or to survive?

MONEY! Once we get over the addiction to money and how it controls our lives, we realise that money does nothing – people do. Money is the thing that stands between people and what they need, and what they want to do. It is the hurdle to progress and the obstacle to human achievement.

Money does absolutely nothing – people do everything. People plant the seeds; grow the food; build the bridges; solve the mathematical equations; build the rockets and design free energy devices; build machines to ease our labour, make clothes and shoes, hold and comfort each other in times of need. People do everything and will continue to do so infinitely if there were no restrictions on them. People are holders of deep emotion and people are capable of infinite LOVE.

Money does nothing – it is the hurdle to all progress and the absolute tool of control and enslavement of the human race.

The space shuttle missions have been stopped not because there is no one to fly them or no one who wants to explore space, but because apparently there is not enough money. But in the same breath the Wall Street Banksters get bailed out for trillions that could have been spent on amazing projects for the benefit of humanity. The size of the global casino the bankers play in is over 1 quadrillion dollars, 20 times bigger than the GDP of the entire planet – yet there is not enough money.

Look around you at the state of disrepair in our towns and cities. Everything seems to be broken, it takes forever to get fixed or replaced, poverty and hunger everywhere... not because there are no people to deal with the problems, but because there is not enough money.

It is the main excuse and topic of debate by politicians everywhere – talking about the money and how the little bit of money that there is should be put to use to benefit the people. But somehow it is never enough to deal with our needs and our problems. Somehow the politicians can never get it right and we never quite get what we want and what we need. Money always gets in the way of our needs and progress.

But the bankers never have any problems. Even when their banks go belly up, they get bailed out – they get saved, while millions of people are left stranded and homeless and hungry with no one to save them, the bankers always get saved. I trust that by now you get the message loud and clear.

The banksters rule the world – and money is their weapon.

THE SOLUTIONS ARE SIMPLE – MONEY IS THE PROBLEM

Most of us have looked at the problems we face as humanity and many of us have come up with possible solutions to these problems. There are billions of skilled people with all the expertise necessary to solve these problems that range from the small and mundane like garbage removal and recycling, to the more scientific ideas like free energy. The fact of the matter is that the solutions to our problems are very simple.

But somehow the politicians and our governments can never get it right. When they do attempt to solve our problems it is always in some way linked to a hidden agenda that benefits someone somewhere and is not really done in full integrity to serve the people. They debate it for weeks and months behind closed doors and allocate budgets that get misappropriated, which is just a fancy word for stolen or lost, while our problems keep multiplying.

That is because politicians are not experts in solving problems, they are experts in making promises and promoting the agendas of their political parties and the bansksters that fund them.

Our scientists, engineers, farmers and ordinary people have all the answers and knowledge to solve all our problems and provide a platform for rapid advancement. Our governments and politicians do not.

If we have a food crisis, let the farmers solve it. Let the engineers deal with engineering problems and the scientists with scientific solutions. Let the teachers come up with creative ideas for learning, and water experts to provide clean energised water for everyone. Because the answers to our problems as the human race are simple – we just have to give it to people who are passionate and have the skills to do it.

But most of the great scientists or researchers work for universities, research labs or institutions that belong to large corporations, who in turn are funded by the bankers. Their research is restricted to the areas of interest that benefit the corporations and therefore we hardly ever hear about groundbreaking discoveries. What we do hear repeatedly is how "new breakthrough research has brought us yet another step closer to finding a cure for cancer" or other similar drivel. This is all cleverly constructed propaganda to keep the flame of "hope" alive amongst humanity while slaving away another day, believing that our leaders are doing the best they can for us. All major new discoveries are hidden from sight – unless they can be controlled for profit.

Scientists should not work for governments with agendas. Independently funded research institutions are the only way to make real breakthroughs that will reach the people of the world, to be converted into devices or technology or be applied in ways to benefit the people. The current system of research only serves those who keep the wool pulled firmly over our eyes.

GREAT MINDS HAVE ALWAYS OPPOSED THE MONEY MAKERS

For millennia, great minds have stood up against the abuse of humanity by money. This is not something new. The fact that we still use money in our lives is an indication how powerful the banksters have been for thousands of years.

In 48 BC, **Julius Caesar** took back from the money changers (bankers) the power to coin money and minted coins for the benefit of all people in the Roman Empire. With this new and plentiful supply of money, Caesar established many large construction projects and built great public works. Rome was healthy, Caesar was loved and the people prospered. But this is not what the money changers wanted, they wanted control of the money supply and we all know what happened to Julius Caesar – he was assassinated. We just never really understood the main reason why – he stood up to the banksters.

As with JFK, Shortly after his assassination came the demise of plentiful money in Rome, taxes increased and so did corruption. Eventually the Roman money supply was reduced by 90 percent, which resulted in the common people losing their lands and homes while the banksters prospered. It seems that history keeps repeating itself, as millions of people lose their property today while the banks keep prospering as they re-finance the new buyers, often buying the properties themselves at the auctions for a fraction of the market price, slowly but surely taking control of the whole world right under our noses.

On two occasions in France, one in around 1710 and the other 70 years later, fiat paper currency was introduced. Both results were such dismal failures and resulted in massive inflation that the banksters began confiscating people's gold and silver to stop them reverting back to the old ways. This didn't work and many people lost their heads at the guillotine. At one point, they even tried to place a price ceiling on merchants to curb inflation. This didn't work so the merchants closed their doors. Sound familiar? So here we are some 300 years later and we still do the same thing over and over again, expecting a different result.

Around 30 AD, **Jesus/Jeshua** used physical force to throw the money changers out of the temple. This was possibly the only time during his life and ministry when Jesus used physical force against anyone. When Jews came to Jerusalem to pay their temple tax, they could only pay it with a special coin, which was the half-shekel. This was a half-ounce of pure silver, about the size of a USA quarter. It was the only coin at that time which was pure silver and of assured weight, without the image of a pagan Emperor. Therefore it was the only coin acceptable to God.

Unfortunately there was a shortage of these coins and the money changers had cornered the market. They raised the price to whatever the people could bear and used the monopoly they had on these coins to make exorbitant profits, forcing the Jews to pay whatever the money changers demanded.

Jesus threw the money changers out of the temple as their actions and monopoly on these coins violated the sanctity of God's house. Apparently these money changers called for his death, days later.

St. Thomas Aquinas was born in 1225 and became the leading theologian of the Catholic Church. He became very vocal about the abuse of money and argued that the charging of interest is wrong because it applies to "double charging" – charging for both the money and the use of the money.

His views followed the teachings of Aristotle who taught that the purpose of money was to serve the members of society and to facilitate the exchange of goods needed to lead a virtuous life. Interest was contrary to reason and justice because it put an unnecessary burden on the use of money.

The truly fascinating thing is that church law during the Middle Ages in Europe forbade the charging of interest on loans and even made it a crime called, "usury".

Ref: Andrew Hitchcock; History of The Money Changers

In the year 2000, there were only seven countries without a central bank. Afghanistan, Iraq, Sudan, Libya, Cuba, North Korea and Iran. In fact, Muammar Gadaffi was planning to reintroduce the gold dinar, which is also the currency in Iraq, as a new currency for the entire region and insist that African countries be paid only in the new golden dinar currency for their oil exports. This would have been a huge psychological and financial victory for Africa, since most of the gold in the world comes from there. But this did not sit well with those who control the supply of money, their governments and their armies. The result was the undoing of Gadaffi's plan and a public execution on the news channels of the world.

The days of the economic hit men are over. A full scale military invasion of an independent country is far more profitable.

Today, in 2013, only Cuba, North Korea and Iran do not have central banks. The Cuban Embargo still stands to this day and no ship or vessel is allowed to travel from Cuba to the USA without special permission. Massive sanctions have been instituted against North Korea and we all know what is happening to Iran – it is under constant threat of invasion and full scale war.

But the most sobering statement made in more recent times was by Thomas Jefferson, one of the founding fathers of the USA, who predicted exactly what is happening today. Private banks and elite banking families have taken control of the world because they control the supply of money.

"I believe that banking institutions are more dangerous to our liberties than standing armies. If the American people ever allow private banks to control the issue of their currency, first by inflation, then by deflation, the banks and corporations that will grow up around them [the banks] will deprive the people of all property until their children wake-up homeless on the continent their fathers conquered. The issuing power should be taken from the banks and restored to the people, to whom it properly belongs." ***Thomas Jefferson***

And this is exactly where we are today. Our children are born homeless into slavery on a planet controlled by the banksters. The banksters have stolen the world from our children.

Those that control the creation and flow of money know exactly what it does to people. It is truly the incurable disease of humanity. And because we have not recognised that it is a disease we cannot heal ourselves. Only once we realise this, will we be able to identify the cure which until now has seemingly evaded us.

On the 27th of April 1961 United States President, John F. Kennedy delivered a speech which referred to the secret dealings of societies and corporations which included the Federal Reserve System and the banking elite. This is an edited extract of what he had to say.

"The very word "secrecy" is repugnant in a free and open society; and we are as a people, inherently and historically opposed to secret societies, to secret oaths and to secret proceedings... Its preparations are concealed, not published. Its mistakes are buried, not headlined. Its dissenters are silenced, not praised. No expenditure is questioned, no rumour is printed, no secret is revealed." *John Fitzgerald Kennedy*

Many people are of the opinion that this was inevitably the speech that got Kennedy assassinated. In essence, he was blowing the whistle on this secretive group of bankers and controllers of humanity, when he realised that he was not really in charge of the path to prosperity of the American people, but that a small group of powerful individuals were in absolute control.

FAMOUS & INFAMOUS QUOTES ABOUT MONEY

Lord Acton: *"The issue which has swept down the centuries and which will have to be fought sooner or later is the people versus the banks."*

John Sherman (1863, Rothschild Brothers): *"The few who could understand the system will either be so interested in its profits, or so dependent on its favours, that there will be no opposition from that class, while on the other hand, the great body of the people mentally incapable of comprehending the tremendous advantage that capital derives from the system, will bear its burdens without complaint."*

Sir Josiah Stamp: *"Banking was conceived in iniquity and was born in sin. The Bankers own the earth. Take it away from them, but leave* *them the power to create deposits, and with the flick of the pen they will create enough deposits to buy it back again. However, take it away from them, and all the great fortunes like mine will disappear and they ought to disappear, for this would be a happier and better world to live in. But, if you wish to remain the slaves of Bankers and pay the cost of your own slavery, let them continue to create deposits."*

Ralph M. Hawtrey, Secretary of the British Treasury: *"Banks lend by creating credit. (ledger-entry credit, monetized debt) They create the means of payment out of nothing."*

British Lord John Maynard Keynes: *"By this means government may secretly and unobserved, confiscate the wealth of the people, and not one man in a million will detect the theft."*

Woodrow Wilson: *"A great industrial nation is controlled by its system of credit. Our system of credit is concentrated in the hands of a few men. We have come to be one of the worst ruled, one of the most completely controlled and dominated governments in the world-- no longer a government of free opinion, no longer a government by conviction and vote of the majority, but a government by the opinion and duress of small groups of dominant men."*

Robert H. Hamphill, Atlanta Federal Reserve Bank: *"We are completely dependent on the commercial banks. Someone has to borrow every dollar we have in circulation, cash or credit. If the banks create ample synthetic money we are prosperous; if not, we starve. We are absolutely without a permanent money system.... It is the most important subject intelligent persons can investigate and reflect upon. It is so important that our present civilization may collapse unless it becomes widely understood and the defects remedied very soon."*

Modern Money Mechanics Workbook, Federal Reserve Bank of Chicago, 1975: *"Neither paper currency nor deposits have value as commodities, intrinsically, a 'dollar' bill is just a piece of paper. Deposits are merely book entries."*

Charles A. Lindbergh, Sr. – 1913: *"This [Federal Reserve Act] establishes the most gigantic trust on earth. When the President [Wilson} signs this bill, the invisible government of the monetary* *power will be legalized....the worst legislative crime of the ages is perpetrated by this banking and currency bill."*

Taken from the Civil Servants' Year Book, "The Organizer" January 1934: *"Capital must protect itself in every way...Debts must be collected and loans and mortgages foreclosed as soon as possible. When through a process of law the common people have lost their homes, they will be more tractable and more easily governed by the strong arm of the law applied by the central power of leading financiers. People without homes will not quarrel with their leaders. This is well known among our principal men now engaged in forming an imperialism of capitalism to govern the world. By dividing the people we can get them to expend their energies in fighting over questions of no importance to us except as teachers of the common herd."*

James Madison: *"History records that the money changers have used every form of abuse, intrigue, deceit, and violent means possible to maintain their control over governments by controlling money and its issuance."*

Sen. Barry Goldwater (Rep. AR): *"Most Americans have no real understanding of the operation of the international money lenders. The accounts of the Federal Reserve System have never been audited. It operates outside the control of Congress and manipulates the credit of the United States."*

President John Adams: *"All the perplexities, confusion and distress in America arise, not from defects in the Constitution or confederation, not from want of honor or virtue, so much as from downright ignorance of the nature of coin, credit and circulation."*

Henry Ford Sr: *"The youth who can solve the money question will do more for the world than all the professional soldiers of history."*

Major L.B. Angus: *"The modern banking system manufactures money out of nothing. The process is perhaps the most astounding piece of sleight of hand that was ever invented."*

Mary Elizabeth Croft: *"In exchange for using notes belonging to bankers who create them out of nothing, based on our credit, we are forced to repay in substance, our labour property, land productivity, businesses and resources – in ever increasing amounts. ...We have been deceived into thinking that we were lent other depositors deposited funds... all you borrowed was monetised credit that your signature created.*

... When mums apply for a birth certificate, the application is registered. The legal title of her baby is then transferred from mum to the state. Mum is left with equitable title of her baby whom she can use for a fee – a 'use tax' – and since the property does not belong to her, she has to treat it in the manner which the owner wants."

Modern money mechanics (Federal Reserve Bank of Chicago):
"The actual process of money creation takes place primarily in banks... bankers discovered that they could make loans merely by giving their promise to pay, or bank notes, to borrowers. In this way banks began to create money. Transaction deposits are the modern counterpart of bank notes. It was a small step from printing notes to making book entries crediting deposits of borrowers, which the borrowers in turn could 'spend' by writing checks, thereby 'printing' their own money.

A deposit is created through lending is a debt that has to be paid on demand of the depositor, just the same as the debt arising from a customer's deposit of checks or currency in the bank. Of course they do not really pay out loans from the money they receive as deposits. If they did this, no additional money would be created. What they do when they make loans is to accept promissory notes in exchange for credits to the borrowers transaction accounts."

H L Mencken: *"The whole aim of practical politics is to keep the populace in a continual state of alarm (and hence clamorous to be led to safety) by menacing them with an endless series of hobgoblins, all of them imaginary."*

Encyclopaedia Britannica (14th): *"Banks create credit. It is a mistake to suppose the bank credit is created by the payment of money into the banks. A loan made by a bank is clear addition to the amount of money in the community."*

Richard McKenna: *"I am afraid that the ordinary citizen will not like to be told that the banks can and do create and destroy money. And they who control the credit of a nation direct the policy of governments, and hold in the hollow of their hands the destiny of the people."*

Sir Denison Miller: *"This truth is well known among our principal men now engaged in forming an imperialism of Capital to govern the world. By dividing the voters through the political party system, we can get them to expend their energies in fighting over questions of no importance. Thus by discreet action we can secure for ourselves what has been so well planned and so successfully accomplished."*

George Bush: *"If the people were to ever find out what we've done, we would be chased down the streets and lynched."*

MEASURE OF SUCCESS

Money is painted as the measure of success in our capitalistic societies. The more you have, the more successful you are. We are taught from an early age that the harder you work the more successful you will become – mostly referring to money as the measure of success. Please see the connection of the word 'capital-ism' to 'capital' as in money; and city of authority; where the control over the flow of 'capital' resides.

We are told that to succeed you have to be the best and you have to get to the top at all costs. We are told that competition is good, but you have to beat your competition and you have to outsmart them in a competitive climate to get to the top. Outsmarting someone in a competitive business climate more often than not means destroying them so that there is no more competition – which leads to a dictatorship with total control.

Because business and commerce is all about profits for the owners or shareholders, by eliminating the competition there will be more money for the shareholders. Therefore the capitalist money driven model for society is fundamentally flawed as it ultimately leads to one giant corporation owning everything while they eliminate and absorb their competitors.

We have seen this happen under the guise of globalisation that has swept over our planet since the 80s. Many people believe that we are still far away from this situation where a few giant corporations own the world – sadly they are mistaken.

Our countries have become the corporations that own everything, including the people. And they are doing everything in their power to protect their interests with their laws, their police, and their armies, while keeping the slaves occupied with mindless, mind-numbing crap, like admin and accounting so that they do not have enough time and energy to figure out the truth.

The world of commerce seems to know no limits when it comes to greed. The hunger for money and power keeps growing and once you get to the top you have to do whatever you can to stay there, because there are a billion people trying to topple you so that they too can get to the top for a while and pretend to be the king of the castle.

It should be very clear by now that this is not a sustainable model for survival, it is however a brilliant strategy to divide and conquer the people. We have been so duped by this money scam that we cannot even see how divided and conquered we have become. All we want is more stuff and more money so that we can have better lives and accumulate more toys, impress more people and inflate our egos until we have a heart attack because we cannot handle the stress of controlling all the baggage we've accumulated or we simply die of old age any way.

And then our children pick up the pieces if they are lucky, and repeat the same insane cycle – or the state takes possession of your assets, sells everything at an auction and the 'corporation'/government benefits again.

Somehow there never is enough money to go around and only a few have accumulated huge amounts of it while the masses have less and less. Sadly there is truth in the expression; "the rich get richer and the poor get babies". And this is exactly how it has been structured for the control of the masses. Money is the absolute tool of control over humanity – it is almost impossible to escape it and live a wholesome meaningful life of bliss away from the madness. Yet there are those who have achieved this. We should all find such people living happily in obscurity and learn their secrets.

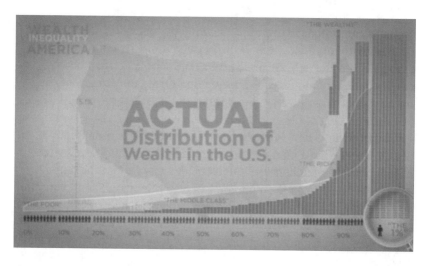

HURDLE TO ALL PROGRESS

All these sentiments are completely in conflict with the core human values which are to love and to create. Instead of competition we should be teaching our children about cooperation for the benefit of all and not just the few.

No consideration is given to our souls, our humanness and our consciousness in this pursuit of money. This is echoed in the legal system and the laws that rule our lives, where pieces of paper called corporations have more rights than people. People are treated as mere 'consumers' and not human beings.

There are many who spend their lives destroying other people's lives as part of their job or so-called career. We have all done that in a moment of anger, or jealousy, or under the egotistic drive that involves any of those other pearly traits called the 'seven deadly sins'. I believe that not too many of us go back to revisit such places to contemplate how our actions may have affected the other's life – sometimes irreversibly.

To make ourselves feel better about what we do to others, the high-flyers go on exotic holidays, do volunteering work, explore the jungles, practice yoga, go on Buddhist retreats, become vegans and chant. Those of us that can do this, do so because they earn loads of money through the misery of others and there always seems to be a justification for what we do. We have become our own worst enemy, prepared to go to war against our brothers because somebody told us to.

Millions of people's dreams are shattered by money on a daily basis because without money it is virtually impossible to do anything, especially starting a business. Millions of loans are turned down every day by banksters, not because people don't need the proposed service or the products in question, but because it is "NOT FINANCIALLY VIABLE".

Not only have we allowed private banks to create money out of thin air but we have inadvertently allowed them to play GOD with humanity. When bankers are left to decide what people can, and cannot do, we display the symptoms of a sick society. These were by and large the privileges of our mothers, fathers, our priests and our teachers but this authority over humanity now sits squarely in the laps of bankers. The bankers decide what we can have, and what we cannot have, as the human race.

- **MONEY IS THE HURDLE TO ALL PROGRESS**
- **MONEY IS A SYNTHETICALLY CREATED TOOL OF ABSOLUTE CONTROL**
- **MONEY STOPS THE NATURAL FLOW OF ENERGY – ENERGY THAT FLOWS THROUGH EVERY LIVING BREATHING HUMAN BEING**

It is insane to say that "money makes the world go round" – the world goes around all on its own. To illustrate the true nature of money, take a look at some of its effects.

- All our lives revolve around chasing money;
- It is the driving force in our world today that controls everything;
- Most of the energy we use daily is in the pursuit of money;
- Money is the cause of most crimes;
- Money causes families to fall apart;
- Money drives people to commit suicide and kill their families;
- Money is the hurdle to all progress;
- It stops the natural flow of energy;
- Money causes gross separation and segregation in society;
- It is the cause for most of the misery on Earth;
- Money leads to absolute power and control;
- Therefore money has been the cause of most conflict and war in the world;
- Money feeds the EGO;
- Money does nothing - people do everything;

Money is the primary cause of the seven deadly sins:

- Gluttony,
- Greed,
- Envy,
- Pride,
- Lust,
- Wrath,
- Sloth

In hindsight, it seems that the so-called 'seven deadly sins' must have been created because of the presence of money in the world. Not the other way around.

JUSTIFICATION OF MONEY

In spite of all the ugly aspects of money, there are still those who desperately try to find excuses for money – try to justify its existence. They say things like "money itself is not evil, it is just a form of exchange, and we have made it evil."

They say that it is not money that is evil, but the LOVE of money that is the problem with humanity. They say that we just need to find a form of 'new' or 'lawful money' and everything will be fine.

All those are just excuses made by those who have not yet truly woken up to the dark side of money and are subconsciously addicted to it – thinking that they can somehow still benefit from it, even if it changes its stripes. I need to imprint this in your heart as firmly as possible:

It is not the LOVE of money that causes our strife...
It is the pure PRESENCE OF MONEY that is the cause of all our misery.

And to find the source of all our problems all we have to do is follow the money. It always unquestionably leads to the primary source of all our strife on planet Earth.

Thinking that money will bring us happiness is as insane as saying that "fighting for peace" will bring us peace – which is what we have apparently been doing for thousands of years.

Just like peace can never be attained through violence or conflict, money can never become a benefit to society because of what it inherently is – a tool of control that causes division among humanity.

Those that seek excuses for money still suffer from the most common side-effect that many of us have not yet diagnosed – FEAR. And suddenly we face one of the most powerful subconscious trappings that hold so many of us back from taking chances in life – FEAR. We live in a world where fear is the primal force that shapes our decisions and one of the most difficult hurdles to cross if we want to escape our economic enslavement.

We seem to fear everything – fear of death, disease, losing our jobs, fear of God, punishment, fear of our neighbours, being robbed, having a car accident, fear of authority, arrest, choking, drowning, fear of failure... we fear so much that we forget to enjoy and cherish life.

This fear tactic is used very skilfully by the global media to control the masses and prevent them from stepping out of line. Banks and insurance companies use fear extremely successfully as part of their marketing campaigns. What if you have an accident... how will you pay for it? Do you have enough hospital insurance? Have saved enough for your retirement? How will your children pay for their schooling? The brainwashing is endless.

Fear is cleverly imprinted in our subconscious minds and constantly forced down our throats on the daily news with constant exposure to war, violence, murder, poverty, homelessness, hunger, shortages, scarcity, financial instability, etc. There is no good news on television and yet we are drawn to it like flies, complaining and moaning about our miserable lives. Remember – it is called "programming".

Even the TV programmes have those undertones on the many reality shows and game shows that fill the participants with hope, but more often than not paralyse them with fear of losing.

LAW OF ATTRACTION – PROJECTING A UTOPIAN WORLD

There is however a far more serious side-effect to the bombardment of fear unleashed on humanity.

Because we watch and absorb the news on a daily basis that constantly exposes us to every possible dark and negative energy imaginable, mixed with snippets of light-hearted nonsense, it all sinks into our subconscious psyche, which becomes our reality and the way we perceive the world – violent dark and dangerous.

We unknowingly become victims of the Universal Law of Attraction and start projecting such a reality for ourselves. If you do not understand these fundamentals of the laws of nature and what we have learnt from quantum physics in the past 100 years, I urge you to do some personal research in these areas to confirm what I am sharing with you here.

We all need to be on the same page to be able to move ahead as a united community of conscious beings that will not allow dark or negative energies to drag us into the void of an infinite Zombie state of mind – the walking dead. In many ways humans have become unconscious walking biological masses of cells that could be described as such. Out of touch with the world around us, out of touch with mother nature, disconnected from our true purpose as living breathing human beings, and out of touch with the Divine Creator.

But we can change all this in a flash. We can use this Law of Attraction and project a beautiful utopian future for ourselves by projecting positive thoughts and images of the kind of world we want to live in – united communities filled with love for everyone, that live in harmony with everyone and the planet, with absolute abundance in every area of human endeavour. That is what I project for my world – I hope you will join me and break the cycle of mind control that keeps us trapped in servitude by our own doing.

We are all living breathing human beings of infinite soul connected to the divine creator through the creation itself. Our primary desire is to love and to create and this is what we should be doing on this planet for all of humanity to benefit from.

Every ancient master and teacher told us exactly this – that we are one with God and that God is within us – and that faith/belief can move mountains and perform miracles. What they were trying to teach us is the nature of the Law of Attraction. We all have the power to do all that, and collectively we can achieve even more.

There is no need to fear anything, as the expression goes, "except fear itself." So stop fearing things and live life to the fullest. It is for these philosophical and spiritual reasons that the UBUNTU Contributionism movement and the newly formed political UBUNTU Party does not seek to govern people but rather to empower the people to govern themselves in united and self sustained communities. No one homeless – no one hungry; everyone contributing their "labour of love" for the greater benefit of all in their community.

"Africa was once GREAT – let us make her GREAT again."

Ref: Wise elder of Africa - Sanusi Credo Mutwa

UBUNTU & UNITY

The UBUNTU Contributionism philosophy is largely based on the ancient tribal structures of the African people and many other native tribes of the world – with adaptations for our times and people accustomed to certain levels of technology of today. For thousands of years the native people of the world lived in united tribal communities, in harmony with mother Earth.

But our society has been segregated and separated on so many levels that we hardly understand the word unity any more. The UBUNTU model will break down the overcrowded urban slum areas allowing people to recreate a unified society consisting of smaller harmonious communities, where people can live by choice rather than forced into economic dependency and servitude.

The UBUNTU model restores this harmonious balance between the people and the land, providing abundance for all, because it is an environment which allows its people to all contribute their natural talents and acquired skills to the greater benefit of everyone in the community.

An environment where their talents are celebrated and supported on every level, at every age. This applies to all areas of our society; from science, technology, agriculture, manufacture, health, education, housing, to every other area that is not deemed to be financially viable under the present capitalistic system.

NEW FREEDOM CHARTER

To begin this journey of transformation, we need to be reminded of our inalienable rights, as the people of South Africa and the world. It is ironic that these so-called new ideas are almost word for word the principles of the Freedom Charter for which many South Africans have died in the past 100 years and brought Nelson Mandela to become the first president of what many believed was a new free South Africa.

The original Freedom Charter was desecrated beyond recognition and conveniently forgotten by our current leaders. The euphoria expressed by the people in South Africa during 1994, when Nelson Mandela was elected as president was short lived, as the people find themselves in dire economic hardship more severe than anything in history.

We must not forget that the incredibly high stress levels people are subjected to because of their circumstances lead to abnormal social behaviour and widespread disease. The increasing rate of cancer and road rage are just two obvious examples of the stress factor.

Today, this call for human rights is no longer applicable to a sector of our population defined by race, as was the case with Mandela, Martin Luther King and many other nameless heroes who remain unsung. This is a unified call by all people who have recognised that all of humanity is enslaved – not just certain sectors.

"Exploitation does not discriminate." Scott Cundill – New Economic Rights Alliance.

The race issue based on skin colour is a deeply emotional one among many, that has caused unimaginable separation and was used very craftily to position large groups of people against each other. This is a wake-up call to all those who believe they are free because of race or class or wealth. We have all been denied freedom and dignity, trapped in a life of servitude to the banking families and their economic stranglehold on our planet – no matter what colour our skin may be.

They say that history has taught us nothing. Well – this is the time when we finally have to learn from history and choose a completely new course for humanity. The New Freedom Charter, at the back of the book, is an updated version of the original call for freedom proposing basic guidelines of honour and integrity for a new social structure.

FUTURE PROSPECTS

There is a very good probability that we will be plunged into a global financial crisis at some stage in the future. The kind of crisis that we have never experienced before and therefore have no experience resolving – not that we have ever resolved the crisis before. Because this time it may not be by choice and humanity may well be forced into it by circumstances beyond our control.

The remarkable thing is, that this potentially catastrophic economic situation presents us with a shining opportunity to consciously change our course and secure our destiny as the human race – a destiny of unity and abundance for all. It may take a catastrophe to save humanity.

There are two primary reasons for a global money collapse. One is terrestrial and the other is cosmic.

1) **Terrestrial:** An unprecedented, unexpected and unavoidable global economic meltdown, that is either outside the control of the banking elite, or carefully orchestrated by them in the hope that they can create "order out of chaos".

2) **Cosmic:** An unexpected and unavoidable cosmic event, against which we have no defences – no matter how much money or technology you throw at it.

If we do not have a plan of action for such events; if we do not know how to respond and how to move beyond such an event, we are already in deep trouble as a species. Even if such a plan sounds crazy in this world today, we should at least have 'a' plan and be prepared to implement it.

To achieve this, we will have to think about our plan as deeply as possible in advance – we will have to talk about it amongst as many people as possible – so that we attain reasonable levels of understanding and consensus for when we need it most. Because when the crisis hits us, it will not wait for us to have executive board meetings or implement strategies. We will need to be ready to implement our plan swiftly when the time comes. Here are a few situations to contemplate.

- What if the money ran dry and tomorrow morning the ATMs and banks were all closed – with no indication if they will open again?
- How would we react – what would we do?
- What if a giant solar flare (coronal mass ejection, CME) fried all the satellites and computer circuits, and control panels in cars, and communication devices, and brought all technology as we know it to an immediate standstill?
- What if you could not drive anywhere, call anyone, had no electricity, no water, no food, no heat, no internet or Wi-Fi...
- What if you were stuck in the city because the trains, planes, busses and trams do not work, and the highways have turned into giant parking lots?
- What if this could not be restored in less than 6 months?
- What if a meteorite shatters in the atmosphere and 100,000 fragments the size of small buildings destroy north America, or Europe, or large parts of Asia and with it blows the global power grid, while the pressure wave rips open all the oil and gas pipes?

As wild and crazy as these suggestions may sound to us now, these are all scenarios that could happen and most likely will happen in the future. They have already happened on a small scale before as a result of hurricanes, solar flares, earthquakes, volcanoes and tsunamis, and the small meteor in Russia during February 2013 in which more than 400 people were injured and many buildings damaged. But luckily for us, we have not had THE BIG ONE for about 12,000 years, what many researchers have called the Deluge or Great Flood.

Supermarkets have no more than three days' food supply, which will disappear within hours under these conditions. The water supply will run dry in less than a week in most cities and so will fuel. It would not take very long for the densely populated urban areas to turn into war zones with people dying in droves not only from the violence but the lack of water first, and then food.

If water is not readily accessible in a city environment, and in the absence of rainfall during this time, within 72 hours the human body will enter a panic state. If this should happen in most cities on Earth, within five days, civilisation as we know it would shatter.

It will become very clear, very quickly, that unless we work together in cooperation for the benefit of all in our trapped communities, we will keep killing each other until there is only a handful of people left. The capitalistic idea that 'competition is good' has no place under such conditions. So why do we allow it to have any place in our lives at all?

If we are to learn anything from history let us learn this. We live on a fragile planet that has undergone many global cataclysms before and it will happen again. If we do not make provisions for this possibility we will have ourselves to blame for our own demise. Many of the messages left for us by ancient cultures in rock carvings and other methods were in fact warnings about such cataclysmic events. Thousands of these carvings that survived global wars and natural disasters are a lasting reminder of past events. Unfortunately such messages in rock are often viewed by ignorant historians as doodles by herd boys while attending to the flocks. A perfect example of the erosion of knowledge and consciousness among humanity through the education system.

So while we contemplate a survival tactic for the possible breakdown of our entire social structure, we also inadvertently prepare a blueprint for a new one, that would have to operate under a completely new set of rules.

One of the first shockwaves that will hit each and every one of us is not only the pressure wave, but the shock of not having money in the world. That one all-important thing that is supposed to make the world go round, money, will disappear from our reality in a flash and yet the world will still be going around.

This is the basic philosophy behind the Blueprint for a New Social Structure – A world without money – A Blueprint For Human Prosperity.

But for now, life goes on and billions of people struggle to survive and pay their bills every day. We keep losing our property to the banksters while the rich get richer in ever decreasing numbers, and the misery keeps rising amongst the masses. How can we stop this stranglehold on humanity? How can we release ourselves from the money trap?

Now that we know that money is the absolute tool of control and enslavement – and that money is the problem – then the answer is quite obvious.

- REMOVE THE MONEY – REMOVE THE PROBLEM
- REMOVE THE TOOL OF CONTROL OVER HUMANITY
- THERE ARE NO HALF MEASURES
- IF WE DON'T USE THEIR MONEY THEY CANNOT CONTROL US
- WE CANNOT REPLACE IT BY ANOTHER FORM OF "GOOD" MONEY
- ANY KIND OF MONEY IS JUST ANOTHER KIND OF CONTROL

UTOPIA – BLOCKED BY A POISONED MIND

It is at this point that many people hit the wall of resistance and simply cannot imagine a world without money. Once again, this is simply an indication of how poisoned our minds have become. Many of us cannot even allow ourselves the freedom to imagine what the world would be like without money. A world in which humanity is truly free, no longer enslaved by the invisible royal-political elite. A world where money cannot be used to manipulate, bribe, influence or kill for.

A complete reshuffling of priorities...
- Where honour and integrity are the foundation of each community.
- Where everyone knows everyone else and respects them for their contribution to the community.
- Where arts and culture are the infinite backdrop that aids everyone to a rapid rise in consciousness.
- Where children are given absolute freedom to pursue their God-given talents as the future contribution to their community.
- Where gluttony, greed or envy knows no place because everyone has everything they need.
- A world where money is as undesirable as a terminal disease,
- Where our infinite diversity and cooperative unity create abundance for the whole of humanity beyond our wildest imagination.
- A world that so many dream of and yet so few are brave enough to enter.

A WORLD WITHOUT MONEY – A NEW SOCIAL STRUCTURE

Some people think that living without money is like going back to the dark ages or living in caves. The truth is that without money we actually achieve the complete opposite. We unleash unbridled exploration, scientific knowledge, sharing the most advanced discoveries in technology, free energy, engineering, design, construction, and every other area of life. By removing money, we remove all obstacles to progress in every sector and release the human spirit to create and discover without limitations.

Once we embrace this simple philosophy we create the space for our visions to become a reality. Where people can follow their natural talents or acquired skills and love every moment of every day, living a truly fulfilled life. The kind of lives we are meant to live as part of this divine creation. Whether we are farmers, scientists, shoemakers, civil engineers, or anything else we choose. The positive energy generated by these conditions is unimaginable to us at present and a great activator of the law of attraction.

THE MIRACLE CURE

The immediate benefits in a world without money are simply astonishing as all the ugly aspects of life miraculously disappear. The moment we remove money from our lives and from the system, everything changes for the better, almost immediately.

- No Crime
- No Hunger
- No Homelessness
- No Greed
- No Gluttony
- No Extortion
- No Hording
- No Accounts
- No Debts
- No Hierarchy
- No Control
- No Obstacles to any kind of progress

This is not utopia – but the **Natural Order of Things** and in a flash, the family of human beings joins everything else in creation that co-exists without money.

QUESTIONS & DOUBTS

It is at this point that the same set of questions usually start to sound from the crowd. It is truly remarkable how we all seem to think alike and how we have been equally programmed to hit the same set of hurdles and ask virtually the same questions. While some believe it is a result of human nature that we ask the same questions, I suggest it is a sobering indication that our education system has brainwashed us all equally.

I can say this in pure honesty because these are the same questions that I had to deal with in the early stages of my exploration of a utopian world without money. Therefore, when someone asks a specific question, I have a very vivid sense of the level they are at in processing the new philosophy, because I've had to work through all those same levels myself.

Here are the eight most frequently asked questions and comments.
1. Human nature won't allow this to happen, people are inherently lazy.
2. Who's going to shovel the crap?
3. If everything is free, I'll just sit on my ass and do nothing and I want people to bring me whatever I need!
4. Great, If everything is free, I want 50 Ferraris and 20 mansions!
5. How are we going to pay for things?
6. Does this mean we are going back to the dark ages – living in caves?
7. Is this a lawless society – who makes the rules?
8. Why should I do something I don't like and why should I give up everything I've worked so hard for?

The answers to these are at the back of the book in a separate chapter with even more FAQ and answers to help resolve the mental turbulence in the minds of some.

Let me put your mind at ease. As part of my own attempt to thoroughly break down the Contributionism system and come to grips with all its components, I had to challenge myself to find answers for as many questions like these, and as many sectors of society, as I could think of.

FIVE POINT MANTRA:

To find the answers we need to repeat the FIVE fundamental aspects of Contributionism – which are:

1. No Money
2. No Barter
3. No Trade
4. No Value attached to anything which makes it more valuable than anything else – because all of our contributions have to be respected and accepted as equally valuable
5. Everyone contributes their natural talents or acquired skills for the greater benefit of all in their community

This is not Utopia - it is the natural order of things that cannot be corrupted or exploited by money. I call it a self-correcting system, because all the decisions are made by the people through their Council of Elders who make the final call on the implementation of the will of the people – on a daily basis. Nobody in this cycle can be corrupted or bribed by money because money does not exist. Everything is implemented for the benefit of the people and the community – not for the benefit of individuals at the expense of others.

So if something is implemented and for some reason turns out to be detrimental to some of the community, it can be corrected immediately, within hours, days, or weeks – by the people and the Council of Elders.

MINORITY RULE – UNITE AND PROSPER

When I mentioned that we need to try a whole new system that has never been tried before, I meant just that. UBUNTU philosophy embraces a principle of *'minority rule'*. As alien as this may sound to most of us at first encounter, it will become clear how we have been conditioned to blindly believe that 'democracy' and 'majority rule' is the best and only way to live our lives. Although the term 'minority rule' does not really describe the system correctly and is not simply the opposite of 'majority rule', it is a good way for our minds to snap out of the state that many of us have been stuck in. The expression itself activates more of a right-brain function of creativity and will force us to think differently about how we should work together for the benefit of all.

The way that democracy has been shoved down our throats is nothing more than a bullying tactic, which suggests that if there are 51 of us – and only 49 of them – we will have it our way and screw the 49 that completely disagree with us and want to have things done a different way.

Minority rule feeds into the philosophy of cooperation and unity rather than competition and division.

It allows the community to benefit from a multitude of options in the UBUNTU Contributionism model, because money does not restrict a multitude of options or possibilities to co-exist for the benefit of all. We don't only have to have two options, or a right and a wrong. We can have many solutions that can all be implemented because money is no longer the hurdle to anything we propose as the people.

The democracy-majority rule model that has been shoved down our throats is just a cleverly disguised tool of control that pits people against each other – divide and conquer – instead of unite and prosper.

Once we realise this, it becomes very easy to recognise the obvious options that we have been denied. The current system keeps the power in the hands of those who call the shots under the illusion that the voters have had their say. And from that moment on we are stuck with the option what we voted for.

The minorities and small interest groups then have to take their gripes and proposals to those who won the majority and we all know what happens to minority groups and their needs. Democracy is not a sustainable model and does not serve all the people fairly. It is a system that subtly promotes a divide and conquer philosophy.

The UBUNTU model provides for all the needs of all the people and allows the implementation of many ideas, options and choices that the people propose. Since there is no need for money to get things done – everything will be done – as long as it does not cause harm to any sector of the community. The Council's task is to look out for the best interests of the whole community, as well as all the people in the community. The more you work through this process the more obvious it will become, that minority rule is an infinitely more conscious way to create abundance. But it is completely alien in a society that functions with money.

Let's get back to those burning questions that everyone raises when first confronted with this new philosophy. To start finding the simple answers for the initial questions I looked at a long list of government departments and formulated a simple solution for each one of those sectors, imagining how it will function in a community without money. A society that is driven by people, their talents and abilities, rather than money.

I must admit that this was by far the most exhilarating part of my journey to embrace the new blueprint for an UBUNTU system. This is why I can truly say that I understand how people feel at precisely the moment they ask a specific question, because I remember exactly how I felt when I first grappled with the same questions.

At first I really struggled to find the answers and I thought that I would end up in a dead-end, having to abandon this utopian dream. It took weeks, if not months, to find answers that resonated with what would be acceptable to everyone in any specific community while keeping in mind the sentiments of individuals.

And then the questions began to pile up and very quickly I had a heap of unsolved riddles to resolve, trying to figure out how we can survive without money. But to my surprise, as the weeks rolled by and I allowed the questions to simply wash over me, one by one, the answers began to appear. And once I had the answers to the first few critical sectors of society, and how these sectors will function in a world without money, it was like an avalanche of revelation had hit me.

The more I resolved, the easier it became to solve the next level, because I suddenly had a set of references from previous questions that guided me towards more simple solutions.

Several years have passed since I began this journey and it took me at least five years to be brave enough to stand in front of a crowd to share the Contributionism ideas. The amazing thing is that the more I share it, the more people seem to understand it. It's as if we have all tapped into the collective consciousness or the quantum field of knowledge. This basically means that the newcomers can simply tap in and get the answers very quickly, if not immediately, from the collective consciousness or the "field". Do not be afraid – ask for the answers and they will be presented to you. Ask and you shall receive. The more people think about it and find the answers, the easier it is for others to find the answers too. The higher the global consciousness, the easier it is for people to get 'it' and embrace 'it'.

So here we are, trying to embrace a new social structure that most of the world would not believe is possible and yet, if I can imagine it; and if you can imagine it; and a million other people can imagine it – very soon the whole world will be able to imagine it. And by now you should know that our reality is created by the observer and the thoughts projected by the observer.

Once a critical mass of people on this Earth share these thoughts, there is no turning back. I believe that we have passed the critical mass and we are approaching the tipping point. It is just a matter of time for our thoughts to become reality on a global scale.

Stop the fear, stop watching the news, and imagine this reality. The more people imagine this utopia, the quicker we will achieve it.

SELF-CORRECTING SYSTEM

I do believe that the UBUNTU Contributionism model provides simple solutions for all our needs. At this stage I have proposed solutions to many sectors of society – but not all of them. As long as we have the cornerstones of the new social structure in place, the rest of the sectors will be restructured by each community itself in the most practical way so that it benefits the entire community. This is after all the simple structure of the UBUNTU Contribution System – people finding their own solutions for their own needs – not being dictated to by laws they did not agree to.

It is so simple, that most of us try to over-complicate it – thinking that it is too simple. This is exactly what our problem has been – we cannot imagine that such a simple system could work, mainly because of the deeply convoluted system we have today – we have been lead to believe that it must be complicated – because our current system has taken thousands of years to construct with the intention to enslave people, with complex rules and regulations so that people cannot free themselves from it. A system that 'simply' does not work for humanity any more. A system that has been designed to destroy anything that threatens its own survival.

The UBUNTU Contribution system is based on the laws of nature – it cannot be corrupted and it cannot fail – from within. Because it functions as a self-correcting system that always reverts back to provide solutions that are for the greatest benefit of the community. As you begin to explore the possibilities you will find that the system always provides the solutions. And if I could find them, so can everyone else.

Since my first public discussion on Contributionism, I have heard thousands of arguments and excuses why this will not work... and why it will fail.. and what about this... and what about that?

Unfortunately all of our current questions are asked from the perspective of the current system we are in – and the set of circumstances that determine how things function today are completely different to the set of circumstances that will shape our activity in the new system. In other words, we have to undergo a complete paradigm shift in our hearts and minds even before we ask the questions. It is very difficult to imagine a 'perfect' world while being stuck in this one.

So before you ask a question to which you expect a simple answer – first go through the set of circumstances that will prevail in the new system and ask yourself how it will affect the entire process; and how it will impact on what it is you are asking about. Imagine how it will work in a world without money – identify the things that will have an effect on what you are asking about and repeat the FIVE POINT MANTRA. Very soon, the answers will come flooding in.

Because we all have the answers within us already, all we have to do is ask the questions and allow our humanness and our hearts to lead us to the answers.

THE SOLUTIONS TO OUR PROBLEMS

The solutions to all our problems are always simple. Ask any ten-year old. They will give you honest and mostly unbiased suggestions on how to solve the world's problems. But we have been conditioned and indoctrinated by our schooling, the media, the politicians and our entire society to believe the opposite.

The lobotomised reporters on the major news networks keep paraphrasing the lies provided by their masters, reminding the masses how tough it is to solve the world's problems. Squinting their eyes and pulling their mouths as they read the teleprompt in an attempt to sympathise with the world.

The politicians keep repeating how hard they are trying to solve the problems. They keep reminding us that they will do what they can to fix the mess that they inherited from the previous regime. It has been an ongoing parade of lies and deception to keep us holding on and hoping for a miracle.

In our hearts we all know that the solution to our insurmountable problems are simple. Give it to the experts in the field – the engineers, the scientists, the farmers, the horticulturists, the bakers, cheese makers, technologists, the inventors, the pilots, the workers...; we the people know what we need and what is wrong with our world and how to solve all the problems.

BUT – unfortunately our solutions do not work for the banksters. Our solutions do not provide for the stacking of the decks, so that the banksters keep control over the people and continue to profiteer off the people. And therefore, as long as they have a hold over the people, the people will never resolve the problems on this planet – because according to the banking elite and the royal political bloodlines we are not meant to solve them. We need to remain suppressed, needy, stressed, ignorant and fearful of authority. This is the status quo that has been dished up for humanity.

Only we, the people, will solve the problems.

THE TRIGGER POINT TO OUR AWAKENING

One of the first questions people ask once they have come to grips with UBUNTU Contributionism is – how do we get there? How do we go from here to there? Because I want to be there now! I want to live in this world you talk about!

The other things people want to know is: How can I get involved – what can I do? Everybody needs to know about this!

The first thing that everyone can do is talk about it. Tell everyone you know or meet about UBUNTU Contributionism - this bright light of hope at the end of the dark and gloomy tunnel. Tell everyone as much as you know and plant the seeds of consciousness in their hearts and minds.

Even if they do not understand it at the time, or if they don't really want to hear your message of hope, that does not matter. Because once they have heard it, they cannot un-hear it. It is forever imprinted in their hearts and minds. This is a critical part of our strategy. Planting the seed of consciousness and a sense of knowing in everyone's lives, even if it dwells in their subconscious for a while.

Sooner or later something will happen that will trigger our suppressed memory and allow us to re-evaluate stored information. No matter who you are or where you come from, or how resistant you are to this information, everyone has their trigger point. The smallest things can trigger our imagination and allow us to process this information from a completely different perspective.

I have seen this happen to thousands of people. From farmers, to city slickers with every expensive toy under the sun; to argumentative teenagers and politicians; to homeless people and street vendors – we all have our trigger point, and I have seen thousands of people's eyes light up with joy at the moment they get it. Miraculously, this includes the banksters, their lawyers and politicians. They too have their trigger points that will wake them up to evaluate the misery they are causing their fellow humans.

I believe that we are all under divine guidance to keep us on the road to UBUNTU. Because the system we are trapped in is in direct conflict with the divine creation. Our primal nature as beings who are part of the great divine creation, is to continue creating. As we realise this, we become part of the 'great awakening' and begin to inspire others – the word 'inspire' comes from 'being at one with spirit'.

This process has already begun and it is impossible to predict how long it will take for the majority to wake up or how long it will take for us to transcend into a utopian life of abundance. But every journey of a thousand miles begins with the first step – the good news is – we have already taken the first step.

TRANSFORMATION

To explain the transition from a capitalist money-driven society to one that operates on the other side of the scale is tricky. This is the crazy thing about our enslavement. In the beginning we will need to use money to set up structures that will eventually allow us to free ourselves from money. We will have to go through transitional stages, in which we will have to accommodate money, while doing many things without money or payment. There may be a need for alternative currencies created by individual communities to protect themselves against exploitation – and many other situations that are hard to predict now. The money controllers will not give up their control willingly, but at the same time they are all human beings undergoing the same rise of consciousness as everyone else. Only a few people at the top know about the lies and deception while the largest majority of people in these industries are mere employees trying to survive like everyone else and provide for their families.

For example, there are only a few bankers who truly understand the process called "securitisation". However, they do not know about fractional reserve banking (ie. loans being made out of nothing) and they have no idea about *seignorage*, which is the money paid to the government by the Reserve Bank as a kind of tax on the value of notes and coins that are minted. You get the occasional banker who understands one of these processes. On very rare occasions you will find someone who understands two of them. Those that understand all three, are extremely rare. They either work squarely for the dark side or they are massive activists desperately trying to bring about change.

Sooner or later many of these people will have their awakening moment when one or more of "the pennies drop". It may come as a result of a question from a child, or a relative making a comment, or seeing a documentary, that becomes their trigger point. Their awakening to higher consciousness will make it impossible to continue doing work of a destructive nature.

But for now, the bankers are supported by the laws that were created to uphold their system; the courts and judges who are paid by the system; the police; the army; and every other organ of state in place. Therefore our aim should be not to confront those in control, but to find ways to convert them to higher consciousness.

The most bizarre aspect of this whole money trap is that we are all suspended in a whirlwind of promises to pay because no one actually ever gets "paid" by the system. What I am going to explain to you now is going to sound extremely complicated, but is actually very, very simple. This is the first step to truly understanding the money system.

Firstly – It is not possible to pay anything because there is no money to pay it with. What does that mean? How is this possible? My wallet is full of money... most will think. This concept was explained in an extraordinary court case in the USA. It was so extraordinary that the ruling by the judge was completely missed by most of us.

"There is a distinction between a 'debt discharged' and a debt 'paid'. When discharged, the debt still exists though divested of its charter as a legal obligation during the operation of the discharge, something of the original vitality of the debt continues to exist, which may be transferred, even though the transferee takes it subject to its disability incident to the discharge." **Stanek vs. White, 172 Minn. 390, 215 N.W. 784**

Typically, this has been written in a legal language that very few people understand. But what it says is this: *you cannot pay for anything anymore. You can only discharge the obligation.*

Let me explain: The money in your bank account is not money. It is merely a "statement" of the bank's promise to pay you money. Money, which was originally linked to gold and silver, does not exist, but instead, bank promises are exchanged by you and me as if they were "money."

Now, when you buy shoes from someone, and you give them these bank promises as currency (what we call money) you are actually trying to settle a real obligation (taking the shoes) with nothing but an empty promise. Because the person you are giving the currency to believes in what you are giving them, they will discharge your obligation to pay them back, but this is not actually a real payment. The paper money in their hand is just an empty promise – with no intrinsic value. They then use the same 'empty promise' to pay someone else and continue the scam – unknowingly.

But it is only the tip of the tip of the iceberg. Never ever forget that the word "credit" comes from the Latin "credere" which means "to believe." If you don't believe in it, or have no confidence in it, the money is totally worthless. As I said before, it is a deeply convoluted system intended only to confuse us and enslave us.

We have to find ways to bypass the economic restrictions on our communities and take control of our own survival. Find new ways of doing things and providing for ourselves with less and less interference from so-called authorities.

Our constitutions and human rights, together with the application of 'common law' will probably play an important role in our attempts to bypass the system in our efforts to create a new system of our own design for the people. We must avoid creating another system of hierarchy that allows a new set of megalomaniacs to replace the existing dictators.

Remember that we are dealing with corporations and individuals that have the highest levels of ego and arrogance imaginable. They believe that they are invincible – that they cannot fail. That kind of belief in itself is a weakness and it will inevitably lead to their own demise.

Because of their unimaginable arrogance, we may be dumped into a sudden and dramatic change of life – without any money at all, when the entire banking and economic system crashes. This crash may be orchestrated by the bansksters themselves to push humanity so low that we will be grateful for any kind of salvation. We must be vigilant and be aware of such tactics and not allow ourselves to fall prey to manipulation of this kind.

The events in Cyprus during March 2013, when banks closed their doors and simply kept as much as 99% of the people's money, may have been a test of the banking elite to see how far they could actually push the ignorant humans before they stood up against the oppressors. A friend of a friend had 22 million British pounds in his banks in Cyprus. When he woke up it was all gone, and I believe that he was left with 100 thousand pounds in his account. This is a sad indication that they can push ignorant humans as far as they want to, because the Cypriots did not rise up in violence against the banks that stole their money.

They protested and waved banners but to no avail. It is unthinkable that any private corporation would be allowed to take possession of our money and not be held accountable or charged with criminal activity – clearly pointing to complicity by the legal system and the government, using the ignorant police to enforce their unlawful agenda. Once again highlighting that the rights of banks are held higher by the legal system than the rights of human beings, and that the banksters are still the ones who ultimately call the shots. I do hold firmly that their arrogance will be their biggest weakness.

But now we are no longer ignorant, we know the game and we know the plan to keep humanity enslaved for as long as possible. Therefore we cannot wait for the system to crash, we have to be proactive and start taking action ourselves that will help speed up the eradication of money from society, by converting and sidelining the bankers into paralysis, until they have absolutely no effect in our lives.

As time goes by we will use less and less money in our daily lives and our communities. The more we develop our new system the faster we will move towards the tipping point, where the balance of scales tips so suddenly that we don't even realise we don't need money –

when we wake up one day and realise that we no longer use money for most things within our communities.

Remember that money does not dig the boreholes, or purify water – people do. Money does not cook the food or make a fire on a cold night – people do. People create, build, invent and have the capacity for infinite love for each other.

Transformation to the UBUNTU CONTRIBUTION system cannot happen in one step. It will happen in incremental steps as we liberate ourselves from the many levels of control. These will be highly liberating and exciting times with limitless possibilities for everyone as we all begin to realise how simple it really is.

THE ANSWERS LIE IN SMALL RURAL TOWNS

The first phase will probably be the slow and steady decentralisation of the urban metropolitan jungles that evolved as a result of the chase for money, as people lose the desire to keep chasing the money and choose an easy relaxed life in the country. The repopulation of the many smaller towns and villages will be the first objective and will probably start happening naturally.

The small towns will receive new blood of innovative thinkers and skilled people and motivators and more.

- All those who are tired of the money trap and are ready to implement something new.
- People who are ready to build communities that are self reliant without the ugly influence of money.
- It will be the reversal of the trends of the past century, where people from the countryside were lured into the cities to seek fame and fortune.

Strong rural and farming communities with a strong sustainable platform will provide the framework for developing future UBUNTU communities in control of their own destiny.

Such boosting of these communities will be accompanied by the first wave of liberties previously unknown to most of us. And once the people have tasted these simple benefits of cooperation it will be impossible to stop the flow towards UBUNTU Contributionism.

A PLAN FOR RURAL TOWNS

This is a proposed blueprint for the transformation of small towns and rural villages into strong, sustainable communities, in complete control of their own destiny. A model that can serve as a template for all small towns to introduce UBUNTU Contributionism to their community.

This model provides the beginning of the 'domino effect' that will be unstoppable – because once the first town is virtually self reliant and self sustainable, it will force all the neighbouring towns to follow the same model, because they will not be able to compete with the 'cheap' produce made available by their UBUNTU neighbour.

These new transition towns will restore the harmonious balance between the people and the Earth because it allows people from all walks of life to achieve whatever they dream of. Their passion for what they choose to do is their contribution for the greater benefit of all in their community. From farmers to scientists, artists to engineers, health workers to craftsmen, and especially community workers. Everyone adds to the abundance of their community.

In some ways these transforming communities will resemble the frontier towns of the gold rush in the mid 1800s. This time however it will not be the lure of wealth and fortune, that very few acquired, but freedom and abundance, which everyone in these new communities will attain. The aspect of education and training play a crucial role in how communities are structured, which will be covered in great detail in a later section.

IMPLEMENTATION – COMMUNITY PROJECTS

The emphasis will be to create as many community projects as possible and slowly reduce our dependency on outside produce, materials and money, until we don't need money at all. These projects must cover as many areas as possible to allow as many people as possible with as many diverse skills as possible to participate. It has to be a social, industrial, agricultural, scientific and cultural initiative that will potentially include everyone in the community.

How will this be achieved?
The knowhow and scientific expertise is available from a variety of great minds to implement every proposed community project

imaginable. Every community has such people, but the present structure does not allow us to mingle and exchange ideas and actually get to know who our neighbours are and what their true talents are. We live in boxes called "apart-ments", specifically designed to avoid any contact with neighbours in the attempt to preserve "privacy."

In the current labour market which includes a lack of "jobs", people's skills and talents are being completely wasted. Most people do not use their natural talents or skills doing what they are passionate about, which means that others do not benefit from their true talents either. It's like a black hole with all the potential energy of the entire community being devoured by the central dark energy of money (the black hole) – that everyone has to chase after. We are all in the same rat race and there is an old saying "only a rat can win the rat race." Do we want to stay in this race? To win what?

Bakers are sweeping streets; engineers are driving busses; architects are designing websites; artists are working in grocery stores; it is completely insane how our system blocks the natural flow of people's talents or the use of our acquired skills.

Countless gifted people work in isolation on amazing projects like: natural eco-friendly building materials; enhancing plant growth with sound; alternative or free energy; solar power enhancement; batteries that never die; perpetual motion magnetic motors; ethanol from fast growing legumes; cars that run on water or air or electricity; treatment for all disease; levitation technology; new materials design; quantum computing; communication systems; stem cell treatment that re-grows organs and limbs; transmutation of elements – that may sound like magic to some people; LASER and SASER technology; and so many more amazing minds that should be making a difference in our lives.

Through the research that I have done for the past several decades, I have been fortunate to meet many such great minds who allowed me to recognise the possibility we have as a species to create abundance for all, if only we start working together.

But for now, these amazing people are being used as slave labour by large corporations, government research institutions and the industrial military complex. Their skills and talents have been hijacked by the corporations and we the people get no benefit at all from their genius. In most cases many of the great inventions are kept locked away, hidden from the global population.

This will be reversed as these great minds join the communities of their choice and contribute their talents to the people rather than to corporations. And so, our towns will be filled with the greatest minds in science, medicine, energy, education, recycling, engineering, agriculture and more to help implement all the proposed plans.

Contrary to what we are constantly bombarded with by the media, the solutions to our problems are simple. There are immediate and effective solutions for most of our needs that can be provided very quickly if the people stand together as united communities. In the following section we deal not with a wish list, but rather a to-do list of achievable objectives.

FIRST STEP – TAKE BACK THE CONTROL

To attain these liberties the communities need to take control of their own needs, services, supplies and activities. It is much easier for small towns to do so than large cities. In South Africa, the real problems lie with local municipalities that are not able to provide basic services to the community.

The existing models of governance in our communities are fatally flawed. Our local councils and municipalities keep disappointing the people they are supposed to serve. Many of the municipalities are on the verge of bankruptcy, failing to deliver on the needs of the people.

In most cases the administrators and mayors were not even elected by the people but appointed by the political party who won the elections. Therefore there is no real connection between the people and the municipality/council administrators, nor is there any real respect for the council by the people. Their main priority is to report to the higher authority of government – not to provide for the people.

The local leaders are unreachable and even when you finally get hold of the right person, or get your letter of complaint delivered to the right person, it takes forever to be evaluated – and in most cases it never gets implemented.

Most of these civil servants have no actual training in the positions they hold, because they are mere political appointments who create havoc in their own communities through their own lack of skills. This is therefore the first area that needs to be corrected. Every community should identify a group of the most respected wise men and women and appoint them to the Council of Elders, to be the true representative body of the community. This is a critical initial step to take control or our own destiny.

THE STRUCTURE OF THINGS

Before I explain my reasons for the proposed structure of the UBUNTU communities and the Council of Elders, I need to explain the fundamental structures that define our reality.

Everything is structured according to what is commonly called "sacred geometry". Some people jump to the conclusion that this is some weird new-age religious cult expression. Those who believe this are simply uninformed and completely misguided by their own ignorance.

Geometry is the fundamental tool of measuring the world and the universal space around us. It is geometry and the infinite relationships between geometric shapes and their respective ratios, that lay the foundation for all of our knowledge in science and mathematics. This applies to everything from the geometry of the macro to the micro – the galaxies and subatomic structure.

Some of the knowledge encoded in sacred geometry include the phi factor of 1.618...; the golden mean spiral; the five platonic shapes; pi; units of measure used in the world today like the mile, Egyptian cubit; metre, 360 degrees; minutes and seconds; all the prime numbers into infinity; quantum fields; Krystic spiral; Katharagrid; cymatic patterns and infinitely more information that we are still discovering today.

Even the quantum levels inside the atom and gravity distortion fields that are created around a vortex are governed by the principles of sacred geometry.

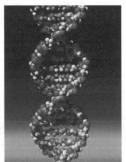

Above: Examples of how everything in creation follows the patterns and spirals of sacred geometry. From the large to the small. From galaxies to our DNA.

The universe and the space it occupies is the geometric seed for all our knowledge. It is the infinite expression of the divine creation by the creator of all. The word 'sacred' has nothing to do with religion or new-age, but is has everything to do with the structure of the divine creation and the natural order of things, which includes everything – including every atom in our bodies.

Some synonyms for the word 'sacred'.
holy, hallowed, consecrated, blessed, divine, revered, venerable, ecclesiastical, inviolable, inviolate, invulnerable, inalienable, protected, secure, unalterable...

The true meaning can be extracted from the last three expressions above - *protected, secure, unalterable.* In other words 'unchangeable or fixed' – as in unchangeable or fixed by the divine creation. The unalterable creation of God.

The study of sacred geometry is one of the most important areas of science we should all be exposed to at school. For those that have studied sacred geometry will know that I am only scratching the surface here and the knowledge is most likely as limitless as creation itself. The lack of this information leaves a huge void in our knowledge base and affects our future comprehension of life and the universe around us.

All ancient rulers, high priests, master artists, builders and philosophers understood the importance of sacred geometry and how it manifests in the world around us. They understood how it influences the flow of water, the flow of energy, the shape of our DNA; the growth of plants – how it forms the shape of our solar system, the movements of the planets, and our galaxy, and everything else in creation. Sacred geometry contains all the 'fixed' rules behind the laws of nature and all of creation. It could be described as the breath of GOD.

The simple structures of sacred geometry contain all the so-called secret knowledge that was held by priest kings throughout the ages, taught in the mystery schools of Egypt, and even the mystery of the 'tree of life' in the Hebrew Kabbalah.

Above: Three overlapping circles inside a bigger circle, create a perfect hexagon in the centre, showing the infinite fractal patterns and the interconnectedness of unity (one); 3 equilateral triangles in each circle; and 6 (hexagon) at the centre that connects it all. Nikola Tesla said that if we understand the significance of 3, 6, and 9, we will know the secrets of the universe. Is this what he was referring to?

Above: The well recognised 'flower of life' pattern, with the 10-point Kabbalah or "Tree of Life" overlaid. This mysterious symbol goes back thousands of years and is said to contain all the secrets to life and the universe. But some researchers like Ashayana Deane, have shown that this is potentially a distortion of our reality and part of our enslavement in a system created by "fallen angelics". The true "Tree of Life" is based on 12 points called the Kathara grid, and is derived from the Krist code, of Christ Consciousness of the universal source matrix. See image below.

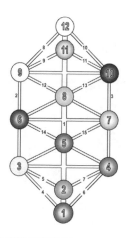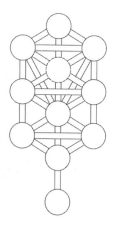

Above: The Kathara grid on the left is balanced at both ends and is based on 12
points of the Krist grid. As opposed to the Kabbalah "tree" on the right which
is not balanced, suggesting that it has been synthetically manipulated to achieve
this shape that only contains 10 points in its structure. This is not a natural
number in sacred geometry, which has the circle or number 6 as its base.

All the great cathedrals and ancient temples of the world are
constructed according to sacred geometry. One of the most impressive
and breathtaking examples of sacred geometry in sculpting, is encoded
in the face of Ramses The Great, in Egypt (see images below).
Christopher Dunn is an engineer and the author of *Giza Power Plant:*
Technologies of Ancient Egypt. He has spent many years analysing and
researching the science behind the Giza pyramids and the giant statue
of Ramses II. It has been shaped with such accuracy, that it cannot be
ascribed to a man with a hammer and chisel, but rather advanced laser
technology.

"What does the face of Ramses have in common with a modern
precision engineering object, such as an automobile? It has flowing
contours with distinct features that are perfectly mirrored one side
to the other. The fact that one side of Ramses face is a perfect mirror
image to the other implies that precise measurements had to have been
used in its creation. It means that the statue was carved in intricate
detail to create precise three-dimensional surfaces. The jaw-lines,
eyes, nose and mouth are symmetrical and were created using a
geometric scheme that embodies the Pythagorean Triangle as well as
the Golden Rectangle and Golden Triangle. Encoded in the granite is
the sacred geometry of the ancients." Christopher Dunn.

A great video clip can be seen here:
http://www.youtube.com/watch?v=h6H13Mi6Kds

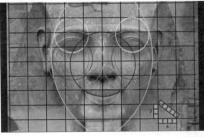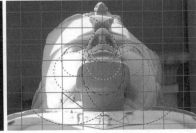

Ref:Christopher Dunn: www.gizapower.com

The great works of art by Leonardo da Vinci, Michelangelo and many others are all deeply encoded with sacred geometry. Many great architects of today still apply this principle in their work. The ancients did everything according to the principles of sacred geometry because it is the infinite expression that lays the foundation for the laws of nature. It is a simple way for us to remain connected to the creation and the creator.

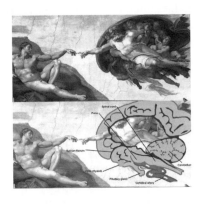

Leonardo da Vinci's Vitruvian Man – shows us the intricate relationship of the human body to sacred geometric principles.

Michelangelo shows us that God is within us – that we can create with our mind – because we are all aspects of God – we are one with God.

Some of the fixed rules of sacred geometry are found in the seven colours of the rainbow, the seven whole notes in one musical octave – where the eighth note completes the octave; the twelve notes in a full harmonic resonant octave where the thirteenth note completes the full scale. That is why so much around us is structured according to this knowledge. We have seven days in a week, and 12 months in a year, twelve disciples around Christ – just to point out the obvious.

One of the great insights into the structure of things was provided by Leonardo Fibonacci, more commonly referred to as simply Fibonacci. An Italian mathematician, considered by some the most talented western mathematician of the Middle Ages. Fibonacci is best known to the modern world for the spreading of the Hindu–Arabic numeral system in Europe, primarily through the publication in 1202 of his *Liber Abaci* (*Book of Calculation*), and for a famous number sequence, called the Fibonacci sequence, which he did not discover but used as an example in the *Liber Abaci*.

The Fibonacci numbers are inextricably linked to the laws of nature, the Golden Spiral and the phi factor of 1.618... but it is not the same as any of these. It is a separate aspect of the great creation that holds infinite knowledge.

1, 1, 2, 3, 5, 8, 13, 21, 34, 55, 89, 144, 233, 377, 610, 987...

Each number is the addition of the previous two. Incredibly, the 12th step in the Fibonacci sequence is 144, which is the only number in the entire sequence with a whole square root number equal to its step. In other words, it is the twelfth number, whose square root is twelve. It is also the first number in the Fibonacci sequence to numerologically add up to nine (1+4+4) which is highly significant in numeric science.

It is also not a co-incidence that all prime numbers (except for 2 and 3) appear in just eight rows of the 24-hour clock, perfectly matching the Maltese cross, used by the early banking societies. The connection between prime numbers and banking is simple – prime numbers are used as the encryption code base used by banks.

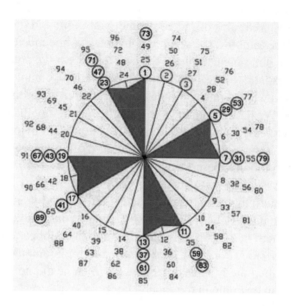

Above: Prime numbers align with specific points that create the well recognised Maltese Cross. Similar cross symbols were used by the Knights Templar and Knights Hospitaller. All of these were associated with money and banking.

COUNCIL OF ELDERS (COE) – WISE HUMANS OF INTEGRITY

The first thing that every community should do is to appoint their own representative body whose primary objective is to look after the interests of the community and all the people. The new council should be a group of people who are known in the community and truly respected for their knowledge and wisdom by the community. I call such a body the *Council of Elders (COE).* I call them elders, but they may not necessarily be older people. This is the first and most critical step to presenting a united front by any community, allowing it to make decisions swiftly on behalf of the people.

We need to follow a natural order of things when establishing the foundation of the UBUNTU communities, using our knowledge of sacred geometry to do so. Apply this knowledge in as many facets of the proposed model for the new community as possible.

If we apply the principles of sacred geometry, this council should consist of thirteen appointed people of wisdom – twelve around one.

Where the thirteen appoint the senior elder among themselves to be the spokesperson for the Council.

These elders will guide, advise and implement the needs of the community on a daily basis from within the centre of the community instead of some unreachable distant ivory tower. The COE will consult with the people every day and hear what the needs are, listen to suggestions, welcome new members to the community, and allocate action to be taken on the most pressing issues. But it will not interrupt or interfere in the flow of life in the community. Only on request by the people.

The council will initiate the implementation of new ideas or projects to improve and upgrade all aspects of the community. Every member of the community must be able to speak to the council at any time, to make suggestions, raise concerns or point out innovative ideas that will improve the lives of the people.

I mentioned before that the concept of democracy is one of the best disguised control systems that was sold to the people as a sugar-coated poison pill. For thousands of years we have tried this 'democracy' – it has not worked anywhere in the world. It has however been used as a very clever disguise tactic to make people believe that they are free and that they have a choice. It is now clear that people of the world, who are in the majority, have no choice in any case. They have options and selections but the true needs are never met. What should be crystal clear to everyone by now is that the governments are imposing their ideas on the people – mostly against their will.

For this reason it is important to remind you that the UBUNTU Contribution system is NOT a democratic system – but rather a system that works on minority rule principles – guided by the Council of Elders. A system that provides for the many diverse needs of many minorities on a daily basis, and not just the needs of the majority – which in fact, are not really catered for under democracy in any case.

This is where the wise men and women of the Council of Elders decide for the benefit of the community. The rapid access to the council by the people will keep the system in check and create a quick turnaround if something has gone wrong or if some sectors of the community are unhappy with something. Keep in mind that in a society where people work together towards a common benefit for all; where everything is available to everyone all of the time; where there is no need for administering bureaucratic control, the levels of unhappiness are probably not going to be nearly as prevalent as they are today.

To initiate the path to transition, the community has to do everything it can lawfully, to take control of its own town councils and management of services. It may be a simple vote of 'no confidence' by the people and appointing the Council of Elders as the representative body.

Remember that this is an interim phased approach to move away from the control of corrupt governments and municipalities who have stolen the land from us – the people. We need a starting point to implement the principles of unity and prosperity of all the people in the community.

FUNDING THE FOUNDATIONS OF TRANSITION

One of the first things that needs to happen during this first phase and transitional period, is for each town to establish a people's bank account into which all taxes, water and electricity bills, or any other money that is normally collected by the municipality, is paid. In other words, stop paying the government and their subsidiaries until they deliver acceptable levels of service to the people.

This should be a trust account protected against unscrupulous raiding by banks or a sheriff or some other unlawful instrument of the illegitimate governments. The trustees are the people of the town/community. If this is not possible or potentially exploitable, the Council of Elders needs to find an alternative way to collect the people's money and put it to good use.

The trustees/people, will instruct the COE to act on their behalf. The new COE must request a collective bill on behalf of all the people for all expenses of the town, to analyse the accuracy of the fees and identify where the wastage is. In South Africa a large majority of bills are grossly inaccurate and the individual people have no recourse against the unscrupulous municipalities. It takes months of slogging and standing in queues at the municipal offices to get anyone to analyse your statements, inevitably claiming that they are correct and you are wrong. In many such cases people do not have the money or knowhow to start legal action, so the municipalities are always on the take. I speak from personal experience in this case.

The COE will pay the collective bill on behalf of all the people and demand corrective action immediately if any mistakes are found. If no remedy is presented by the current municipality, the COE can simply withhold the entire payment until the faults/mistakes have been corrected. The municipality will not be able to survive any mistakes and most likely not be able to continue operating the inferior service of the past. They will have two options: either step up and start providing acceptable service OR hand over the management of services to the COE.

To take over the governance and management of the town, the people can raise a vote of no confidence in the mayor and the town council ensuring that the management is handed over to the COE. This sounds easy in principle, but will take determination and guts to achieve in the bureaucratic system with draconian rules. But we have to start standing up for our rights and unite in these situations. Our strength is our unity. The trust and trustees must be used with cunning efficiency where possible – it is a powerful tool if we know how to use it.

The municipality has funds available for upgrades, repairs and other activities. The COE must get into a position to receive either a portion of the funds or all the funds from the municipality every month and allocate it to the approved UBUNTU community projects.

In addition to this, everyone in the community who wants to participate in the new UBUNTU projects must commit some cash every month to the people's account. Those who simply cannot contribute any cash can contribute their time to receive benefits from the projects. There will be those who contribute cash; time; and both. Distribution of benefits will be proportional to everyone's contribution at the start.

The aim is for the various projects to involve the entire community in various ways and provide the first FREEDOMS as soon as possible to its people. The initial focus must be on projects that will provide the cornerstones – water, food, electricity/energy and housing. As one town succeeds, the others will follow their example to emulate their success.

Keep in mind that this is a temporary solution and an initial transitional phase. The existing money system is not a long term solution, but an intermediate plan is required to get the towns self-sufficient and "off the grid."

STEP-BY-STEP

There are several steps to reaching complete UBUNTU Contributionism in the towns and ultimately in the whole country. Keep in mind that this new social structure will bring new laws and guidelines that will be established by the communities themselves under the guidance of each Council of Elders.

Every community will in essence be an association of sovereign human beings who choose to live in united sovereign communities benefiting each other, making new laws for themselves and their community, based on the needs and morals of the people.

The new lawful structures will be outlined in a separate detailed section but the foundation for everything is the common law of the people. Three very simple principles that govern the sanctity of life that every human being can relate to.

1. **Do not kill or cause anyone harm**
2. **Do not steal or take that which is not yours**
3. **Conduct yourself honestly and honourably in all that you do and say**

We have to wipe the slate clean to begin something new and untarnished by the existing laws that enslave us – which are just statutes outlining corporate rules. A brand new set of laws needs to be created by the people, for the people, involving a critical input from the youth if they are to have any future at all.

NEW LAWS AND GUIDELINES

Every community will create new guidelines and additional laws for their own needs which will be specific to the activities of that community. For example, fishing communities will have a different set of guidelines and laws that are specific for fishing, boats, rivers, beaches and so on. While communities that have a high percentage of computer geeks will have a different set of laws.

We have to view every sector with brand new eyes of unlimited opportunity, not restricted by the availability of money. It is therefore also imperative to keep reminding ourselves that everything is possible and everything is achievable, because everything is available

– because money is not a hurdle. It will however take several stages of using money to liberate us from money itself. The objective is for communities to become completely self sufficient in as many fields as quickly as possible to shed that need for money.

The initial phase will see the growing of food which is a critical ingredient for self sufficiency. The production and manufacturing of goods and produce across a broad spectrum of human activity should include light industry that may already be present in various forms in the community. Like building materials, doors, windows, furniture, metal works, etc.

These products and services will become a good interim revenue generator for the community while in its transition stage to full Contributionism. The funds generated will be used for launching new community projects deemed to be most necessary by the Council Of Elders, for the benefit of the people.

PARTICIPATION BY THE PEOPLE

This new social structure is called Contributionism for very specific reasons – people contributing their time and their talents. The launch of new projects will require the participation of as many people as possible from the community. There will undoubtedly be those who sit on the fence to see what happens, without getting too involved in the initial phase. But only those who participate will benefit from the goods produced.

The success is based on everyone contributing a few hours per week to one of the projects they choose. This will provide thousands of work-hours per week, which under normal conditions is simply not possible – because companies or municipalities do not have enough money to pay so many people for their labour. It should be evident how quickly we can create abundance in every imaginable sector of our communities, by simply applying this principle. There are many people who have special skills and talents that are not being utilised in their community – this will be a perfect platform to use such skills.

The early stages of transition will be tricky as we try to create new communities that function without money and create abundance for all – while we are still stuck in the capitalistic world of slaving away to earn money to survive. This is why the initial stages of establishing the diverse community projects is structured as outlined above. It is realistic and achievable, because it only requires everyone to contribute 3 hours per week to one of the projects – even people with jobs will have spare time to do this. Collectively they will create a solid foundation for income generating projects that belong to the community and benefit the community, and allow the community to keep growing and adding new projects at a rapid rate.

These funds will also be used to upgrade public areas, sporting facilities, arts and cultural activities that will enhance the lives of the people. To utilise such enhanced facilities people will have to contribute their 3 hours per week to one of the projects.

Slowly but surely, more and more people will be able to leave their jobs and take on full-time positions in the areas of their special talents or skills within their own communities. This will be the true beginning of the transition phase to full UBUNTU Contributionism.

And so we will experience the snowball effect as the projects multiply, become more profitable in the transitional phase, providing more and more benefits to all those who contribute. The key emphasis is on producing 'abundance' in every sector. This will allow the people to obtain the products and services at a very low price, reaping immediate benefit, while the rest of the produce is sold to outside communities at higher prices, but still much cheaper than what is available at the supermarkets.

As this system grows and evolves we will use less and less money within our own communities and eventually the need for money will simply fade away on its own, without much fanfare.

COMMUNITY INCOME GENERATION DURING THE TRANSITIONAL PERIOD

Every community project launched during the initial phase must have some kind of short-term financial aspect to it, while providing long-term solutions towards self sustainability. Here is a suggested list of the products and services that the community should be able to sell and trade, while moving towards full Contributionism. The money should be used for continued improvements and upgrades on all levels of the town/community.

Bread, milk, cream, butter, cheese, eggs, chickens, vegetables, fruit, seedlings, fish, spring water, furniture, windows, doors, other building materials, bricks, fertiliser, compost, camping and recreational activities, water activities, home industry products like jams, chillies, biscuits, art works, clothing, fabrics, shoes and many more products that may already be manufactured or produced in the community.

The primary revenue generator will most likely be tourism and hospitality related services as people will flock from all regions to experience the UBUNTU spirit and learn from what the community is creating.

There are many obvious areas that must be developed in each community, as the initial foundation for self sufficiency. The implementation will differ from town to town. Each one of these activities will create many off-shoots and give rise to more opportunities for the people to prosper.

LABOUR OF LOVE – NO JOBS, CAREERS OR SLAVING AWAY

In UBUNTU communities there are no jobs or careers or corporations. You will never again have to slave away from sunrise to sunset just to stay alive. Working in disgusting factories for some corporation exploiting you for its own profit. In a world without money nobody earns a 'salary' or gets a 'pay cheque' because there is no money to pay anyone. Instead, everyone has a Labour of Love (LOL), and everyone follows their passions and uses their God-given talents as we were meant to. Everybody does what they choose to do for their community, because they love doing it and they are good at it. And the community honours and respects them for their valuable contribution, from which everyone benefits. And because of their contribution, they have access to anything and everything at all times, just like everyone else.

And so, this allows everyone to wake up with a smile on their face, every day, as they look forward to putting their passions, skills and talents to good use. The expression 'workaholic' will take on a very different meaning. Because all our efforts will result in infinitely higher productivity, our model shows that we will only have to perform our LOL for 3 hours per day – otherwise there will be too much stuff. Too many bridges, too many shoes, too many computers, too much crockery, too many candles and too much food that goes rotten.

This poses a problem, because once you have finished doing what you love to do, for your community, you will have another 18 hours in the day to do what you want – without restriction or any cost to you. To follow your hobbies or other passions, go fishing, horse riding, grow seedlings, paint or sculpt, or build a kit-car. This is a good problem to have. It allows people down time, and quiet time, during which they explore their own consciousness. Nobody will ever have to feel enslaved again. The number of hours we will have to contribute daily is just a guideline and will most likely change based on the needs of the community. It may end up being only be a few hours per week, because there will be too much stuff available for everyone.

FIVE AREAS OF PRIMARY IMPLEMENTATION

These are the ultimate goals in the first two years.

1. Free Water
2. Free Energy – Includes: electricity, lights, heat, gas, methanol, and others
3. Free Housing – Includes building materials
4. Free Food (Agricultural land optimisation)
5. Free Education – Creating an alternative education system

There are brilliant members in every community who have access to knowhow and technology to add greatly to the implementation in each one of these five sectors. They range from farmers, water scientists, teachers, engineers, inventors, tool makers, cheese makers, architects, designers to builders... the list is endless. The community under the guidance of the Council of Elders must ensure that the skills of these individuals are used to the best of their ability.

To initiate these projects may be challenging, but it is up to the people to find a way. As explained earlier, people should deposit a small monthly amount into the Community Trust account to be used to set up the first critical projects as suggested above. The other option is to pay all the monthly fees normally payable for rates, taxes, electricity and other services into the community trust account, forcing the municipality to play ball in establishing some of the initial projects, instead of going into the pockets of corrupt council workers that use the funds for their own benefit.

Once the infrastructure for the above services has been established, there should only be a small monthly fee payable by the people, for maintenance and improvements, to continue providing the many services needed by the community. Once this has been achieved some things will become free almost immediately, while others will be available at a very low cost during the transition period.

FREE WATER

The water belongs to the people – not the government. The community needs to do whatever it can to find the cleanest and purest source of drinking water and use the experts who know the natural treatments of purifying and energising water – not by adding chemicals, especially not fluoride.

One of the latest scare tactics imposed on the people of the world is the future shortage of water. This is just another evil scare tactic and scam by the controllers who have started to take control of our supply of water. Our governments are privatising our rivers, lakes, dams and even rain water. In some places it is illegal to collect rain water. This just adds to the FEAR factor among humans and keeps many of us firmly caught up in the prison matrix.

The world is full of water. There is NO shortage of water. It is the most abundant element in the world and it should be clear to any sober person that the authorities initiated a slow and sinister disinformation campaign some years ago to confuse us into believing their lies.

There is however the issue of increasingly contaminated rivers, wells and underground water sources, caused by mines that have been given free rein to do what they want by our governments. But because the large corporations like the mines, pay the government huge amounts of money, they are not held accountable and we, the people, are being taxed and charged to clean up the mess they created. This is a huge global problem that was created by corporate greed, which will be eliminated by the removal of money from society.

Towns near clean rivers or mountains have no problem with water. There is so much water coming out of many mountains that nobody should be without water, and everyone should have free fresh energised water supplied to their home.

Coastal towns have the oceans that can provide all the water they need. Reverse osmosis converts salt water into fresh water and creates salt as a by-product. Because this process loses massive amounts of water, and alters the molecular structure of water, it should be used to supplement fresh underground water, rain water, or spring water. Since energy and money are no longer going to be a problem, the production of reverse osmosis water will be no problem either. Humid coastal areas can extract water from the air by a well established process which is in essence condensation of water out of the hot humid air.

- All water must undergo a natural process called "energising" which makes the water healthy and even helps to prevent and cure many kinds of diseases. This is based on our knowledge of sacred geometry as described earlier.
- Water from the mountain streams can be utilised for drinking and other needs.
- The water reservoir can be upgraded to receive clean mountain water and distribute it to the houses.
- Water wells will provide clean and pure water where possible.
- Eliminate any kind of centralised grid system that causes a mass water cut off when there is a problem. As in the supply of energy we should replace all grids with localised supply that cannot go down and plunge everyone into darkness or without water.
- It may be a good option to create smaller water tanks that supply several homes at a time, to prevent water shortages if the main supply is damaged in some way.
- Sewerage and drain water must be purified and energised with advanced green technology. This can be used for agriculture and in need of shortages, for drinking too. Effective Micro-organisms (EM) are the primary solution to this problem. They are readily available and cost almost nothing to brew. Because they are brewed naturally, the centralised powers have not promoted this knowledge, which is why EM still goes mostly unnoticed.
- Scientists know that structured and energised water improves the growth of plants and will be beneficial for seedling and plant nurseries created by the community as part of the agricultural initiatives. When water is combined with Effective Micro-organisms, poor quality soil can rapidly be rehabilitated for organic growing.
- Contaminated ground water will be treated by experts - those who know how to treat water – not with chemicals that cause secondary diseases and feed the pharmaceutical corporations, but with well understood natural processes like EM and others.

FREE ENERGY

Energy is possibly the most powerful tool of enslavement that has been used against humanity and therefore the most fiercely guarded sector. Guarded against new or alternative energy of any kind. And because electricity drives the wheels of industry, it pretty much runs the word. Many people can no longer afford a permanent supply of electricity and are forced to use kerosene and other dangerous and toxic substances in their homes.

Those in the know are aware that we are not far from receiving real FREE ENERGY from the many brilliant inventors that have already created it. They have been waiting for the right moment to share their creations with the world. All previous such inventions have been removed from society by the energy giants, oil corporations and banking mafia like JP Morgan. Inventors have been silenced, bribed, tortured and killed for their creations.

Many have been working secretly in hiding to avoid the same fate. The UBUNTU Contributionism system provides these inventors with a platform to finally release their free energy devices to the world. But until this happens we have to utilise every other way to get free energy, or cheap energy to the best of our ability.

There are many sources of energy for our different needs like light; heating; cooking and baking; and other needs for industry and farming, like diesel or petrol.

As we strive to find one powerful source of free energy that can cater for all our needs, we have to use the most appropriate sources for different tasks. All these are attainable by every community to free themselves from the stranglehold of the energy giants.

- Solar
- Hydro-electric
- Wind
- Geothermal
- Magnetic
- Gas
- Ethanol
- Methane (bio-gas)
- Tidal motion... and more.

- Solar energy is the most obvious source for providing light in homes, factories, schools and everywhere else that light is needed. Low wattage LED lights are almost indestructible and use very little energy.
- Where there is a river or a waterfall, there is free energy. This is a continuous energy source just going to waste. A hydro turbine placed in the river, in a waterfall, or under a bridge will not pollute the river nor use up any water. There are many rapids and smaller waterfalls that can be used for multiple hydroelectric power generators or water wheels to provide the whole town with all the power it needs for free – with minimal maintenance.
- If necessary a basic dam wall with a turbine can be built across the river in an area that will not affect the environment and benefit the community.
- A methane gas plant at the sewage dam or land-fill site, will provide many with free methane gas for cooking, heat and even light. Cow dung from the dairy should be used not only as a compost ingredient, but also to add to the methane gas production.
- Geothermal options are very real and have been implemented successfully all over the world, especially in the Philippines.
- Wind turbines can be erected in large numbers to add to the supply where necessary. These can be designed and manufactured by engineers in the community and do not have to be expensive as some towers are.
- Geo-magmatic options are also possible and need to be investigated.
- Silent magnetic motors that run perpetually and generate a high voltage output have been demonstrated and could be used in every home effectively for various electrical appliances. These are part of the Free Energy devices that we all await.

FREE HOUSING & INNOVATIVE TOWN PLANNING

Everyone must have a home – not a shack or a mansion – a beautiful home that suits the needs of the individual or the family. No-one hungry; No-one homeless. Everyone who is an active member of the community and contributes their LOL (labour of love) will have all the comforts they desire – within the limits that prevent anyone from exploiting another. To achieve this we will embark on some very exciting restructuring of our towns.

- Before any structures are erected or upgraded under the new Council of Elders, we have to evaluate the layout of our towns and use the best town planners, environmental experts and civil engineers to redesign the layout of the town for maximum benefit to the people. This must include the vision of future growth, provide for industry and agriculture and be in absolute harmony with nature. Designed by those who understand the flow of energy, incorporating sacred geometry into all our designs. This is very beneficial for the health of the entire community as it allows the free flow of energy throughout the entire community. Remember that when we are not at "ease" with our environment, we are in "disease" and we get sick. The current layouts of our towns are mostly based on grid systems. Grids can be related to nets – that are designed to trap fish, birds, animals and also humans – without even realising it. The so-called technology that is supposed to set us free, actually creates an invisible energetic trap as part of the matrix. Much of our technology today is based on grids that are controlled from central control towers. If the grid goes down, it affects large sectors of the population. It is not an effective model. Electricity is a perfect example of this.
- Embark on an extensive building material production. Using natural building materials that are available in each unique environment like clay/straw/lime/ thatch/wood/stone/and more.
- Utilise experts in creating such materials and use this as an opportunity for training people who are attracted to this sector. Working with natural materials like clay, soil, sand, stone, wood and grass is highly invigorating. Homes built from natural materials last for thousands of years, are easy to repair and withstand natural disasters more effectively than modern homes. Just think of some ancient homes found by archaeologists that are 6,000 years old with walls and roofs still intact. Imagine what your modern home would look like if it was deserted for a decade. In places like Yemen, there are six-storey buildings built from mud, surviving better than fancy modern buildings.
- Obtaining free or cheap stone and sand from the surrounding mines and quarries.
- Use our initiative and imagination to make and create all kinds of materials necessary for building houses, factories and agricultural structures needed by the community.
- Allow the artists to create materials that add an artistic, creative flavour to the building process.

- Lobby the forestry companies for wood that grows in the area. This wood can be used to build log houses, furniture, doors, windows, and more. After all, the land belongs to the people and all the trees that are planted for the benefit of private corporations do not benefit the people. As time goes by these forests will become managed by the people and will morph into more diverse forests that provide a wide variety of woods to the people. At present much of the wood in South Africa goes into creating paper, which is exported and that the people cannot afford.
- Establish a saw mill and wood factory where the carpenters can perform these tasks and a training centre for new carpenters. The factory can also be used by other community members to build their own products if they wish.
- Establish a basic but effective metal welding workshop for the basic manufacture and production of a variety of metal goods needed by the community.
- All those who participate in the various activities or services to the community will immediately be eligible for maximum benefits in all the basic needs like housing, water, food and electricity.
- Everyone will benefit based on their contribution to the community. The more you contribute – the more you benefit. Everyone is required to contribute 3 hours per week in any of the community projects to become eligible for benefits.

THE TOWNS BELONG TO THE PEOPLE

The current financial crisis should be dealt with in such a way that the banks are prevented from continuing their unlawful activity of extortion and be rapidly converted into "lawful banks", issuing interest-free money that is managed by the people. The UBUNTU model intends to follow the model of Iceland as part of the transitional phase which means that all home and car mortgages will be reversed and the bankers made responsible for all debts created from the blood and sweat of the people.

This will liberate people from their mortgages and other debts that are strangling most of us, giving us more time to participate in community projects as part of our LOL (labour of love) contributions, which will help initiate many projects.

Keep in mind that land ownership will fall away as people are free to move and settle in communities of their choice. Everyone will have a home – will be able to move to another community whenever they choose and contribute their LOL. Land will be allocated to everyone based on what they are doing for the community, by the community COE.

This means that if you want to farm you will be allocated as much land as you need to farm for the community and fulfil the farming needs of that community. If you want to breed fish, you will be provided with all the needs to do so, and so on. This applies to every sector of society and nobody can abuse the system for their own benefit at the expense of others.

The towns belong to the people who live there and contribute to its abundance. Towns are an association of sovereign human beings who choose to live in a community of other sovereign beings. One of the fundamental principles during this period will be to introduce everyone to this new lifestyle and let us realise that we do not need to horde things and store things in the garage because everything we need is always available to everyone.

THREE TIMES PRODUCTION PRINCIPLE

This is where the full UBUNTU principle really begins to show its true colours of unity and sharing. Not every community will be able to produce all the basic needs for its own survival because of climate, elevation, terrain, natural disasters, unforeseen events and more.

Every town/community should therefore produce three times as much as it requires for itself. This will allow each community to support all their neighbouring towns that may be in need of certain produce. This applies predominantly to agricultural produce and food. Other areas of industry and manufacturing will depend on other factors which I will outline in a separate section.

There will be a vibrant movement of goods, products, food and services between communities, ensuring that everything is provided to those who need it for activities that benefit the respective communities – not individual greed and hoarding. The respective Councils of Elders will play a critical role in this distribution and supply of goods between towns and across the country.

THE CONTRIBUTIONISM ASPECTS

The most crucial part of UBUNTU Contributionism communities is captured in the name – contribution by everyone. Everyone above a certain age – probably 16 years – which is the age at which "education" will end, must contribute 3 hours per week to one of the many community projects. The chapter on education outlines the beautiful experience that learning will become and why we will stop formal learning at the age of 16. Everyone who contributes will immediately be eligible to benefit from the proceeds of such projects. These projects will also be a good training ground for people to learn new skills that were previously denied to them, or they could not afford.

Initially, those that cannot contribute time, will have the option to contribute cash to make their contribution. The Council of Elders will determine how much they need to contribute to equal the labour contribution by others. Some will choose not to get involved at all – by doing so they will not be eligible to any of the benefits from the produce and other projects generated by those who make it work. Three hours per week is not a tall order and will hopefully allow everyone to participate.

I do believe that those who choose to sit on the fence will wake up very quickly when they see their friends getting their daily needs for a fraction of the price they have to pay at the supermarket. These benefits will grow quickly as more people join and the number of community projects increase. Within a relatively short time we should be getting most of our daily foods for virtually free from our own community – like bread, milk, butter, cheese, cream, fruits, nuts, vegetables, fish, eggs, chicken, and more.

Everyone is required to contribute 3 hours per week towards community projects. People can choose in which area they want to contribute, or the council of elders will allocate people to various tasks based on their ability OR the most pressing needs in the community at the time.

This means that in a town where 1000 people are eligible to contribute their skills and time, there will be 3000 labour-hours dedicated to community projects per week. 1000 people x 3 hours per week, per person. This means that every day there will be on average 143 people working for the community on various projects. There is no town council which represents a community of 1000 people that can even remotely afford to pay 143 people's salaries on this basis.

In return for their participation, people will pay a fraction of the normal cost for all the foods and goods created by the community projects, until eventually, everything will be freely available to the active community members. It is instantly visible how the community will benefit from such participation from the first day of implementation and how towns with this kind of public participation will grow and flourish in every area imaginable.

FREE FOOD

The world we live in today most people work, to make money, so that they can buy food. When people are homeless, jobless and hungry, they will do anything to get money so that they can buy food, even turn to crime. Currently the sad situation is that a lack of money turns good people into criminals. More and more people face harsh conditions finding themselves without work and without hope of survival in the future.

During March 2013, police in the USA acted on the instructions of a bank that foreclosed a food store, to prevent hungry and homeless people from taking the food put out on the sidewalk by the disgruntled store owner. The police stood by, preventing the people from taking any, while the food was loaded on to trucks and taken to a landfill. The video clip can be viewed here: http://www.youtube.com/watch?v=4eZmczK2UKM

This is the kind of behaviour that will eventually make police officers realise that they are working for the 'devil' while oppressing their own fellow human beings.

Food is so expensive that the little bit of money people have available hardly keeps them sustained. Bad diet leads to bad health and an unhealthy mental attitude leads to bad decisions. This is the spiral of social degradation that is clearly visible in the world today.

In many parts of the world the governments are removing people from their land, where they grow food to sustain themselves. These removals are maliciously premeditated, to force people to work for money, to keep the bankster corporations in control.

The production of food, together with the supply of water, are the very first activities that need to be implemented in every town, to make each community self reliant on its own food supply as quickly as possible and give everyone back their dignity as human beings.

We must not underestimate the attempts by Monsanto and other GMO giants to take control of our food supply. They will do everything they can, to stop communities from achieving self sufficiency in food supply.

Self sufficiency in food supply will make such towns highly desirable to live in and they will experience a rapid flow of people from the overcrowded cities. It is also the catalyst that will start the domino effect, causing the neighbouring towns to adopt the same way of life. Because it will not take long before all the people from the neighbouring towns start buying all their goods from the town where all these goods are available at a fraction of the price, compared to their own town – which still operates on a normal capitalist system.

It is important at this stage that the community not "fall" into the temptation of becoming a profitable and capitalistic enterprise. The Council of Elders must be mindful not to increase prices or jeopardize the UBUNTU Contributionism principles for the lure of money.

These activities will allow all the people to live well in the town/ community, needing very little money, if any. Very soon the people will realise that they hardly use any money at all while at home in their own community. The real spending applies only when people travel and they have to interact with other towns or buy items not available in the UBUNTU town. As part of the phased approach, it is imperative that the following projects are implemented with immediate effect.

- All possible support must be given to the farmers to produce as much organic non-GMO food as possible for their own community and other communities in their area.
- Utilise the idle municipal land and reach agreements with farmers to use their land in the surrounds for all agricultural activity.
- Establish a communal dining hall as one of the first projects to gain the confidence of the people. To show that this is not just another empty promise by the government. Provide one good meal a day for the hungry, the homeless and those out of work and all those who cannot afford food. Especially the orphans and the aged.
- But to qualify for a meal, the people have to do 3 hours of community work per week, towards creating the meals. I am not talking about hard labour or slave labour or even child labour. Those are expressions closely associated with a capitalist system

where people and children are exploited. I will deal with the role of the children in other chapters, especially the education section. There are many things that children and the aged can do for the community that are linked to learning new skills while providing a diverse number of benefits to their community. Even some cultural activities create products for the community. The aged can contribute their experience and knowledge in almost every area. The number of meals provided to such participants will increase as the system gets refined and can provide the extra meals.

- Utilise one of the empty municipal buildings in town to create a functional kitchen with tables and chairs and get some of the jobless people with the right skills to do the cooking. This can eventually escalate to 2 and 3 meals a day when the community projects have become really productive.
- The funds for the kitchen can come from the recycling of the rubbish dump, the agricultural activity by the community, the income from selling the long list of products and services by the self-sustained community, and also the interim community account that is controlled by the Council of Elders on behalf of the community. Remember that during the initial stages there will be money going into the community trust account every month instead of disappearing into the bottomless coffers of the municipality.
- A community bakery must be upgraded to bake a large number of breads every day to provide all the people with bread at a low cost. Not just the boring government loafs, but all kinds of nutritious breads that can also be sold at the farmers' market, restaurants and 'exported' to neighbouring towns. Those that contribute will get free or very cheap bread, based on the situation of the community.
- Dairy for production of milk, cream, butter and cheese. This can become a very lucrative part of the first phase towards self sustainability.
- Free-range chickens for eggs and meat.
- Growth tunnels for vegetables and herbs all year round.
- Bee hives and bees, to pollinate the plants and trees and provide honey. Each bee hive can produce an average of 15 – 30 kg honey per year.
- Fruit, nuts and citrus orchards – will also have many spin-off products.
- Fish breeding – an average size fish farm can produce millions of trout, bass, catfish and other fish in the dams and abandoned

factories/farms, for consumption by the community and for selling to neighbouring towns.

- Bottled water from the natural springs to sell on the open market to distributors and also passers-by on the freeway.
- Experts in each activity can advise on how large that sector should be to provide enough for everyone and comply with the 3-times production principle.
- These are just some of the most obvious activities that can to be implemented to create a self sustained community with food related produce.
- The production and supply of food to the community will provide a good model for understanding of how to implement the same in other sectors of industry and manufacturing.

OTHER BENEFICIAL ACTIVITIES DURING THE TRANSITIONAL PHASE

Using specialists and experts for the benefit of our communities.
- Processing the sewage into fertiliser will generate income for the community and allow us to fertilise our own lands.
- Using the sewage plant to generate gas – use for cooking and more.
- Making compost from cow dung and all other organic material.
- Plant seedlings of all kinds for own use and external sales.
- Utilising fast growing invasive species of trees like wattle for manufacturing wooden items.
- Use discarded wood from forestry activity and other wood for mulch/wood chips.
- The various working farms will be promoted as tourist attractions to city children to learn about life and mother Earth.
- Set up community manufacturing of all kinds of products needed by the community. These can also be sold to outsiders as income in the early stages of transition.
- A regular or permanent farmers' market to attract people from the entire region and passers-by to the town. All the goods manufactured and produced in town can be sold for the benefit of the community. This will include: Fruit, vegetables, seedlings, plants, herbs, meat, fish, butter, milk, cheese, bread, wooden products, bottled preserves, jams, art, fabrics, etc.
- Setting up effective literacy classes for children and adults with

available teaching tools by members of the community.

- Create day-care and learning centres where children from an early age begin to explore, while learning the important things in life as opposed to the current system of indoctrination.
- An alternative education system must be initiated immediately to allow our children to grow up with open minds – open to all possibility. To learn meaningful skills for life and be allowed to express their natural talents. There are many great teachers who have already left the current schooling system, frustrated by its shortcomings, desperately looking for new alternatives. I cover education extensively in the Education chapter.
- Upgrade and restructure the roads and parks and schools and sports grounds for the benefit of all the people.
- Plant trees, including fruit and nut, along all the roads, schools and parks.
- Create and plant food forests in public areas, parks and other places.
- Build a small smokeless factory for converting used tyres into charcoal and generating energy from the heat. This is also a huge solution for the pollution aspect of used tyres. This technology exists among many other technologies not used by the current councils.
- A well planned recreational area for promotion of arts and culture. This should include a well stocked art studio for painters, sculptors and more.
- A music school with as many instruments as possible – giving the students the platform to do regular performances for the community.
- Allow artists to create works of art that are displayed along the streets to beautify the towns.
- Art gallery to display all kinds of art and crafts and other hand-made goods by community members.
- Clothing factory where tailors inspire each other, where material is also dyed into beautiful fabrics.
- Shoe factory – using leather and tyres for new innovative strong, practical and lasting shoes.
- Turn the town into a haven for tourists to marvel at the industrious and artistic nature of the people.
- Where possible utilise the river/water front as major attraction.
- Promote fishing activities and competitions.

- Promote all the activities and attractions in the town with a well planned and ongoing PR campaign - as an example of UBUNTU Contributionism.
- Turn your town into the most beautiful town in your country that attracts people from all over the world.
- The people and the Council of Elders will come up with countless more ideas to benefit the town and its people.

NOTICE: These points should only be seen as ideas and not a list of absolute instructions.

TOURISM

Global tourism has changed dramatically and people no longer just want to travel as observers like visitors to a zoo. More and more tourists prefer to become involved in the communities they visit. This should be used as new tourism approach – the way people go cherry picking for fun – people love to learn new things for fun too. We need to provide an environment for tourists to get involved in a multitude of hands-on activities – like milking cows or making cheese, or ploughing the land, planting seedlings, creating ceramics and pottery and art, designing fabrics, making shoes, feeding the aged and orphans, building new eco-friendly homes, etc, etc.

Build beautifully attractive accommodation for tourists and make it available at a low cost to attract active tourists to your town. People that will love the participation in the various activities while they help to create more abundance for your community.

When people do what they are passionate about, they radiate very positive energy. These are simple scientific facts. This invisible positive energy generated by each happy and fulfilled individual feeds others around them with positive energy. It is infectious and exponential. It can be felt when you walk into a room of happy people, doing what they love to do. This is all connected to those laws of nature which I covered earlier. Whether it is cooking, farming, engineering, washing, making shoes, creating art, or even solving the sewage problems. It is this positive energy that fills the hearts of the people in their UBUNTU communities and infects everyone around them.

ALTERNATIVE LOCAL CURRENCY - INTERIM PROTECTION MEASURES

Once the first town has become self sustained and produces all the basic foods and other goods mentioned before, it will be impossible for surrounding towns to continue operating on the old capitalistic model. It will create a domino effect that will influence every aspect of our lives in ways that are impossible to predict.

What we have to do, is keep an open mind to deal with the unlimited possibilities that we have never had to deal with before. The neighbouring towns must be treated as brothers and sisters and an extension of the greater UBUNTU family. They should never be seen as competitors or the 'dark side' which still operates a capitalist system.

What will most likely happen in the initial stages is that the people from surrounding towns will start to buy all their necessities from the UBUNTU town. Then the greed issue will begin to play a role and someone will attempt to buy all the goods from the UBUNTU town at a reduced price, so that he can re-sell it in his own town at the full price.

Or – someone will try to get one of the production factories in the UBUNTU town to produce items for him to sell outside of the town, for his own enrichment. There will be many attempts by selfish individuals to exploit the UBUNTU community's ability to create things virtually for free. As always this greed aspect comes down to money which we need to guard against in the initial stages of transition. Always keep at the top of your mind our united intention: *a world without money*.

It is imperative that the communities are acutely aware of this and ensure that the Council of Elders is in a position to prevent such exploitation of its own people and resources. It may be necessary to create an alternative local currency for the town to prevent such exploitation. As the community progresses towards higher levels of self sustainability and Contributionism, all transactions in the town will be done with the town's own currency.

It can be in any form imaginable, as agreed to by the COE, but it would be crazy to repeat the money printing exercise that has already caused all the problems. The most obvious solution lies in electronic cards that can be streamlined for all the activities in the community. There are existing sophisticated electronic currency card systems available that have been tested and are ready for use with minimal initial cost to the community. They can be programmed to allow different people to benefit according to their contribution to the community.

These are not linked to banks in any way but simply create an electronic form of payment. This can be controlled by the Council of Elders to ensure that no outsiders can exploit their town. It must remain uncomplicated as opposed to what we have endured in the financial sector until now. Everything that is made, traded, bought or exchanged in any way within the town, will be done with the currency of their own community.

The external sales of goods and produce to outside towns, tourists, or anyone else, will be done at markets or specially arranged events controlled by appointed people by the Council. These will generate the regular currency used outside of the community, which will be used by the community for acquiring the materials and other goods not produced in their own community and in so doing replenish the materials needed to keep the community projects going .

As this external funding increases, the community will be able to build more factories and initiate more projects to produce other items to benefit the community. A good example of such community models are the many kibbutzes in Israel. Some of the kibbutzes have become great success stories in their own right, by manufacturing products that they export to outsiders, amassing large amounts of money for the members of the kibbutz.

By the year 2013, Community Talent Exchanges have been operating for more than a decade with amazing success, and without any money at all. This simple system will be an intricate part of the early transition phase. This will be a particularly attractive alternative to city dwellers with diverse skills, allowing them to move away from using money. Although it has strong aspects of bartering, these talents or skills that people exchange will eventually become their LOL that they contribute to their communities. I have interviewed some people who claim that they have hardly used any money since they joined the Community Exchange system. It is a well managed online system that provides very diverse skills and services by thousands of people. This will be a perfect solution in the initial transitional stages making people accustomed to not needing money.

There will also be those who sit back and watch the process unfold without getting involved or too excited. That is to be expected given our schooling. Many people will not wish to work three hours a week because it interferes with vital television time. They will not believe that this will work and will keep falling back into the old system, while they watch the abundance around them grow. This should be tolerated because sooner or later they will see the benefits and will not be able to resist them. What must not be tolerated is any attempt by them to sabotage the plans either vocally or practically. Non-contributionism is acceptable in the short term, but anti-contributionism must be avoided.

FINAL DESTINATION – TOWN BY TOWN – COUNTRY BY COUNTRY

The ultimate goal is to convert the whole country into a Contributionist UBUNTU society that functions without money, excels in arts, culture, science and technology, allowing the people to live where they choose, do what they are passionate about and succeed in abundance on all levels of their lives. There will be a vibrant exchange of food, goods, products and services between communities – supplying those towns that cannot produce certain items on their own.

But what happens once our country is a fully Contributionist UBUNTU community? How will we interact with other countries? This is where it gets really interesting as we realise that Contributionism is a true utopian seed of unstoppable growth towards abundance across the whole planet.

To explain this will require that we stretch our imagination and allow ourselves to be projected into the new system – fully developed into every sector of our society – fully implemented and fully functional. Do not try to trip yourself up while going through this exercise and do not try to imagine possible stumbling blocks or insurmountable hurdles – just go with the flow and imagine what may still seem to be impossible to some.

SPREADING THE UBUNTU BUG

As an example of this I will use the motorcar manufacturing sector in South Africa to demonstrate how things unfold and evolve, the moment we remove money from the system.

South Africa manufactures all the major brands of cars for the global car market. Mercedes Benz; BMW; Toyota; Mazda; Ford; VW; and more. We export these to the rest of the world and yet, South Africans pay amongst the highest prices in the world for cars, based on the average income. The vast majority of people cannot afford to buy a new car. How is this possible?

In truth, this example is not realistic because in a Contributionist society where money is no concern, we will probably not drive cars the way we do today; we will have free energy for everything we do; there will be a brand new transport system for people and goods that is hard to predict at this stage; we will not use fossil fuels; we will probably have levitation devices that until now have been suppressed by the oil giants; the production of the new cars or transportation devices will happen completely differently to how it happens today; every aspect of our lives will change for the better.

BUT – for the purpose of this explanation, let's stick to the car manufacturing sector and let us imagine that the production lines in the car factories are filled with car enthusiasts who love cars and everything about them – it is their choice to contribute their 3 hours per day towards building cars for their community and extended society. They do it with love and passion, producing the most immaculate hand made cars that we can imagine. From the engine, to the interior, to the body and the paintwork. Every car a masterpiece.

Where do they get all the materials needed to make the cars?

From the people who make the individual components for the cars – with equal love and passion because that is what they have in turn chosen to do for their community – 3 hours per day. Every single item that makes up the car will come from those who make those parts.

And where do they get the materials to make the engine; the seats; the dashboard; the gear stick; the wires; carburettor; the paint; the tyres; etc? From those who make that – and so on, and so on. The amazing thing is that the diversity in human passion and interest is infinite. There is always someone interested in something that others have not even heard of.

Keep in mind that under the Contributionism system all these materials and items are made and delivered to the car production line for free – because every step in the chain is part of the Contributionism system. I need to qualify the word "free". Since there is no money in the system, things are not really free. They are simply made available to everyone all the time – in a never-ending chain of supply to create abundance for the people. Nothing is 'free' but everything is made available to everyone as long as they are contributing members of the community. It is that simple.

The result is that when the BMW rolls off the production line it will be made at no cost – for free. This poses an immediate problem for the manufacturer and the community they are a part of. Do we give the cars to the German corporation for free? Or do we charge them money for it?

BUT the problem is that we don't use money... which means that their money is completely useless to us and of no benefit at all to the community and country. So, what will we want in return from the German corporation for building their cars? Something that will benefit the people of the country. As is it stands, it seems that there is nothing that the BMW corporation can offer the people of South Africa in return for building their cars.

This opens up a few interesting possibilities. We can offer the cars to China, or Russia, who may be able to trade the cars for a rare material/mineral that we desperately need for some reason or another. This will give China or Russia a distinct advantage because they will be getting the cars virtually for free and therefore be able to sell the cars to the global market at greatly reduced costs and create a big problem for BMW. Very soon BMW will be bankrupt and we will probably stop manufacturing their silly cars anyway, because it would be like building ox wagons when we use levitation devices powered by zero-point energy - for free.

It is quite evident from this silly example that as soon as one country becomes a full Contributionist entity, it will force all other countries to follow the same route, otherwise their entire economy will collapse. And once all the countries become UBUNTU communities there is no need for borders, passports, interrogations and treating people like terrorist suspects, the draconian control that restricts our freedom and liberties, and many other aspects of our lives that are controlled for one reason only – to control commerce by controlling the money. We will have complete freedom to travel and live anywhere we choose on our planet that we are born on – FREE and sovereign.

In this simple example we can recognise the reason why the global bankster syndicates have been forcing their private money supply on the people of the world for hundreds of years. They simply cannot allow any country to break away from their complete financial control.

This is why economic hit men have been sent to deal with countries that in the past showed too much independence and where the leaders had their own ideas of working for the benefit of their own people. These are seen as rogue states that could potentially threaten the stability and growth of the bankers' global empire.

Please take a while and let this sink in – herein lies the weakness of the bankers and their money. It provides the opportunity for the people to regain their freedom from global economic slavery. For those who are new to this information I suggest reading the spine chilling *Confessions of An Economic Hit Man* by John Perkins, to get an insider's story on unimaginable manipulation of politicians and governments around the world by the Illuminati bankster mobs in an ongoing attempt to control every country.

So, the domino effect of Contributionism will start with one town, eventually liberating the entire country. Once one independent country achieves this status, it will affect other countries very quickly, as people all over the world share the same desire for freedom. It can happen very quickly – seemingly overnight, like the Russian and French revolutions. And all it may take to topple this money gangster empire, is one small town in some country, out of sight and out of mind, while the banskters focus their attention on the big cities.

As soon as people realise that the banks actually have no money at all – because they create it out of thin air every day – a simple event like a bank-run will expose their fraud and cause the banks to close their doors – and in effect become insolvent in a flash. This may end up being one of the strategies used by the people to expose the unlawful and criminal activities of the banksters. Ironically, this is almost precisely what happened in Cyprus at the end of March 2013, but the people did not realise what they had achieved. The general ignorance of the masses prevented them from publically declaring the banks insolvent and using the necessary legal structures available to enforce a court ruling, to declare them insolvent. The banks are after all companies.

The people should be prepared for such future events and have a plan ready to declare the banks and central bank insolvent, and implement a new currency of the people as soon as this happens. Since the currency that belongs to the insolvent private banks has been withheld from the people, the people could invoke a vote of no confidence in the existing money and launch a new currency of the people – by the people. I leave the rest up to your imagination.

THE INTERIM PHASES – CREATIVE MONEY

We cannot go from zero to hero in one step – as much as most of us would probably like to. There will be a number of transitional steps to move us from where we are today to full UBUNTU Contributionism, unless something dramatic happens. We may have to create interim alternative currencies of what some call "lawful money" or "asset backed money", or simple credit/point creation in a responsible way, compared to what the banksters have been doing, and so on.

We will have to be as creative as possible to provide a platform for a smooth transition – avoiding the creation of more problems and situations that can be exploited to the detriment of the people. We have to put those days behind us.

Linking money to gold or some other valuable commodity for a short period is probably not a good option. It only perpetuates the problems of the past and opens it up to potential exploitation by those who still want to hold on to control over others.

The one critical thing that needs to happen in every country, is the closing of the unlawful privately owned central banks and replacing them with a PEOPLE'S BANK – that creates money for the people, by the people – interest free and tax free. This is what Abraham Lincoln and JFK did before they were assassinated. So do not take this lightly. The banksters will go to any extremes to prevent this. It will cut the bankers off at the knees and remove all their financial control over the affairs of any country.

The obligation of the new PEOPLE'S BANK will be to make money available for the people as and when it is necessary in all areas of the economy, to stabilise the financial sector and remove all the financial hardships from the people.

BUILDING – INDUSTRY – MANUFACTURING

Everything that is needed by the communities and the people will be manufactured and produced as long as it is of benefit or necessity to the community – and not because of individual lust or greed. This means that the tools required to do so also have to be created. And so, we will develop a new supply chain that is not the consequence of brand strategy, marketing campaigns or attempts to increase market share, but the true needs of society.

Presently, every cycle of production delivers goods that are cheaper to manufacture to increase profits, and less durable, to increase the likelihood of being replaced in the near future. All to keep the industry monster expanding.

The entire sector that comprises industry and manufacturing will take on a very different face in a Contributionist society, because money is no hurdle to progress and new materials that are eco-friendly, biodegradable and recyclable will be used. Everything will be made to the best possible quality so that it lasts as long as possible and never has to be replaced or fixed.

Hundreds of thousands of people working in large factories, hired as cheap labour, will be able to follow their passion and choose other things to do, and probably move to other smaller factories or workshops where their expertise will be utilised more effectively for the benefit of their community. For example, many of the thousands of workers in the production lines for NIKE or BATA shoes could become shoemakers in their own right, and in their own communities, providing a highly necessary specialised service.

Every factory or workshop will have a master craftsperson overseeing the activity. From the bakery, dairy, glass making, forestry, farming to engineering and more, supported by many other highly skilled people. Such masters of their skills will probably also be the master teachers in their sector, where children will come to attain practical experience and knowledge, as part of the new education system that teaches true skills for life as opposed to useless theoretical knowledge.

The huge mining operations will be reduced dramatically to only mine what the country and its people need. Foreign ownership of mines and mineral rights will revert back to the people of the land and minerals will not be exported or exploited on any stock markets to create wealth for only a few. The hundreds of thousands of people slaving away for mining corporations that contribute very little to the wellbeing of the people, other than paying them a few lousy dollars to buy stuff with, will become productive members of their communities applying their LOL, contributing greatly to the abundance of each community they live in. Each one of the miners has special skills of some kind, that have been destroyed by the capitalistic beast and the need to earn money to survive.

Mining is one of the most critical industries of the world because it produces the raw materials used in almost everything we use in our daily lives. At present, the mines dig out as much mineral wealth as they can get from mother Earth, ship it all over the world to drive the global industry, to manufacture stuff to be sold to the people; stuff that people don't really need, but think they need, in a capitalist consumer society, to continue surviving and feeding the monster called the economy, which uses money to stay alive and continues to enslave the people in this insane cycle of consumption – all to keep the banksters in control.

Below: An extraordinary example of this are the "ghost cities of China." Entire cities, housing as many as five million people lie empty all over China. These cities were built for one primary reason, to show the world that China is experiencing economic growth. The amount of resources that were wasted to create this insanity is testimony that the time for Contributionism as an alternative reality has arrived.

The minerals that are not gobbled up by industry are sold on the international markets to enrich only a small percentage of the world, while enslaving the people in the process. This applies to all our natural resources. Just think about what has happened to water in the last decade. We used to be able to drink water from a tap – now many people only drink bottled water that is shipped all over the world. The governments and giant multinational corporations have taken ownership of these minerals against the will of the people. When ordinary South Africans dig for gold or diamonds, they are guilty of a criminal offence and are given harsh sentences.

The mining and minerals industry is one of the first sectors that must be rescued from the unlawful pirates that have hijacked our land, and must be returned to the people of the country to whom it belongs.

This will dramatically affect all the components we need to manufacture everything imaginable. The supply of metals like steel, iron, aluminium, and other building materials like wood, bricks, stone cement, sand – will be provided to those manufacturers that have been appointed by the communities through their Council of Elders. This obviously also extends into the field of radioactive elements or related activity like research on such substances.

The truth is, there is no need for humanity to use any of these dangerous materials in any way. There are other alternatives that are safe and infinitely more effective. There is already an explosion of new energy and free energy technology that will be available to the whole world without much fanfare. This free energy will change the way we do everything in our lives in ways that we cannot imagine today. Especially in the field of industry and manufacturing.

Once we realise that all this mining activity is not really necessary to create abundance for the people and that it is only a tool to keep the wheels of industry turning so that the money can flow and keep people enslaved in this relentless cycle, while keeping the banksters in control, we will put a stop to it immediately.

Scientist, inventors and ordinary people have all the solutions we need to create abundance on all levels without raping our planet for minerals. There is an abundance of renewable sources for everything we need to live fulfilled lives.

A major development drive will be structured across all sectors of industry to design and manufacture everything locally, to the best possible quality which is not possible under a capitalist system. Remember that money is no longer a hurdle to progress. This means that every country will need very little, if anything, from any other country to be self sustained and allow its people to live utopian lives. But by this time, there will be no borders and every community will be able to get anything it needs from those who are already doing it.

And since money is no object, the central Council of Elders will provide everything needed by each and every producer and manufacturer, by utilising the mineral and natural wealth of the country. Every production or manufacturing plant will get whatever they need, to do what they do for their community and more. Keep in mind that all this activity is not for profit or greed, but only for the needs of society – therein lies a huge philosophical difference.

Communities will consume a fraction of things we use today – and everything will be reusable; recyclable; biodegradable; as practical as possible and as durable as possible so that it only has to be made once. The concept of 'obsolescence' will be erased from our memory. This is a despicable legacy of capitalism in which corporations manufacture things to only last a short while before it needs to be replaced. Most things in our lives today are structured to keep the money monster alive and keep us, the consumers, consuming more and more. Contributionism will allow us to build everything to last as long as possible.

One of the best short documentaries that shows this insane consuming mentality is the *Story of Stuff* – by Annie Leonard. Please view it here: http://www.storyofstuff.org/

Conclusion

- The UBUNTU CONTRIBUTION SYSTEM is a blueprint for human prosperity and a new social structure in which everyone is absolutely free and equal.
- Communities of sovereign humans who choose to unite for the greater benefit of everyone.
- A society that functions without the concept of money, any form of barter or trade, or the attachment of value to material things.
- Where everyone's contribution to the community is treated as equally and infinitely valuable.
- A culture where each individual is encouraged to follow their passion and contributes their natural talents or acquired skills to the greater benefit of all in the community.
- A society with a new set of laws based on the needs of the people.
- Where everything is provided to everyone because they contribute their Labour of Love.
- A society where everyone is cared for and loved from the womb to the day their soul leaves their body.
- A world where there are no jobs, careers, corporations, unemployment, homelessness, hunger or any other negative aspects of the past.
- A society which promotes the highest levels of scientific and technological progress because there are no financial restrictions.
- A society in which arts and culture flourishes allowing people to experience life to the fullest.
- A society in which spiritual growth of its people through the explosion of arts and culture will allow the rapid rise of consciousness to fully embrace the concept of unity.

- A system that provides unimaginable abundance of all things on all levels, impossible to imagine by those trapped in the capitalist, consumer-driven environment of today.

MOVING FROM TOWN TO TOWN

What happens if people get itchy feet and want to travel or move to another town up in the mountains or closer to the sea, or closer to a family member or some other place that has suddenly caught their attention? This is one of the regular questions asked by people trying to process the UBUNTU philosophy, simply because those who are new to the idea of Contributionism still think about the money, and how they will get things without money, and how they will be able to travel. Keep in mind that everyone can choose to live in any community – OR – families can choose to live on their own in a remote area.

All modes of transport are available to everyone all the time and travelling anywhere is free. There will be many modes of transport that are difficult to predict. People can choose to relocate to another town any time.

Because of the different social structure and the closely integrated community, people will notify their fellow workers of their intention to move, just in case there may be a replacement required for that specific skill in the community. But because of the completely different structure of UBUNTU communities, it is highly unlikely that there will not be someone who can perform such a function. There will most likely be a whole host of highly skilled people only too eager to perform the task in question.

Let me also remind you that in UBUNTU communities everyone knows everyone else, they know their skills, what they do, where they do it, where they live, how to get in contact with everyone, how to get anything you need, how to get things fixed or built or designed and so on. These are fully integrated communities where everything and everyone is taken care of. So when someone chooses to leave an UBUNTU community, it will probably be a major event and result in a festive occasion in the form of a farewell party.

Let me take you through a sequence of events that will most likely transpire when moving to a new town. This will also outline some finer details of the structure of our new communities and how effortlessly they function.

I arrive in a new town with the intention to settle there, whatever my reasons may be. I go to the visitors building to announce myself. This is most likely attached to the community centre where all other community activity is planned and where the Council of Elders sits. All new settlers or visitor to the town are required to announce their arrival the way we do when entering a nature reserve.

Michael: "Hello my name is Michael and I am here to settle in your lovely community."

John: "Welcome Michael, my name is John, I am one of the community skills coordinators, so nice to have you here. Please write your name in our community book. What is your labour of love (LOL) Michael?"

Michael: "I am a sculptor... I make ceramic pottery sculptures."

John: "That sounds amazing... you will make a great new contribution to the arts and culture of our town. But at present we don't have a need for another sculptor – what other skills do you have, Michael?"

Michael, after thinking for a while... "I love growing seedlings or planting trees."

John: "That is fantastic because we have a very active program of growing seedlings which involves the small children as part of their learning process. Our seedlings are used by six of the neighbouring towns for the farming and forestry projects. They will be very happy with your contribution."

John turns to the community projects page...
"Now... what community projects would you like to participate in as you weekly 3-hour contribution, Michael? "

Michael: "I love chemistry... is there anything that I can get involved in where I can learn more about chemistry?"

John: "Yes, our water and sewage recycling team is doing amazing work with chemistry, making new discoveries all the time."
John enters my skills and talents into the community contact book.

This is also done on a sophisticated computer, with open source software of the highest level technology possible, which immediately identifies where my skills or talents may be required. I have agreed to contribute three hours per day, five days a week, to growing seedlings, and three hours per week in a community service while learning about chemistry at the recycling plant.

After my LOL for 3 hours every day, I still have 18 hours of the day left to do my sculpture work at the best equipped sculpture studio imaginable – where all the materials are provided for me as a contributing member of the community.

John: "Where do you prefer to live Michael, in the valley, by the river or up on the mountain?"

Michael: "I prefer the mountain."

John scans the computer for homes on the mountain. "It seems that there are no vacant homes on the mountain at the moment, but there are several lovely homes by the river. I will give you the map so that you can go choose the one you prefer, while we start planning your new home. Here is the community contact list with the names and skills of everyone. I will contact the town planners and architects so that they can start planning your home on the mountain with your input."

I take a ride on the free public transport to view the homes by the river and choose the one I like most. Notice that I was not given a key, as keys and locking things is unimaginable in UBUNTU communities. I love the interiors of the house but I am not mad about the dining table. I scan through the contact booklet to see where the furniture makers are and take a ride to the furniture warehouse to choose a new table. I meet the carpenter who arranges to deliver the table I have chosen and uplifts the old one – so that it can be used by someone else or remodelled into a new piece. I have the rest of the day off.

That evening I am introduced to a large crowd that gathers to meet the newcomer. This happens in the town square or some other communal gathering place where such events take place. People are free to ask me questions about my talents and get to know me in the process. This is accompanied by festivities, dancing and music and food for everyone. The next day, I have the day off, to move around town and meet as many people as I can and become familiar with their skills and talents. I meet the people with whom I will be 'LOLing' with (labour of love-ing) in the seedlings project and learn about the process.

The following morning I start my LOL contribution for the community. I choose to LOL from 7 to 10 a.m. because I am an early riser. By 10 a.m. I stroll over to the park where the community art centre is located and establish a workspace for my ceramic sculpting. I order all the materials I need from the master teacher who oversees the activity at the sculpture centre.

Over the next six months my passion for seedlings reaches new heights while I continue to create a wide variety of sculptures. The master teacher is so impressed that she asks me to teach some classes in the afternoons to the 12-year old children as part of their education. In the meantime my sculptures have become highly desirable by people in the community and I cannot keep up with the people's demand for my new works of art. So much so, that after six months several members of the community approach the Council of Elders with a request that I be appointed as a sculptor for the town.

This is supported by one third of the people – which is in line with the minority rule principle and the sacred geometry ratio of 1/3 or 11/33, that is used to follow the laws of nature. The Council calls me in and suggest this request from the community to me. Everyone is very excited about me having more time to create my breathtaking sculptures. I accept the appointment graciously and the next day I take may place as the respected appointed sculptor for the community. My sculptures align the streets and parks and are the pride of my community.

In the process of sculpting I am also appointed as master sculptor by the existing master sculptor. This affords me the opportunity to teach children as part of the education process – where they will sit in on my sessions and learn from me as I work.

OR

I decline the proposed appointment as town sculptor because in the past six months I have developed a deeper passion for seedlings and forestry and I want to become more active in that area.

OR

When I present myself on arrival in my new town they instantly recognise my skills as being superior to anything available in the community. I am offered a home of my choice and the following day the Council of Elders decide, upon the advice of other masters and teachers, to offer me the position of master teacher in the area of my expertise – because there is no one with this ability. But like everyone else, I have to choose a community service, towards which I contribute 3 hours per week. If I am confused and cannot choose – I will be temporarily allocated to one of the projects that are in need of more people, until I make up my mind. The community projects work on a rotation basis every few weeks, so that the people don't get bored but rather keep experiencing a wide variety of activities.

This is a basic example of how simply anything can be accomplished when money does not stand in the way. This example will apply to every aspect of our community – all the different talents and skills imaginable. It is a self correcting system that will present a solution for every challenge.

HOLIDAYS & VACATIONS

People take holidays and vacations because they have been working like slaves for a whole year and they need to recharge their batteries before they come back and do it all over again. Holidays are not human rights, they are privileges granted to citizens by our employers and the corporations we devote our lives to. A large percentage of the world's population don't have official employment, or the kind of work they do, does not even afford them a vacation. While people in official employment get on average between 2-4 weeks off work per annum. This is a big deal and some people plan their holidays years in advance to make the most of it. It is truly a sad situation.

In UBUNTU communities where people live where they choose; do what they love; have access to everything they need; have access to art, culture, sport and any hobbies they may have; enjoy their life to the fullest without any stress or worries about anything, people will not think about 'holidays' or 'vacations' the way we do today.

Annual vacations will probably not be part of our thought process at all. Nor will holidays or long weekends or time off work and other such luxuries that are extended to us by our superiors in a hierarchical society. We will be in complete control of our own time and destiny. We can move around as we please within the guidelines of UBUNTU structures.

Transport is freely available to everyone and people can travel anywhere, anytime. Upon arrival they will announce themselves at the community centre, state their reason for arrival – vacation – and choose a LOL or community project to contribute to as is the norm under the Contributionism model. In return for contributing their 3 hours daily, five days per week, they will have access to all the facilities in the community, sports, arts, culture, and all the food they can eat. This will allow the people on their so-called vacation to sit on the beach for 18 hours a day if they wanted.

This model applies to travellers or holiday makers or anyone else. It is simple and cannot be corrupted because there is no money to corrupt any part of it.

Even those who are born travellers will be catered for. Travellers, even though they only stay for a short term, are considered honoured guests of any community. Travellers contribute stories, news, and a wide perspective on life, the world and the universe, that will be new and intriguing to the people in the community. Often, they bring gifts and talents from faraway places that ignite the desire within others to explore and learn and grow. And since everything is free, the gifts they bring are always breathtaking. And so they will have to be, because in a free society where everyone has everything they need, your gifts will have to be truly unique.

COMMUNITY FOOD HALLS – RESTAURANTS – COOKING AT HOME

Keep in mind that food is available to everyone all the time in UBUNTU communities. If something specific is not available in the community, the master teachers or master craftsmen in that sector will obtain it through the Council of Elders, which would be the basic process to obtain anything needed by the community, and create a constant supply for the future. This applies to chefs just like everyone else. Wasting food will be severely frowned upon by all in the community, therefore people will not waste food. Furthermore, there is no need for hoarding food or storing food in large quantities if fresh food of all kinds is available every day.

Chefs and cooks who have a passion for cooking and who have been appointed by the community as chefs, will play a key role in the eating habits of the community. The way we eat and prepare food will change dramatically. It is common knowledge that we eat far too much poor food. In Contributionism, people will eat far less, but the nutritional values and enjoyment will increase substantially.

Our classic 21st century family units are structured so that the man goes to work, the wife stays at home and cleans and cooks. But because of harsh economic times both parents have to work to keep up with the bills. The end result has been more money, but higher inflation. Now we are stuck where both parents must work in order to survive. This places a major stress on the entire family but especially the women if they are expected to come home after a long day at work and prepare a delicious meal for the family.

Many women who are caught up in this situation are not necessarily good cooks and by the time they come home from work tired, frustrated, stressed and expected to cook a delicious meal, the net result is that the food is not made with love. Those that have studied these finer aspects of science which includes the flow of positive energy, will know that the water we drink and the food we eat holds the thoughts and the energy projected into the water and the food.

Dr. William A Tiller, has done massive amount of work in this field with startling results and I highly recommend that you find his papers on the internet for a thrilling education on thought projection and the effects on water.

"For the last four hundred years, an unstated assumption of science is that human intention cannot affect what we call physical reality. Our experimental research of the past decade shows that, for today's world and under the right conditions, this assumption is no longer correct. We humans are much more than we think we are and Psychoenergetic Science continues to expand the proof of it." William A. Tiller, Ph.D. (Professor Emeritus Stanford University)

Dr. Masaru Emoto of Japan is probably the leading expert in capturing the images of projected thoughts of people into water and the effect it has on the water. His many books and spectacular photographs of such experiments have opened up a whole new area of scientific study into water, how it responds to the environment and its profound influence on life as we know it. His work shows how the crystalline structure of water changes from beautiful geometric shapes, known as structured water, that sparkle when exposed to loving and positive words and thoughts, to dirty globules of unstructured water when exposed to words and thoughts of hate and violence.

Experiments with such unstructured water have shown, that not only does it not nourish plants but in some instances, the plants actually die when watered by such specimens. The spectacular photographs of structured frozen water crystals that Dr. Emoto has become famous for, indicate its alignment with sacred geometry.

While in Cape Town, South Africa, Dr Emoto visited the UBUNTU Healing Centre created by Ian and Dawn Macfarlane, where he performed one of his experiments at the sacred UBUNTU Tree in the courtyard. He tested the effect of the word UBUNTU on the structure of water. The result was astounding, producing a perfectly symmetrical crystal, which became the symbol of the healing centre. This was the first time ever that Dr. Emoto donated his special crystal photograph to any organisation, with the condition, that they would use its energy to imprint healing projects for all sentient beings in Africa and beyond.

The shape created by water when exposed to the word UBUNTU is a beautiful hexagon crystal with a simple hexagon and circle at its centre.

This is what Dr. Emoto has to say about this spectacular image. "A beautiful circle appeared inside the crystal. I believe this circle is UBUNTU itself. It signifies that everything is in perfect harmony. Only when everything is in harmony and accord, all the beings will attain true happiness."

Ref: Dr. Masaru Emoto.

According to Plato the number of a circle is six. A hexagon is associated with a circle because there are six sides to a hexagon and when you extend each corner into the centre of the circle, it forms six equilateral triangles. This ratio is unique to the relationship between a circle and a hexagon. In sacred geometry the equilateral triangles arguably represent the fundamental structure for matter in the physical form. This is where architects took their lead from, using triangles or tetrahedrons, when constructing towers or bridges that need to be really strong.

Plato also said that six is a perfect number and the circle is a perfect shape. The fact that UBUNTU is represented by the perfect number and the perfect shape encoded in structured water, that gives life in abundance, is telling us that UBUNTU is the perfect system of abundance for humanity to thrive. This may be a phenomenal coincidence or simply just an indication of how everything is connected. If we know where to look in the perfect creation of the Divine Creator, we will find all the answers.

The result is that, if we make food under duress because we have to, while angry or stressed or frustrated, the food will carry that same energy. It will lose much of its nutrition and could even make us sick. This is the fate of much of the world today. Millions of people in urban areas have resorted to eating junk foods and take-out food that is devoid of any nutrition. The bad food we eat is one of the major contributing factors to the declining health in society today.

- UBUNTU communities will not have such problems.
- The food is organically grown
- Using energised water
- People have no stress or anxiety about their jobs or survival
- UBUNTU people love their lives
- When they prepare food they do it with love in their hearts

Those that cannot cook or simply do not like to cook will never have to cook again because their town will be full of small restaurants and community dining halls run by master chefs who love to cook and prepare the food with love. Restaurants and communal dining halls will become gathering places for the community to meet and interact and be merry. People will not have to cook if they do not have the skills, or if they do not want to. Our entire custom of eating will change dramatically.

PLAN OF ACTION – SECTOR BY SECTOR

To convey a new philosophy about a world without money is a complex task. Some people get it immediately while some take a little longer to digest the information and work it out for themselves. And then there are those who fundamentally struggle with the simplistic concepts and fight it with every ounce of conditioning that most of us have been victims of in some way or another.

In the chapters that follow I outline a number of key sectors and how they will most likely change in a moneyless society. These are by no means rules or instructions but merely ideas and possible guidelines that have evolved over several years of contemplation. I do not cover every possible sector of life because that is just not possible – but as long as we have the cornerstones in place and an idea of how to start implementing them, the rest of the activities will evolve naturally – guided by the people, for the people.

More importantly, as long as we have the united intention to create this new world, then it will be, and so it is. This is after all the lesson we have learnt from quantum physics since the early 20th century. We are the co-creators of our own reality. Visualisation and intent is key to manifestation.

This brings us back to the words of Jesus/Jeshua; "with faith, you can move mountains." What he really meant by this was not for us to worship him, but to comprehend another clue he gave us that "god is within you". By this he really meant that we are responsible for our own reality, our own hologram, and the particles responsible for making up our reality are under our control. Because God is within us, and we are one with God, we are meant to be co-creators of our divine reality.

We will not create a utopian world by repeating any of the mistakes of the past. It is impossible to predict exactly how our lives will change and how we will do things differently, but one thing is for sure – to survive as a species we have to lose our fear, initiate the change and do things completely differently. We can no longer wait for someone to save us – we have to save ourselves. We cannot solve our problems by applying the same logic that created them.

We need to re-learn the basic principles of unity and equality, which may be difficult for many because of the system we were born into and indoctrinated by. We are a product of a system designed to make us addicted to stuff, and the accumulation of stuff, believing in some twisted way that the more stuff we have when we die, the more successful we have been.

The philosophy of slavery is well evolved on our planet. People have been enslaving each other for thousands of years. But to keep people enslaved physically, you have to house them, feed them and clothe them. Through the introduction of money as a tool of enslavement, people have to work; feed themselves, clothe themselves, and house themselves. To do all this, people need that stuff called money, which is controlled and supplied by those at the top. What a brilliant and simple scam to keep humanity enslaved – money.

Our education system is cleverly used to create separation and hierarchy. The system puts those with the highest degrees obtained from the system on a pedestal, and makes everyone believe that they are wiser than the rest and for that reason they deserve to get more than the others. But sadly, I am not the only one who found that it is often those who are more educated and have risen to higher levels of respect through their 'higher education', who are more resistant to change.

It is the subtle indoctrination and disinformation that we acquire through our so-called education that prevents us from accepting new ideas, new information and new truths, about our unimaginable enslavement as a species. Many people simply believe that they are too smart for anyone to have pulled the wool over their eyes so severely.

Many of these highly trained and educated individuals have become the most vicious protectors of their slave masters and the prison matrix that Morpheus describes so well. The bankers and their governments have cunningly conned the educated into a false sense of superiority, believing they are defending their freedoms and privileges in a free society – a society where those who are smarter will succeed. And so instead of opening our minds, our education becomes the first pyramid of hierarchy and separation.

If we want to liberate the minds of our children and all future generations we have to start by completely restructuring the education system. We have to discard the old one and invent a new way of learning skills for life – not skills for finding jobs and developing careers.

As you read through the various sectors along with the UBUNTU plan of action, it will become blatantly clear how we have been deceived and manipulated for the benefit of our governments and other giant multinationals that control our lives. This is a crucial part of the awakening process, which we all have to go though, for humanity to realise what we have to do to free ourselves. Since we know that we are co-creators of our own reality, then let us consciously do just that and create the UBUNTU world.

EDUCATION AND LEARNING

Our school system, and how we continue to teach our children, is largely responsible for our mental and cognitive conditioning that prevents most of us from breaking free from many years of indoctrination. Some researchers like David Icke, have called this "the left brain prison" that has been imposed on us over the most important and formative years of our lives. The sad thing is that most of us never get out of this prison for the rest of our lives and many of us end up defending this prison and force our children into the same prison.

"State schools are failing and government mandated education forces everyone to learn the same and often useless material despite the unique interests and learning styles of each individual. The curriculum is designed more to serve the purposes of corporations and the government than those of the student." www.thrivemovement.com

Restructuring our education system is probably the most critical thing we have to do if we want to liberate ourselves from the prison matrix and the never-ending struggle for survival. It is through the current education system that we become the prison guards to the very prisons that have captured our own immortal souls and our humanness.

We look around us, at how things work, how things are done, and how we live from day to day, and we believe that this is the norm – that this is how things are done – that this is progress and we are part of this never-ending wheel of progress. And yet life gets tougher every year, every month, every week. But we believe that maybe if we hang on for a little bit longer, things will get better.

After more than 120 years of enduring the current education system, we are all products of this system and we are all equally tuned and calibrated by this system to endure its consequences – without any questions. Most of us now believe that this is the norm – and that this is the best way of educating ourselves and our children – and that there is no better way – because if there was a better way, the authorities would have implemented it. Blindly we continue holding on to distorted slivers of hope that our leaders will do something to answer our cries for remedy.

We see the education system as giving ourselves and our children a chance in life. The better our education, the better our chance of having a successful life – getting a good job – having a good career that will earn us loads of money. It is ironic that the indicator of success among living breathing human beings is not their ability to love others, their compassion, creative achievement, contribution to society, but most of the time the emphasis is on money, as an indicator of our success.

We quickly forget that we are all born equal and we should all have a wonderful life, not dependant on the level of education that we can get for our children. And so, without most of us giving it any thought, the schooling and education system becomes the first tool of separation and division among all of us from the very first day of school.

Remember that history is written by the victors, and our education is manipulated by those who impose their control on our society. The victors have a vested interest in holding onto power and therefore teaching their conquered subjects whatever it takes to stay in power. We are forced to place our children in schools at the age when they are most vulnerable to outside suggestion and influence – in the hands of strangers, who get their instructions and teaching manuals from some invisible department in the government.

Our schools are also used by the draconian authorities to commit mass genocide in the form of forced vaccination of children who in turn are compelled to go to school. This is a malicious plot to infect all of us with diseases that will affect us for the rest of our lives – and keep the drug companies in business. As far-fetched as this may sound to those who are new to this information, this is the reality we have to face and change. It is very difficult to obtain entry into South African schools without appropriate vaccinations. In many cases, children line up like cattle to receive the latest shot, completely trusting in the decisions of their parents and teachers.

These teachers, most of whom have honourable intentions, and in most cases are just too happy to hold down a job, have to follow orders and teach what they are told in the style and fashion they are told to teach it. If they do not follow these orders they get fired from their teaching jobs and lose their income and become undesirable as teachers in any other official educational institution.

For twelve years of our lives we are made to sit in classrooms, separated from mother nature, while we are forced to cram information into our heads, so that we can regurgitate it during an examination – so that we can get an 'A' on our school report – so that our parents can brag to their friends and so that we can try to impress our future employers – so that we can get a good job and earn as much money as we can – because we had good marks at school in subjects that we will never ever use in our daily lives.

If we can regurgitate this information really well, we are allowed to go to university where the indoctrination and brainwashing reaches even higher levels, with even greater corporate sponsorship. Those who are privileged enough to reach these levels take on a certain level of pride and arrogance, because they see themselves as special. Because they have worked hard and regurgitated well. And by being able to regurgitate, they have elevated and separated themselves from the masses.

And so, without realising it, the graduates become the quiet promoters and defenders of the system that creates hierarchy and separation amongst humanity.

From the first day of school we are exposed to academic competition and a hierarchy of intelligence that we are forced to conform to. When we do not understand the subjects or if we do badly in our exams, we are laughed at, mocked and reprimanded to work harder. We are told that if we do not get our "act together" we will amount to nothing and that we will end up on the street – that nobody will give us a job and that our lives will be wasted.

From the first day at school we are exposed to continuous stress in many forms. The stress and pressure to succeed – to be the best – to get to the top – to have the right answers. We are made to believe that this is all normal and part of life and that competition is good and that this is the way things are done in life. My friend Scott Cundill has an 11 year old son, Cameron. Cam was asked to write a poem for school using three instances of the word "exhaustion" - three in the positive and three in the negative. He wrote *"It is not exhaustion in the sense that you have been running for miles. It is not the exhaustion of gym for three hours and not the exhaustion of not sleeping for four days. It is the exhaustion of trying to please; it is the exhaustion of caring what people think of you; it is the exhaustion of people bringing me down."*

Ironically, it is these experiences that are supposed to be "character building." These experiences are supposed to condition children to be able to handle the big wide world and the "knocks" they will have to face. These experiences are encouraged by our schooling system – why?

The stress of passing exams and not failing, is one of the most cruel forms of subtle mind control we can imagine. We willingly expose our children to this cruel system of stress for most of their young lives. It is this subconscious, relentless stress, that finally spills over and becomes the cause of antisocial behaviour experienced by many teenagers. Many adults carry psychological scars well into their middle ages purely because of the lingering nightmares of exam stress.

We send our children to psychiatrists, feed them drugs like Ritalin and punish them for failing or behaving badly, not realising that it is the system, and not our children, that is out of our control. We never stop to think about this indoctrination because we believe that this is the norm in life – because we have gone through it ourselves and look how well adjusted we are – because it comes from higher levels of the pyramid of hierarchy and authority. We do not question it and simply accept it – and plan how we will become "successful" in life. These subconscious scars stay with for most of our lives.

By now we should all clearly see that the current education system does not work. It has nothing to do with true learning, or teaching our children real skills for life, or inspiring children to follow their dreams and to use their god-given talents to give true meaning to their lives. But instead, our education system has everything to do with continuous indoctrination and subtle mind control of young minds to follow orders, obey authority, and even fear authority. To believe in a pyramid of hierarchy that controls all aspect of our lives, but especially to follow and obey orders when given by a person of higher authority in this pyramid of hierarchy.

All of this is done under the pretence of freedom and personal choice that does not actually exist because if we do not conform to the controls of the establishment, we will be seen as opponents of the system. In some countries it is now compulsory to send your children to school, to submit them to this inhumane treatment. Parents that do not conform will be charged and prosecuted under the legal system that upholds these laws and brutal treatment of our children.

In an attempt to teach us about our origins as human being, spirituality, and our immortal souls that all come from the same source of the divine Creator of all things, we are taught about man-made religions that have been enforced by man, that divide us even more. Religious division that has caused most of the conflict and suffering on our planet. And so the suffering continues, deeply buried beneath many layers of deception, our own ignorance and brainwashing.

Most of what we are taught in school is theoretical information with very little, if any, practical knowledge of how to do things, how to create things, build things, fix things and how to think outside the box – because that would be seen as being antisocial and not conforming to the norms of society – in other words: *the normally accepted behaviour of those who have already been indoctrinated by the education system to stay within the boundaries of the matrix.*

These boundaries of accepted norms include every sector of our society, especially the commercial, financial and political sectors, that have somehow taken control of our planet.

Please ask yourself: What exactly does our education system provide us with when we leave school, other than a piece of paper or a degree that makes us feel special, and makes us believe that we will find a good job. Our education has nothing to do with learning, but everything to do with preparing us to get jobs and have successful careers. And what do jobs do? They allow us to earn money. In the end, it is all about money. And therefore, those who control the money will continue to control the education system.

It is a well documented fact that governments have been manipulating and controlling the content of school textbooks for the distinct benefit of those in power, so that they can maintain their control over the people. For example, the majority of research in the medical field that is consequently included in the medical textbooks is funded by pharmaceutical companies who fund the research and the printing of the textbooks. So much so, that being a doctor is not about healing, but about prescribing the right drug.

We are taught exactly what they want us to believe so that we can regurgitate their deception to others. The young minds that come out of medical school know very little about diagnosing and healing; about resonance and the laws of nature and how all disease can be cured and has already been cured in the past, because that would be counterproductive to the bottom line profits of the pharmaceutical giants. Schools have become prisons for young minds who want to create and explore without restriction. It is up to us to change it.

A NEW WAY OF LEARNING – FOR A NEW WORLD

Our approach to educating will change completely in a new social structure where the focus is on providing abundance for our communities while expressing our own creativity and talents. The typical school prisons that we have become accustomed to will disappear and there will most likely be no classrooms as they morph into more appropriate locations to teach and learn. Theoretical teaching will be reduced to a minimum while majority of learning will take place in the actual environment specific to the subject. These learning centres will be constantly adaptable to the everyday requirements of those who have been appointed as teachers.

The insane custom of cramming information into so-called 'periods' that last 30 min to an hour, enforced by a sharp piercing bell that rings with clinical precision in most cases, will fall away as learning takes on a true experiential style and allows teachers and learners to truly explore each subject in depth.

All teaching and learning will be done by master teachers who are appointed by the community because they are respected and honoured by the people of the community for their specialised skills, talents, abilities and craftsmanship. This means that communities will have many masters with an infinite variety of skills across many subjects. Because part of the lifestyle in the UBUNTU communities will be a long list of new things that people do, which is unimaginable to us at present. People will create and participate in many activities that were previously not possible for the lack of money or because it was simply not financially viable. In UBUNTU communities, everything is possible.

As it stands right now, the best teachers become private tutors. Realising a gap in the market, they focus on extramural private lessons because that is where the most money is. They know that teaching a class of 40 children is not very productive, so they unwittingly perpetuate a form of exclusive education only for the rich.

Millions of children and adults are constantly denied the opportunity to learn new skills and participate in hobbies or sports because they cannot afford it or it is not available close-by. Not to mention that after the excessive amount of homework that children are loaded with by their teachers, impacts not only on the lives of the children, but also on their parents, and leaves very little time for anything else. This situation will no longer apply.

In today's society, the skilled artists/artisans who should be the teachers of our children are ignored and marginalised – creative expression and art is undermined in favour of scientific and financial achievement. Millions of talented artists and artisans are simply discarded by the world as we know it – until such time that they become a financial benefit to those who rule the roost. We have all witnessed how dead artists are celebrated by the rich and famous and their works are collected as tokens of achievement and status.

And yet most of the things we do in our lives are actually skills and crafts that have taken time, commitment and attention to master. Some skills take many years to learn while others only a few minutes. From typing to shoemaking, to architecture, rocket science, bee keeping, baking, sewing, engineering, lawn mowing, farming, painting, sculpting, driving, sailing, flying, plumbing... the list is endless. Even washing dishes and sweeping the floor are skills that need to be attained. In the Shaolin Temples, kung fu monks learned body connection, power, control and focus by turning menial tasks into highly advanced training methods.

But to become a master you need passion and commitment. In his highly illustrative book, *Outliers – The Story of Success*, Malcolm Gladwell demonstrates that those who have achieved the highest levels of mastery in their craft have applied 10,000 hours of commitment to do so. The social structure of the UBUNTU communities will allow everyone such freedom, to become masters of their skills, making tremendous contributions to their community by doing so.

Japanese Master Sasaki, for example, focussed his training only on the 'kiai' – or 'scream'. Realising that the human body is mostly water, and water can resonate pulses of sound and therefore energy, he has mastered this art so well that he can drop an opponent just by shouting at him. He can also ring a gong from across the room with his voice. The impossible is possible, provided money is removed from the system.

The beautiful thing about this approach is that there are as many skills and passions as there are people. In the UBUNTU system all teachers will be appointed by their own community and through the Council of Elders. Only those who carry the respect of the people and are deemed to be masters of their skills will be appointed.

Every subject and skill that is taught by master teachers will have a very unique flavour and therefore has to be taught in the environment in which it is normally performed. The normal classroom is a synthetic environment separated from the natural processes that take place in a myriad of things that people do. You cannot effectively learn how to make cheese in a classroom - you cannot learn how to grow seeds in a classroom – you cannot learn how to build a free-energy machine in a class room. In fact, there is very little that we can truly learn in classrooms. Each skill must be experienced in its own environment to be truly absorbed by those learning it.

STARTING OUR EDUCATION – Young Children

Children growing up in UBUNTU communities will actually belong to the whole community in the sense that the community takes extra special care of their children. There are no homeless children, hungry children or uneducated children. Children are loved and cherished by the community and protected against any harm. All children get the same opportunities from the earliest age possible. Therefore, kindergartens and crèches will take on a different look, feel and function.

Community day-care and night-care centres will be the foundation of learning for young children. In these centres they will also receive unlimited healthcare and the best nutrition possible while in their most vulnerable years of life.

These centres will be managed by many people who are highly specialised in their respective fields like nutrition and healthcare, and appointed by the community to care for the children. Among these skilled people will be developers of educational material who will develop such materials without restriction of any kind. Remember – money is no longer a hurdle to progress or success of any kind and therefore those who have been appointed by the community to develop educational and learning materials will have no restrictions.

Early learning will take place in the form of interactive games and other innovative techniques yet to be discovered. While Plato and many other great teachers of the past indicated the importance of 'play' and having fun during early development, we have completely negated this advice in modern times.

Fun and games have been removed from our schools by the controllers for obvious reasons. The current regime seems to believe that children should pay attention and listen to authority – not play games and have fun.

Anyone who has ever taught young children will know how much information they retain and how much they learn by playing simple games or participate in fun interactive play. They will also know how scared they can become and how easily their self-belief or self-esteem can be shattered by the wrong environment.

This early learning will include a wide variety of toys, tools, books, instruments and also technology like interactive video and informative programmes shown in a controlled environment while children are still too small and young to move around too much. The use of such tools has been extremely effective in giving young children important and basic knowledge about a large variety of subjects – before they venture out to learn about them on a practical level.

Special attention to artistic skills like drawing, painting and learning about musical instruments – experimenting with different instruments to activate their creative talents is critical. During these first formative years children will learn all the basic skills like reading and writing but the most important thing they need to learn is to love and respect our planet, mother Earth.

Learn about soil, water, air and sunlight – learn how things grow and why they grow – learn about the animals, plants and insects – learn how to plant and grow seeds – where food comes from and how it is grown or made – learn about compost and earthworms – the cycle of nature – ignite their curiosity with as much diversity as possible.

As they learn this basic knowledge from the age of around six years, they will start to participate in short half-day workshops and hands-on practical activities to learn the skills in greater detail. These practical experiences must include being exposed to as many different activities and skills as possible to keep their minds stimulated and wanting to learn more. They will visit as many masters as possible to stimulate their imagination and open their minds to unbridled possibilities.

Physically, children should be introduced to yoga and martial arts from the day they can walk. They will be strong, fit, flexible, focussed, confident, energetic and above all, extremely healthy. On the mental front, children become so adept under the right conditions, that it takes no motivation to get them learning and it is difficult to hold them back – which is the way it should be.

At this early age children love to watch people do different things and everything is exciting to them. Most of the time they are inspired to somehow get involved – often they want to participate or imitate. They must be provided with all these opportunities and never denied their natural creative outburst of talent. Their exposure to what people do must be as wide as possible. From farming, baking, woodwork, building, engineering, sowing, music, arts, how chickens lay eggs and cows create milk – how cheese and butter is made, how cotton is spun and carpets are woven, instruments are crafted and everything imaginable. This will also help the children to activate and recognise their own natural talents at an early age.

Planting and growing seeds and food and taking care of the young plants and trees must be an ongoing part of early learning for the first few years. Children could be the source of all the seedlings and young trees that are used by the community. Especially the large number of herbs and medicinal plants that have been marginalised by the pharmaceutical industry. These will be used to great effect by traditional healers and natural healers who are masters of true healing.

These activities must include vegetables, fruit and nut trees of a wide variety to provide an abundance of food and health in years to come. This way children will develop bonds with what they grow and also develop mutual respect for what others have grown and cultivated – which will also include respect and love for mother nature. By the age of seven, a child growing up in the Amazon can recognise 2,000 individual plant species.

In UBUNTU communities there is a strong emphasis on participating in a wide variety of sports and cultural and recreational activities. Learning about music and playing instruments – painting and drawing and sculpting –all forms of art will be explored in abundance. After all, humans are creative creatures that are the expression of the Great Creation – and therefore our desire to create is insatiable and infinite. It is only the restrictions that have been placed on us in life by society, the economy and those who attempt to control us, that prevents us from continuously creating, developing, building, making, inventing... implementing.

Music schools and musical performances by children will most likely be a huge part of our cultural activity. The same applies to all forms of art and artistic expression – many such new forms will evolve in the UBUNTU communities because there will be no restriction due to a lack of money.

Sport and recreation will take on a similar evolutionary phase – some sports we participate in today will fade away, while new kinds of sports and games will be developed by communities as part of their creative expression.

Children will be encouraged to come up with creative solutions to the challenges of the community. Their ideas will be evaluated by the Council of Elders and implemented if it presents a benefit to the community. Young uncluttered minds often come up with the most brilliant ideas, but our society does not recognise or utilise these talents in any way today.

All knowledge of all things known will be captured and stored on computers and other durable technology that will be available for children and adults to search and to learn from. A comprehensive educational and information database of all master teachers of all communities.

CONTINUING OUR EDUCATION – Older Children

As the children get older the duration of experiential, hands-on learning and workshops that they participate in will become longer. They will go from half-day; to full day; to several days in a workshop; to a week; then two weeks; a month and so on.

The Tekos school in Russia is a great example of a new approach to learning. This remote forest school completely redefines the word "education". Here the children have designed, built and decorated their entire school campus without adult supervision. They cook their own meals, do the administrative work, write their own textbooks and teach each other. They cover the entire high-school math curriculum in one year and get Master's degrees by the time they are seventeen. These students come and go as they please and their parents pay no tuition fees.

In this kind of creative and open learning environment, children will start to recognise their natural talents and skills very early in life. They will naturally steer towards their preferred abilities or talents and what they are truly interested in. Therefore, by the time children are 12 years old, they will already have a pretty good idea what they are really good at, what drives them and excites them and what they want to do in life to contribute to the abundance of their community, while satisfying their own creative needs.

Between the ages of 12-14 the hands-on learning and workshops will keep getting longer. From a week to a full month or even more. The number of skills will be reduced and become more aligned with the abilities, skills and preferences of each child. No child is ever forced to do anything they do not want in the learning arena. Everyone is given complete freedom to pursue only what they are attracted to.

From the age of 14-16 the children will only have a few chosen skills they continue to master. These can now be seen as mini internships with master teachers, during which time the skills of the children will truly be refined. Once again – this can be anything the child has chosen for themselves and it can vary from farming to mathematics or sewing, to playing the violin.

Leading up to this point every child will also have spent many hours teaching young children. No traditional cultures ever segmented children to the extent we do today. Older children teaching younger children is an absolute requirement of any system of learning.

In their 16th year, every child will do their final so-called internship of their preferred subject with a master teacher. By the time the children are 16 years old and have gone through thousands of practical learning experiences and workshops and internships with master teachers, on many levels, they will know more about life and all its secrets than all the academics in the world combined today.

And so, every child and every member of the community will have the knowledge and practical experience we can only dream of today. They will be able to build a rocket; milk a cow; solve mathematical equations; grow food; weave carpets; build bridges; make butter and cheese; create free energy machines; play various instruments; excel in sport; and so much more.

More importantly, they will be completely independent. They will not have the uncertainty issues about their future that many young people displayed today, and that many carry through to adulthood. At the end of this final internship the children will go into their chosen "labour of love" (LOL) and become valuable contributors for the benefit of the entire community. Cherished and honoured for their skills by everyone.

Some people may see this as some kind of life-long commitment or slavery from which there is no escape. This is not the case but merely the residue of our poisoned minds still trying to throw hurdles in our way on the road to complete freedom. I need to remind you that the UBUNTU Contributionism model suggests that everybody only contributes THREE hours per day with their chosen "labour of love".

The reason for this is quite simple. If we spend more than three hours per day creating and producing abundance, there will simply be too much stuff. Too much food; too much electricity; too much fuel; too many shirts; plates; tables; houses; soccer balls; rockets; carpets, chickens; cows; milk; bread; etc, etc.

Because we will no longer chase money and spend 90% of our lives in the pursuit of money in some form or another, instead we will be creating abundance in everything we do. All our efforts and all the things we do in the UBUNTU community and all the energy we spend is to create abundance for the community and therefore ourselves. It is almost impossible for us to imagine this kind of abundance in the current capitalistic world we live in today.

Remember that everyone in the community will also contribute three hours per week towards one of the many community projects or activities. Whether it is mowing the lawn in the parks; dealing with sewage removal or conversion; creating free energy; transporting materials; fixing the street lights; planting seedlings; looking after the aged, etc.

So, after we spend three hours in the day doing what we love to do as our LOL contribution to the community, we still have 21 hours left in the day. Since we have no stress or worries about survival or where we will get our meals each day, we will engage in other activities that we are passionate about and that we have become really good at because of our training. People have various hobbies and sometimes many passions that they will be able to pursue without restriction. No matter what we do or participate in, everything will ultimately be of some kind of benefit to ourselves and the entire community.

Everyone will be able to undergo any kind of training or additional learning at any stage. Remember that only master teachers that have been appointed by the community will be able to do advanced skills training. When the children leave their final internship at the age of

16, they will do their LOL under the supervision of a master who is already active in that specific field. When the master determines that he can no longer teach the student any more – or that the student has attained the highest level of skills that the master can teach, he will appoint the student as a master himself. This is how the respect of the community gets passed onto new people who have mastered their skills and it keeps expanding the number of people who can take on the important role of teaching the children to become highly skilled and clear thinking individuals.

THE LAW – OUR LEGAL SYSTEM – COURTS AND JUDGES

We, the people, are lead to believe that we live in a lawful society and that the legal structures are constantly evolving for the benefit of the people and the country as a whole. Nothing could be further from the truth.

Since we now know that our countries are registered as corporations, and the CEO/president of the corporation appoints the judges – means that the courts and judges are instruments of the corporation. They are there to uphold the laws that will protect the corporation above all, and will not do anything that may cause the corporation serious or long-term harm. Therefore the people will never get justice under the existing legal system.

SELLING OUR CHILDREN INTO SLAVERY

Colonel Edward Mandell House (July 26, 1858 – March 28, 1938) was a highly influential American diplomat, politician, and presidential advisor. Commonly known by the title of Colonel House, although he had no military experience, he had enormous personal influence with U.S. President Woodrow Wilson as his foreign policy advisor.

House helped to make four men governor of Texas and became a close friend and supporter of New Jersey governor Woodrow Wilson in 1911, eventually helping him win the Democratic presidential nomination in 1912, after which he assisted in setting up Wilson's administration. House was offered the cabinet position of his choice but chose instead "to serve wherever and whenever possible." House was even provided living quarters within the White House.

In the 1916 presidential election House was Wilson's top campaign advisor. It is said that "he planned its structure; set its tone; guided its finance; chose speakers, tactics, and strategy; and, not least, handled the campaign's greatest asset and greatest potential liability: its brilliant but temperamental candidate." (Hodgson: *Woodrow Wilson's Right Hand: The Life of Colonel Edward M House. 2006*)

House played a major role in shaping wartime diplomacy and Wilson had House assemble "The Inquiry" – a team of academic experts tasked with advising efficient post-war solutions to all the world's problems. In September 1918, Wilson gave House the responsibility for preparing a constitution for a *League of Nations.*

House helped Wilson outline his *Fourteen Points*, and worked with the president on the drafting of the *Treaty of Versailles* and the *Covenant of the League of Nations*. House served on the *League of Nations Commission on Mandates* with Lord Milner and Lord Robert Cecil of Great Britain, M. Simon of France, Viscount Chinda of Japan, Guglielmo Marconi for Italy, and George Louis Beer of the United States, as adviser. On the 30th of May 1919, House participated in a meeting in Paris, which laid the groundwork for the establishment of the *Council on Foreign Relations* (CFR).

In the 1920s, House strongly supported U.S. membership in the League of Nations and the World Court, the Permanent Court of International Justice.

Edward Mandell House was clearly a cunning man with a special vision for the world. Who that vision was driven by, remains a secret for now, but in his private memoirs, during a meeting with Woodrow Wilson, Colonel Edward Mandell House, is attributed with giving a very detailed outline of the plans to be implemented to enslave firstly the American people and thereafter the rest of the world. For this Colonel Edward Mandell House was featured on the cover of *Time Magazine* on June 25th, 1923.

"Very soon, every American will be required to register the biological property (that's you and your children) *in a national system designed to keep track of the people and that will operate under the ancient system of pledging. By such methodology, we can compel people to submit to our agenda, which will affect our security as a charge back for our fiat paper currency.*

Every American will be forced to register or suffer being able to work or earn a living. They will be our chattels (property/cattle) *and we will hold the security interest over them forever, by operation of the law merchant under the scheme of secured transactions. America, by unknowingly or unwittingly delivering the bills of lading* (Birth Certificate) *to us will be rendered bankrupt and insolvent, secured by their pledges.*

They will be stripped of their rights and given a commercial value designed to make us a profit and they will be none the wiser, for not one man in a million could ever figure out our plans and, if by accident one or two should figure it out, we have in our arsenal plausible deniability.

This will inevitably reap us huge profits beyond our wildest expectations and leave every American a contributor to this fraud, which we will call 'Social Insurance'. Without knowing it, every American will unknowingly be our servant, however begrudgingly. The people will become helpless and without any hope for their redemption and we will employ the highest office (presidency) *of our dummy corporation* (USA/RSA) *to foment this plot against America."*

When the Federal Reserve Act was implemented on behalf of bankers in the United States in 1913, Congressman Charles Lindberg warned the US Congress in a Congressional Record dated December 22, 1913 (vol. 51) that an inevitable consequence of instituting the Federal Reserve system was that, by using their power to inflate and deflate an economy, corporations would take control.

The **South African Reserve Bank**, privately owned and part of the American Federal Reserve System, is the central bank of South Africa. It was established in 1921 after Parliament passed an act, the *Currency and Bank Act* of 10 August 1920 and by so doing set the stage for taking complete control of the people.

The Federal Reserve and *birth registration* or *birth certificate* systems were incorporated into South Africa between 1921 and 1923 through the *Children and Child Care Acts* of 1923 and the *Reserve Bank Act 1921.* From that point *South African* citizenship was regulated by the *Children Acts & Child Care Acts, 1923,* through birth registration, allowing the Government to assign a commercial value to each 'citizen'.

WHO'S COURTS ARE THESE ANYWAY?

Anyone who has ever had any experience with the legal justice system will know that the system with all its laws and courts and bureaucracy, has nothing to do with protecting the people and dispensing justice and fairness. It is all about procedures; knowledge of court rules; and collecting money. In the High Court it's all about bowing to some guy dressed in a black robe, sitting on an elevated bench, and calling him "my lord".

Even our Constitutional Court in South Africa, which is held in such high regard by many, is not truly there to help the people, because the people who experience gross and unimaginable hardship on a daily basis do not have access to the Constitutional Court.

Obviously it pretends that everyone has access to their constitutional rights but the court hides behind its complex rules, structures and procedures. The courts are supposed to be the people's courts and everyone should have access all the time to get justice – this is not the case. I was bluntly told by the judge in the Supreme Court in Johannesburg during February 2013 that "this is not a people's court."

The questions is then – whose courts are these?

The founders of the UBUNTU Contribution system have a great deal of experience trying to get justice for the people in various attempts to expose the unlawful activities of the banks, but in the process we discovered that the courts and the banks are inextricably linked, and that the courts seem to be protecting the banks.

YES – in the end, it is all about the money. The majority of ordinary people will never get any form of justice because they do not have money for lawyers and advocates to represent them in court. We do not have the knowledge of the infinitely complex rules that govern the procedures, or how documents are to be presented and "served", and what may be argued and what may not be argued – it is an infinite quagmire of deception.

And so, very soon, it becomes very clear to everyone who has experienced the justice system, that this is not a justice system – it is a control system.

Most people do not realise that courts have "cashiers" to take payments and settlements on behalf of their "clients." These are just banks in disguise.

Corporations, that are fictional entities, pieces of paper, have more rights in our courts than living, breathing human beings. New laws are being made and passed every week by the invisible lawmakers, without the knowledge of the people, constantly adding to the bottomless pit of complexity that will never benefit the people in any way.

It is a deeply unjust system aimed at keeping the masses under control while creating the impression that they have rights and a justice system created to protect them. This is completely unacceptable to any moral society that has a fundamental belief in honour, integrity and fairness on all levels. But once again, only we, the people, can change this – it will not be handed to us on a platter.

CORPORATIONS CANNOT FORCE THEIR RULES UPON PEOPLE

Some people still think that this is all some kind of conspiracy against the government. Quite the contrary - the government has conspired against its people.

Time to wake up and realise what is going on in the world – take control of our minds and our ability to reason for ourselves. We are living, breathing, human beings - NOT juristic persons, legal fictions, or other synthetically created entities, spawned by the corporation REPUBLIC OF SOUTH AFRICA and its laws.

And the deception starts with the first sentence of the preamble to the highest law of the country, the CONSTITUTION OF THE REPUBLIC OF SOUTH AFRICA.

CONSTITUTION OF THE REPUBLIC OF SOUTH AFRICA 1996

Preamble
We, the people of South Africa; Recognise the injustices of our past; Honour those who suffered for justice and freedom in our land; Respect those who have worked to build and develop our country; and Believe that South Africa belongs to all who live in it, united in our diversity. We therefore, through our freely elected representatives, adopt this Constitution as the supreme law of the Republic so as to Heal the divisions of the past and establish a society based on democratic values, social justice and fundamental human rights; Lay the foundations for a democratic and open society in which government

is based on the will of the people and every citizen is equally protected by law; Improve the quality of life of all citizens and free the potential of each person; and Build a united and democratic South Africa able to take its rightful place as a sovereign state in the family of nations. May God protect our people. Nkosi Sikelel' iAfrika. Morena boloka setjhaba sa heso. God seën Suid-Afrika. God bless South Africa. Mudzimu fhatutshedza Afurika. Hosi katekisa Afrika.

The clever deception starts in the wording of the preamble above, which clearly states that South Africa belongs to all those who live in it. We need to be vigilant and recognise the twisting of words and sentences. "South Africa" is a physical land with a geographical location defined by its neighbours and borders – it is not the same as REPUBLIC OF SOUTH AFRICA – which is a corporation, registered on the US Securities & Exchange Commission, with its own set of laws that governs the corporation only.

Our constitution applies to THE REPUBLIC OF SOUTH AFRICA, a corporation, not the land of South Africa. Therefore the constitution protects the rights of the corporation, not the human rights of the people, who are living breathing human beings who live in the land of South Africa. It tells us further that the "citizens" are entitled to rights, privileges and benefits of citizenship – not human rights. This is so twisted and perverted that most people simply run away from this information – and this is exactly the kind of ignorance the corporate governments feed on.

A corporation is a piece of paper, with 'limited' rights enshrined in its title – PTY LIMITED. Contrary to that, living breathing human beings cannot live in a corporation which is just a piece of paper. People live on real land, physical land and breath air and have the capacity for infinite love. Corporations cannot do that. Citizens belong to corporations because they pledged allegiance and are awarded right and privileges in return for their citizenship.

Contrary to that, people or human beings are born free on the land, with human rights, inalienable rights, without having to be granted such rights by anyone – they are our God-given rights. We are all born free, without commitments or obligations to anyone, sovereign humans. Nobody may enslave us or force us into servitude of any kind.

Remember, corporations can only remove rights. They cannot give them. If we are born free, then any document we sign MUST, by pure definition, erode this freedom.

Remember that just as KFC cannot force you to follow their rules and regulations unless you work for KFC, neither can any other corporation force you to do so. That would be called slavery and servitude. So think for yourselves - what exactly is the corporation called REPUBLIC OF SOUTH AFRICA doing to every one of us who live in South Africa? It is a corporation posing unlawfully as the government of the people of South Africa.

Where did our original government go? Just ask our tribal leaders. Today they stand helpless having been placed in quasi-positions of synthetic power.

Please become comfortable with this information and expressions because these are the words that control our lives in the unlawful courts that have claimed authority over us. Our so-called independent judiciary is part of the corporation RSA; the judges are appointed by its CEO – the President; the judges are paid by the corporation to uphold the laws made by the corporation RSA. This has nothing to do with a land called South Africa, a physical landmass, occupied by human beings – that have been conned into believing they are the same as corporate pieces of paper like ID documents and passports – juristic persons or citizens.

What are we going to do about it? Let us stop watching the news and soap operas and do something for ourselves. Let's start educating everyone, especially our children, and start standing up for our HUMAN RIGHTS. The land belongs to the people – not to the corporation RSA. Their laws only apply to their employees. The amazing thing is that the constitutions tells us this – but in such a clandestine way, by repeatedly confusing South Africa with the REPUBLIC OF SOUTH AFRICA, and "people" with "citizens", that it makes me wonder if the authors are consciously allowing the people to figure this all out for themselves, as they wake up from their unconscious state of being.

HUMAN LAWS versus CORPORATE LAWS

The first laws applicable to human beings is Common Law with its three basic principles.

1) Do no other harm and do not kill;
2) Do not steal or take what is not yours;
3) Conduct yourself honourably in all that you do and say.

But sadly this is not applied in our courts, unless we stand up for our rights and demand it from the judges. Our laws have not evolved from the wisdom of the aged, instead our laws and courts are enforced on us by colonisers who impose Roman-Dutch Law, English law, and other draconian laws with political agendas, so out of place and so complex that it cannot be of any benefit to the people.

Our entire legal system is structured around commercial law, contract law and statutory law. These laws have nothing to do with common law and the rights of people, but rather the rights of corporations and fictional entities.

It is important to realise that each and every one of us has also been turned into a fictional entity, or a piece of paper, a "juristic person" stripped of our humanity, the moment we are given a birth (berth as in naval vessel) certificate. This is usually followed by some kind of identification document and an ID number, followed by a passport that carries our picture linked to the numbers that appear on the documents.

From that moment on, you have two entities. Your true self – a living breathing human being of flesh and blood and infinite soul, with inalienable rights that no one may take away from you;

AND secondly;

a piece of paper, often referred to as a "straw-man" or "juristic person" or even "natural person" that is identified by a picture of you and an ID number of some sort.

The two are NOT the same, but all our lives we are lead to believe that they are one and the same and the human being is made responsible for the legal fiction that was attached to its being at birth and in a strange and complex legal way has become the property of the state who issued those numbers. These documents belong to the 'corporation' or country that issued them and this corporation has laid claim to you.

You will notice that all your fictional entity legal documents carry your name written in CAPITAL LETTERS. This is the first mark of distinction to look out for. This came as a result of the *Cestui Que Vie* trust act of 1666, when the people of the world were declared "dead". Only legal fictions were recognised and if a legal fiction / corporation happened to have a muted gimp (human being) helping to administer it, then that was fine as long as the gimp followed the rules given to it.

It is crucial for everyone to truly comprehend this great deception that has been poured on all of us. Our human sovereignty and absolute inalienable rights have been desecrated against our will and without our conscious consent.

Our laws and court systems come from a slow evolving control structure of the royal political elite, and is based on Admiralty Law or Maritime Law. As strange as this may seem at first, the oceans that are referred to in these laws do not restrict themselves to the ocean of planet Earth, but extend to the oceans of space throughout the universe. But while we still live on Earth, this is why we all have "passports" and we have things like "ownership, internship, partnership..." I hope you get the "drift"?

Perhaps it will come to you as you drive your *registered vessel (car)* in the correct *lane, navigate* an *island* to finally reach your *destination* where you may drop off your *insured passengers* and *cargo*. It may not come to you then, but if you don't pay a fine, or your business is no longer *afloat* and you are *going under*, you may be called to *insolvency* court. Perhaps it will make sense to you then, when you stand in the *"dock"*.

Or you could just look up the word "human being" in *Ballentine's Law* Dictionary, the only legal dictionary that has a definition for human being. Under the definition of human being it sates: *"see monster."* Either way, be careful which *course* you take – always make sure that everything you do is *above board.*

Black's Law Dictionary is the modern Bible of legal dictionaries and is used by the entire legal industry. There is no definition or entry for *human being*. It conveniently jumps from HULK to HUNDI, all written in capitals, briefly mentioning human beings under HUMAN RIGHTS, but never defining what a human being is. It is equally disturbing that the same dictionary does not define human rights, but rather vaguely suggests that *"according to modern values (esp.at an international level), all human beings **should be able to** claim as a matter of right in the society in which they live."*

This system that controls our lives involves incredibly complex layers of deception so cunningly crafted over thousands of years that nobody can say that they truly understand it. Its main objective is to retain absolute control over the "vessels" or people, who believe they are free, but in fact are subjects owned by the king or the state, or the country. The word *register* comes from *regis* which is the crown – when we register anything, we submit or surrender to the crown in some way or another.

Attached to this immaculate deception is the whole body of legal language that was designed to confuse and entrap trusting human beings, called by those in the know as "legalese". These are words that mislead us and deceive us – but we all think we comprehend their meaning.

For example if any official figure of authority like a judge or a police officer asks you: "do you understand?" It really means "do you stand under my authority". And if you agree, then they can do with you what they want, because you have submitted to their authority. It is truly a masterfully designed deception that makes us willingly submit to their authority and give up all our rights.

The people deserve a new legal system, designed for the people, by the people.

In a world without money, a convoluted legal system such as ours will simply vanish overnight. Almost every legal action in all of the courts of the world today can in some way be linked to money – I urge you to think about this carefully. Because once you see this link, it become very easy to recognise the web of deceit that permeates the financial and legal systems we are trapped in.

As it stands now, the courts, judges and lawyers that act against the people in favour of the unlawful banks or government corporations are committing crimes against humanity. How their crimes and actions will be dealt with under an UBUNTU system, with new laws written by the people, will be up to the people to decide. We need to implement a complete overhaul of the entire legal system that is based on the principles of Common Law – Human Law, created by the people, for the people.

OUR NEW LAWS – THE UBUNTU PLAN OF ACTION

1) All existing laws, Eurocentric, Roman, Dutch, English or any other laws that are in any way opposed to the will and the needs of the people will be abolished.
2) Everything that the people want to attain must be possible.
3) There shall be no one homeless; no one hungry; and no one sick without the best possible care.
4) New laws and new governing structures will be created based on the will of the people, starting at local levels;
5) The reintroduction of African tribal structures (native tribal structures) consisting of a Council of Elders will be implemented to guide and advise communities;

6) These Councils will be voted for and appointed by the people from each community,

7) They will consist of the wisest elders from the community to guide the community and therefore respected by the community.

8) The Councils will be voted on by the community every year or as often as the people deem necessary.

9) These new Councils of Elders will adopt the fundamental principles of UBUNTU Contributionism to enhance their ability to guide and advise the people in their community.

10) These Councils Of Elders will be available to deal with all the matters of the community – including legal issues. We will depend on the wisdom of the aged to guide and advise the people – not lawyers, advocates or judges who are out of touch with the real needs of the people, but instead uphold the ideals of the corporation.

11) The governing structures will be decentralised and communities will have absolute control over their own well being, as long as it does not infringe on the rights of other communities around them, or undermine the greater well being of the nation as a whole.

12) There will be a centralised Council of Elders that will be represented by a chosen elder from each community, province or district. These structures will be developed as we embrace and implement the simplicity of UBUNTU.

13) These are living laws that will grow according to the needs of the people and the guidance of the Council of Elders of each community.

14) The foundation of all our new laws will be based on Common Law and Unity Consciousness where every individual's actions should contribute to the greater benefit of all in the community.

15) If it's not good for everyone – it's no good at all.

"Africa was once great – Let us make her great again." Sanusi Credo Mutwa. Elder of integrity and wisdom – spiritual icon of millions around the world – living treasure.

Please see the *New Freedom Charter* at the very end of this book for a more detailed outline of a proposed lawful structure which is based on the original Freedom Charter – for which many have sacrificed their lives in the struggle for freedom in South Africa.

LAWS AND WORDS THAT ENSLAVE US – Part 1

<u>The Unlawful Deception</u>
Our entire legal system is underpinned by Maritime or Admiralty Law, that very few people are even aware of and is guarded by the highest levels of our legal system. It is a great trick of deception that has been played on most of humanity, keeping us entangled in a web of confusion about who we really are and our rights as living breathing human beings, while we are literally treated as numbers by our so-called authorities.

This is a deeply convoluted system that has been evolving for thousands of years. It has nothing to do with justice for the people but everything to do with the control over human beings who are all sovereign and have inalienable rights that they do not know about. It's about keeping us ignorant so that we can continue to be treated like cargo and possessions.

Most of us are filled with utter shock and disbelief when we first stumble upon this information and many people choose to simply reject it as utter nonsense. I urge you to read this carefully and then do your own research to verify what you find. Share this with everyone you know, because we can only free ourselves from the unlawful control of our people by becoming informed.

Knowledge is power. Let us use this knowledge to free ourselves from the unlawful oppression and financial tyranny imposed on the people by a small number of individuals.

Part 1:

Words ending in **SHIP** include ownership, custodianship, partnership, receivership and of course citizenship (see all 218 words here: http://www.morewords.com/ends-with/ship/). The vast majority of these terms are used commercially because commerce originated from shipping merchants, who extended their rituals and practices from the **sea** onto the **land.**

This is why you must SHIP your furniture from Vegas to Dallas, even though there is not a drop of water in sight. This is also why you need a pass**port** to travel. There are even ports in the air, known as air**ports** which are clear extensions of the laws and rituals of the sea. It is all about money and commerce.

When driving on a road, one uses a left and right **lane**. These lanes are symbolic of shipping lanes. Strangely, common city streets have **islands** which need to be **negotiated**, just like ships negotiate difficult waters. The person sitting next to the driver is called a passenger. Passengers are paying people who are taken from one place to another on commercial **vessels** for money.

The assumption is made that you are always doing commerce when driving on a road. Commercial vessels need to insure their **cargo**. That is why passengers are insured because they are literally considered cargo. Who owns the cargo? Research this yourself to find out just how deep the rabbit hole goes. Even the word currency that we use to describe money, originates from the current of the sea: current-sea.

The word "person" means **corporation** and a person is therefore considered **cargo**. If a person cannot maintain their commercial integrity, the corporation **sinks**, the business cannot stay **afloat** and they are declared **insolvent**.

A solvent is a liquid in which something can be dissolved. If you have too many **illiquid** assets, you are **insolvent**. This is why the word liquidity is used in commercial affairs. Everything is about water and the sea because commercial laws of the sea is about commerce and cargo.

It's about turning real solid things on land, into liquid trading commodities such as money, commercial paper and negotiable instruments. How the illiquid (the real assets) are linked to the liquid (money) is the most masterful of deceptions and why lawyers are paid huge amounts of money NOT to investigate this.

In summary, it works like this: unless you specify otherwise, **YOU ARE THE STATE'S CARGO.** However, if you specify to someone who has no idea what you are talking about (like a traffic officer) that you are not cargo, they will look at you very strangely, and possibly lock you up for the night.

See how clever this is: a ship **berths** in a **canal**, and its cargo is offloaded into a **delivery room** where it is accounted for by way of a **certificate** with a **title**. Certificates are evidence of ownership and commercial value like a share certificate.

Is it a coincidence that babies are also born from a **birth canal** in a **delivery room**? And a doctor then signs a manifest of live birth and issues a **birth certificate** in their name? The baby is then **registered** and it, the baby, now has a commercial value as **property**. The word *register* comes from Latin *rex regus* – "for the crown".

This property (cargo) has been gifted to the crown (ie. the

government's estate). The state now has a vested commercial interest or **share** in the value of that property / cargo. That is why your human baby is stripped of all **rights** and given a commercial value to be traded as part of the national corporation.

Please see the evidence on our website that the SA Government is registered as a Corporation on the US/New York Securities & Exchange – allowing it to sell the labour of its people into slavery to invisible shareholders around the world. http://www.ubuntuparty.org. za/2012/08/sa-government-is-registered-as.html

If you take a look at your birth certificate, you will see that it does not say *what* you are – ie. a human being. However, if an animal is born, it gets a certificate specifying "bovine" or "feline" or "equine" or whatever the case may be. Put simply, when a human baby is born, a **shadow corporation** is formed in the baby's name. The baby's name then becomes it's **title.** This cute little corporation only has those rights which the state chooses to give it.

Ask yourself – is a baby born with any natural rights at all – like the right to food and water? Or does it only have those rights which are **granted** to it by the state? Well, the state can intervene at any time in the life and education of that child can it not? It can if the child is their precious cargo. This is why the state has the right to remove children from their parents at will, making any excuse it chooses as its legal reason.

Remember that a flesh and blood human being has no natural "legal" standing, only it's shadow corporation or "juristic person" does. This is why the word "human being" is not in Black's Law Dictionary, and Black's Law Dictionary contains just about every word imaginable.

However, if you want a definition of a human being, go back to 1930 and read *Ballentine's Law* dictionary where next to Human Being, it says *"see monster."*

Ships require navigational instruments to negotiate through rough waters. Instruments used to negotiate the seas of commercial law are negotiable instruments and are used as money. Banks do not use 'money', they work with negotiable instruments like Bills of Exchange and Promissory Notes – NOT Money. Money is a fancy word used to keep people happy on the other side of the counter.

Just like ships use negotiable instruments, so do merchants (bankers, lawyers and judges) use negotiable instruments <u>between themselves</u>. This is why they always threaten to take a "**course of** action." This is very important because if you understand the concept of negotiable instruments, the banking and court systems begin to unravel and make more sense.

For example, a "draft" is not a pint of beer. A draft is a bill of exchange which is an order to pay money. An order to pay money, like a promise to pay money, in a world where money is not backed by any physical resource, the draft is, quite literally, the money itself.

(In memory of Dr. Johan Joubert, who dedicated his life to bring us this volume of research and knowledge. This is an edited version of one of his many articles.)

LAWS AND WORDS THAT ENSLAVE US – Part 2

The government is itself a legal person or **juristic person** which means that it is a **corporation**. Just like most governments of the world, the South African Government is a Corporation registered on the US Securities & Exchange – allowing it to sell the labour of its people into slavery to invisible shareholders around the world.

The only asset this corporation really has is its **people,** which is a collection of persons. This property (the people) must be given a value so it can be used as **collateral** to make loans, so they need to calculate how and what they can **repay**.

The word **repay** does NOT mean to pay something back. It simply means to pay something over and over and over again. Be careful of this word "repay", for it is very tricky. Just another 'legalese' word that is intended to confuse us.

A regular census of the people gives the government the data it needs to calculate how much its property is worth. This is how countries are able to **borrow** money. They borrow, and use the people as **surety** to pay it back. In actual fact they do not **borrow** money because money is created by central banks out of thin air.

Remember, the word **loan** in the legal sense does not mean 'loan' as you and I know it. This word lies at the root of an incredible deception. Banks do not make loans, they **extend credit**. The difference is vital to the future of the world at a very pivotal time in history.

Natural resources belong to the planet and are cared for by the **real human people** of the land. However, real human people are not recognised in commercial law, only their legal person / corporation is recognised. The real human being was tricked into giving up all their rights when the "berth of their vessel" (corporation) was registered with a **birth certificate**.

Therefore, the land and natural resources have been gifted (presented) to a **corporation** called the government, which acts on their behalf. But to be part of the government corporation, one must first **pledge** ones **allegiance** to it. Nobody in their right mind would ever pledge their allegiance to the government, at least not knowingly. Of course it should be the other way around. When you pledge your allegiance to something, you admit that it is more powerful than you and therefore you grant it **authority** over you. In other words, you are a submissive **slave**.

Here is the key: look up the definition of a **"citizen"** in Black's Law Dictionary. It is defined as *"one who pledges their allegiance to the state in return for benefits and privileges"*. If you are in the army, you are given the privilege of going home for a weekend. However, that privilege could be revoked at any time.

It is the same with **citizenship**. You were tricked into giving up your natural rights in favour of benefits and privileges granted by a superior authority. You are now a corporate entity subordinate to another **corporation**, the state and government. The state is, of course, subordinate to whomever it owes money to. Our governments owe money to other private corporations known to us as the central banks. This is why when the central banks bail out the country, the people have to pay it back. This is an insane deception of the grandest proportion. In the end, it all comes down to the banks and the money.

So then, are you a citizen of your country? Of course you are – we all are.

In case you are still confused, a **citizen** of a country is **property** of that country, by way of: **1)** a birth certificate; and **2)** voluntary citizenship registration. If you join the military, you are no longer an ordinary citizen and are now part of a new **legion**. In essence the soldiers have been **re-legioned**. Churches used to have a completely separate legal standing called *piae causa*.

If you cannot pay a debt, you will need to appear before a **Judge** in a **court**. In the old days, priests and ship captains could **marry** people. Commercial judges can therefore be associated with priests and ships' captains which is why they can **preside** over commercial affairs and why **black robes** are worn.

Judges in the high court are called **"my Lord"** and everyone is expected to bow down to them. Take a look at any court document and you will see parties literally **praying** for judgment from the **lord** on the podium. This entire system is a cleverly disguised ritualistic sequence designed by those who created this legal control for us, thousands of years ago. But we are waking up to its lies and deceptions.

What is the similarity between a church prayer and legal prayer? In both cases, you are voluntarily submitting to a higher authority. Everything that goes on in commercial law is about **submission.** Every court document you submit and sign is purely about getting you to **submit** to a higher authority.

When you appear in court, you are required to stand in a **dock,** which is another reminder that we are dealing in shipping terms. But first, you need to enter through a small fence called a **bar**. This fence, often with a little gate, represents coming aboard a **ship**. You are now in maritime admiralty law and are no longer bound by the natural or common law of the land.

When lawyers pass the bar exam, they are able operate **above board** (another shipping term) as a registered officer. This is opposed to being **below board** which is where the **cargo,** slaves and criminals are kept. The holding cells in the courts are often below the floor level and the accused are brought up above board into the dock.

When you place your **signature** on a piece of paper, the line below your signature represents the horizon line and below that line is your name (usually in capital letters). You have just been tricked into relegating yourself from a flesh and blood human being living on the Earth endowed with Creator-given natural rights (represented by your signature), to that of mere cargo / property / chattel / slave / criminal, and you are now bound by the terms and conditions of that agreement.

In the law of the sea (maritime or commercial law), all cargo must be labelled with a name and a **title**. Do you have a name and a title? Of course, we all have e.g. Mr, Mrs, Miss, etc. And therefore you are property, without ever realising it.

Try this: try signing all agreements with the words "all rights reserved" below your signature. This tiny little act will create absolute havoc. Why? Because you are stating that YOU HAVE RIGHTS. Heaven forbid you should have rights.

(In memory of Dr. Johan Joubert, who dedicated his life to bring us this volume of research and knowledge. This is an edited version of one of his many articles.)

LAWS AND WORDS THAT ENSLAVE US – Part 3

The "money" that you are forced to use by the banks and the money that the banks use themselves are different. Banks use *promissory notes* and *bills of exchange*, and all this is clearly outlined in the Uniform Commercial Code (UCC) which is the international Bible for doing business and commerce. Some countries including India, Australia, the UK and South Africa use the Bills of Exchange Act.

So this is what money really is – pieces of paper with signatures on them. The Bills of Exchange Act, which originates from the UK, is common to almost every country in the world. For example, an **inchoate instrument** is defined across the globe as any blank piece of paper containing a signature. An inchoate instrument can be filled up as a bill of exchange to the value of any amount. Be careful what you sign.

Both UCC and the Bills of Exchange Act, talk about "capacity to contract." Look at the words: Capacity (a volume of liquid/ity) to **contract** (to shrink back to zero). This means that all of us can 'contract' any bill back to zero, because our 'money' is no longer backed by any physical resource.

Think about the concept of capital. The president of the United States (which is actually a trading name, the corporation name is actually the "Virginia Company") lives on "Capitol Hill". Every country has a "capital." All things capital, like capital letters, relate to all things commercial and that means everything comes down to money.

The Romans had three classes of people:
1) *capitis dimunitio maxima,*
2) *capitis dimunitio media* and,
3) **capitis dimunitio minima**.

You can read all about this in Black's Law Dictionary. Slaves are *capitis dimnutio maxima* which refers to "maximum loss of rights". Slaves had their names spelt in capital letters. Official grave stones have names spelt in capital letters because those buried there are legally dead. Clever reading and understanding the *Cestui Que Vie Trust Act of 1666,* which was passed while everyone was focusing their attention on the Great Fire of London, declared everyone legally dead.

The assets of all the dead people were put into a trust and are held by the state. This still applies today – you do not own property, you only think you do. Read your title deed carefully, it says that the state reserves all its rights. Are you dead? Yes, which is why your name is spelt in block capitals on all legal documents.

Have a look at how diplomats have their official names written/ spelled: half the name is in capital letters and half of the name is lower case. This is *capitis dimunitio media* and refers to medium loss of rights.

When slaves won their freedom, they were given a title. The slaves were very happy, but they had no idea that their title simply meant **"slave."** This just highlights the important aspect of how this convoluted language or 'legalese' is used to deceive humanity.

More evidence that death abounds in the legal and banking world can be seen in the word '**mortgage**', which, like the word '**mortuary**' is related to death. Even the word 'attorney' comes from the word 'attorn', which means to take from one person and give to another, while keeping a nice chunk for yourself of course.

Attorneys cannot **see**, they can only **hear** because everything must be in writing which is why you have a court hearing, not a court seeing. We can therefore confidently state that justice is blind. In fact, the entire court room is contained in the piece of paper – the *contract*.

In court, *contract* is everything. Writing is the language of the corporation because in the past when these clever tricks were established, very few people could read or write. When they learnt to read and write, the legal language was still very different to the language used on the street, even though the words sounded the same.

The legal and banking world is completely two dimensional with no heart and no soul. Certain judges have the power to grant remedy, but even their hands are tied because they are playing out an **act**. They are bound by the script of the act (the statutes) and there is not much room for improvisation.

You will notice that Judges always operate in **honour**. They are always referred to as being "honourable." But being "in honour" and being "with honour" are completely different. This is one of the many misnomers about legal language. Legal words and English words are NOT THE SAME THING.

Honour simply means "balanced books" or that the "debts are paid." The Judge is a banker and his books are always balanced. Another classic example is the word "security" which does NOT mean what you think it means. Security is more or less the pledge on a negotiable instrument.

You pledge your "security" to the instrument so the instrument (or debt) is then "secured." A secured instrument is one where a "person" puts in their sweat and energy into insuring that it gets honoured (paid).

Remember, the Judge sits on a **bench** and the root origin of the word "bench" comes from the Latin word **"banca"** because merchant bankers would sit on a bench in the market places. If they were caught cheating, the naughty banker would have their bench smashed in public and from that day forth, they were **bankrupt**.

Judges are always **in honour**, because to be in **dis-honour** would mean to be insolvent. Judges books are always balanced / their debts are always paid because they represent the **bank**. A bank's books must, by definition, always be balanced, which is yet more proof that they do not really lend money.

You will learn this when you learn about banking – the bank is merely a debit / credit computer system that operates on your instruction. When you wake up and realise that you can instruct the bank differently, and enough people do it as well, then everything will shift. It's all about knowledge and enlightenment – let us make this our pledge to the people of the world.

(In memory of Dr. Johan Joubert, who dedicated his life to bring us this volume of research and knowledge. This is an edited version of one of his many articles.)

LAWS AND WORDS THAT ENSLAVE US – Part 4

The word **act** is a very interesting term. An 'act' is something that is played out on a stage. Shakespeare said "all the world's a stage, the men and women merely players." This could not be more literal – and the royal political elite who understood the full meaning, must have laughed out loudly when they heard it.

Today, when an act of parliament is signed, it then becomes just that, an **act**. Of course none of the people or the police who enforce this have any idea that this is a complete game of charades and that they are mere instruments enforcing an unlawful act against their own people. This is why there will be more and more support from the police, army, traffic enforcement, lawyers and other agents of governments around the world, for the people in protest, as they begin to wake up to the unlawful activity they have been conned into by their governments.

You may wonder why you always have to sign contracts in black ink. The usual argument is that it is easier to see, but that is utter nonsense. The more logical answer is that only wet ink (original) signatures have value as negotiable instruments. When these structures were originally implemented the colour of the ink was black.

When your instruments (ie. documents containing your signature) are traded amongst the lawyers and bankers, they must use the 'black' wet ink signature. They endorse it (sign it) over to other parties in exchange for other kinds of money or rather, negotiable instruments. This happens behind the scenes in the banks all the time.

Banks are selling our signature on the negotiable instruments that we sign into the derivatives market and we have no idea that this is going on. We actually think that we owe the bank money which is why we continue to pay them every month. Think about the word 'repayment'. Does it mean to "pay back something you have borrowed" or does it mean to keep re-paying, over and over again?

By using black ink, it is very difficult to know where the original document actually is. Some banks in the USA have been caught forging signatures on mortgage documents so that they could foreclose on people's houses. There was a big expose on 60 minutes about this. I have no doubt that this is case in South Africa and every other country in the world. After all, banks are nothing more than organised crime syndicates that work in fancy offices and have fancy buildings and control governments – they will do anything to get their way.

Black ink also has a more sinister connotation. It represents death. Black robes in court represent death because they are not dealing with real people, they are dealing with corporations, or *characters in a play.* That is why we are called a *legal character, legal fiction,* or *juristic person* which is not a human being, but the title of a corporation or a stage name.

It is also another reason why you have a court *hearing* and not a court *seeing* and why justice is blind. The symbol for justice is the goddess "Themis" who is blindfolded. Why would the symbol for justice be a blindfolded goddess? Why even use a goddess at all? This is part of the ancient ritual that is continued and upheld today without anyone being aware of it. Most people believe that only the ancient cultures had rituals relating to gods and goddesses. They are wrong in their belief.

The bottom line is that if you sign a contract, you are relegating yourself to be subordinate to a higher authority. However, even the word contract is misleading. A contract used as a noun is merely an agreement. The verb, to *contract*, means to get smaller, like a balloon *contracts* when the air comes out.

Because our currency (current/sea) is no longer backed by gold or any other natural resource, the only reason it stays afloat (like a business is floated before it sinks), is because it is backed by the confidence of the people.

That means, the people have the full, inalienable right to *contract* (the verb) any agreement and bring the amount owing (pledged, or promised) back to zero. Yes, you heard correctly, you have the power, using your signature, to eliminate any debt that exists in the world today.

Our unlawful governments have very skilfully turned brother against brother, father against son and mother against daughter in the grandest web of deceit that has ever befallen humanity.

(In memory of Dr. Johan Joubert, who dedicated his life to bring us this volume of research and knowledge. This is an edited version of one of his many articles.)

JUDGE DALE SPILLS THE BEANS ON BANKS, COURTS AND GOVERNMENTS

During May 2012, a retired United States Judge released an article in which he exposed the entire banking and corporate government scam and how it is linked to the laws and courts that uphold it. Let this serve as an example to all honourable judges everywhere. Let them realise that they are human beings first – judges second, and that they are being used as instruments of an unjust, corrupt system, which is enslaving their brother and sisters, and all other human beings, to a global corporate beast. The information in this article is meant mainly for people who live in the USA, but is applicable in most countries with minor adjustments based on their local legal custom. Since virtually all countries are corporations, they all fall under the internationally applied UCC (Uniform Commercial Code) the Bible of global commerce.

'Judge Dale' is his pen name, since the retired judge who is now in his 80s, had been threatened many times in his career even while still

active on the bench and after going into retirement. I have had many contacts with him and confirmed that he is what he claims to be.

<u>PREFACE: By Judge Dale (Retired)</u>
I didn't plan on writing a PART 5 but given the global movement in play to collapse the fiat financial dominance historically created and controlled by the Vatican; European Royal and Elite plus the retaliatory efforts by the United States Corporation to recoup their control of America; I felt a need to point out the flaws in their CORPORATE PROCESS.

You probably identify with this CORPORATE PROCESS as LEGAL PROCESS but it really isn't about what is legal or lawful because all process is about the enforcement of CONTRACTS or the imposition and enforcement of CORPORATE REGULATIONS called STATUTES. The best advice you will ever receive is to: AVOID THEIR COURTS WHENEVER POSSIBLE. There is NO justice to be found in those Courts unless you are a member of the Vatican; the Royal or Elite, or have purchased Diplomatic Immunity!

1) THE COURTS:
The only Constitutional Court in America is the International Court of Trades, which was created because no Foreign Nation Government would Trade with the Corporate United States, until they provided a way for these Foreign Nations to enforce their Trade Agreements with America.

NOTE: Historically, the World Court was created to provide Nations with a venue to enforce their Trade Agreements but the Corporate United States refused the Courts invitation to participate because they were denied control over the Court.

All of the other American Courts are pseudo courts or fictions and simply are Corporate Administrative Offices designed to resemble Courts and all of their Judges are simply Executive Administrators designed to resemble Judges.

The purpose of these pseudo Corporate Courts are only to settle contract disputes and since George Washington's government was military in structure; if either party refuses to participate, these Courts cannot become involved and the dispute is dead in the water! My use of the term "dead in the water" is not a canard because these pseudo Courts are unconstitutional Courts of Admiralty, the International Law of the Sea!

The Washington Monument was completed in 1884, as a tribute to George Washington and his military government, which is actually a sea-level obelisk that infers that all of America is "under water" and thus subject to the Laws of Admiralty as opposed or contrary to the intended Constitutional Civilian Government under Common Law.

The pseudo Judges of these pseudo Courts have NO powers without the Consent of both the Plaintiff and the Defendant. [AND] In every case the Judge must determine that he has Consent; Personam and Subject Matter Jurisdiction before he can act or access the Cesta Que Trust.

NOTE: All tradable Securities must be assigned a CUSIP NUMBER before it can be offered to investors. Birth Certificates and Social Security Applications are converted into Government Securities; assigned a CUSIP NUMBER; grouped into lots and then are marketed as a Mutual Fund Investment. Upon maturity, the profits are moved into a GOVERNMENT CESTA QUE TRUST and if you are still alive, the certified documents are reinvested. It is the funds contained in this CESTA QUE TRUST that the Judge, Clerk and County Prosecutor are really after or interested in! This Trust actually pays all of your debts but nobody tells you that because the Elite consider those assets to be their property and the Federal Reserve System is responsible for the management of those Investments.

Social Security; SSI; SSD; Medicare and Medicaid are all financed by the Trust. The government makes you pay TAXES and a portion of your wages supposedly to pay for these services, which they can borrow at any time for any reason since they cannot access the CESTA QUE TRUST to finance their Wars or to bail out Wall Street and their patron Corporations. The public is encouraged to purchase all kinds of insurance protection when the TRUST actually pays for all physical damages; medical costs; new technology and death benefits. The hype to purchase insurance is a ploy to keep us in poverty and profit off our stupidity because the Vatican owns the controlling interest in all Insurance Companies.

You may receive a monthly statement from a Mortgage Company; Loan Company or Utility Company, which usually has already been paid by the TRUST. Almost all of these corporate businesses double dip and hope that you have been conditioned well enough by their Credit Scams, to pay them a second time. Instead of paying that Statement next time, sign it approved and mail it back to them. If they then contact you about payment, ask them to send you a TRUE BILL instead of a Statement and you will be glad to pay it? A Statement documents what was due and paid, whereas a TRUE BILL represents only what is due. Banks and Utility Companies have direct access into these Cesta Que Trusts and all they needed was your name; social security number and signature.

2) CRIMINAL LAW:

There are NO Criminal Laws in America because Criminal Laws would imply that the Corporate United States Government are Sovereign that have absolute power over all living, flesh and blood Americans, which of course is not true because a corporation is a fiction and therefore cannot be Sovereign. Man is Sovereign and is in control of his own destiny and one day he will finally wake up and realize this to be true!

There is however Criminal Contracts being enforced against us and with our Consent, which are surreptitiously called: Criminal Statutes. Our Consent has been obtained by them visa vie our silence and failure to act or protest, which under law is defined as: Tacit Procuration.

(e.g.) Tacit Procuration: If someone accuses you of theft in writing and you fail to respond or deny those allegations in writing, your failure to deny or act is considered an admission of guilt! (or) You receive a Bill for goods or services that you never ordered or received, and you fail to deny those allegations, your omission represents the truth of the matter, which imposes an obligation to pay! Collection companies frequently use Tacit Procuration to establish indebtedness to them on a discharged debt they had purchased from some corporate business.

"Now you're probably thinking: No Criminal Laws? Well, that can't be true? A whole lot of people have been tried; convicted and are doing time in American Jails for breaking Criminal Laws!"

And my response to that is: True, they are in Jail because they unknowingly accepted the Criminal Contract on behalf of their Birth Certificate and consented to be imprisoned as a condition of their conviction and punishment. Their lawyer didn't help any because he reinforced that situation by and through his Notice of Appearance to represent you. It is the Birth Certificate that is under arrest, which I will explain shortly!

NOTE: Criminal Contracts are graded according to the

severity of the crime alleged and that grading is identified as either: Summary; Misdemeanor; Felony or Capital offenses.

The Criminal Process usually begins with a Police Officer issuing a Citation [or] making an arrest with or without a Warrant [or] the Police Officer [or] County Attorney prepares a complaint based upon a sworn affidavit or an information, which is presented to a Judge and a Warrant is then issued. The defendant is subsequently arrested and is brought before a Judge for arraignment.

The Complaint and Warrant will reflect your [BIRTH NAME] or identify you as a [JOHN DOE], if your name is unknown, which is typed out in all capital letters! This is not a mistake on their part because it is your Birth Certificate that is under arrest and not your living, flesh and blood person. The hope of these pseudo Courts is that the flesh and blood person will be intimidated enough to accept responsibility for the Birth Certificate! Sounds crazy but nothing is what it seems: "It's all Smoke and Mirrors."

Most Police Officer's do not know or have these details and believe in what they are doing and believe the lawyers who counsel them in law like they are Gods! Big mistake on their part because just like everyone else, they too have been vigorously lied to! You can't trust lawyers to be inherently honest!

Police Officers are instructed to always print or type the Defendants Name in capital letters but they are never told the reason why! As a precaution, you should always carry a copy of your Birth Certificate with you as part of your identification papers, which I will explain in the next paragraph.

At your Arraignment or Trial, the Judge will ask you if you are the named individual [ALL CAPS BIRTH NAME] on the complaint and your natural response will be to answer in the affirmative but that is exactly what you don't want to do!

Remove your Birth Certificate and respond to him by stating: I am making a Special Limited Appearance on behalf of the defendant who is right here and [hold up your Birth Certificate!]

Then state the following: *As I understand this process Judge; the County Attorney [or] Police Officer has levelled a criminal charge with the Clerk and against the TRUST, using the ALL CAPS NAME that appears on this BIRTH CERTIFICATE! The use of capital letters is dictated by the US Printing Style Manuel, which explains how to identify a CORPORATION. The Clerk, who is the ADMINISTRATOR of the CESTA QUE TRUST, then, appointed you Judge as the*

TRUSTEE for the TRUST and since neither of you can be the
BENEFICIARY, that leaves me and therefore you are MY TRUSTEE!
So as MY TRUSTEE, I instruct you to discharge this entire matter,
with prejudice and award the penalties for these crimes to be paid to
me in compensation and damages for my false arrest!

NOTE: The Law of Trusts dictates that an Administrator; Trustee and Beneficiary cannot serve two positions in a Trust. So a Trustee cannot be a Beneficiary too!

The TRUSTEE Judge has no alternative but to honor your demands but you have to get this right and act with confidence! You really need to know this information well, so that you can't be hoodwinked or confused by either of them! They will or may attempt to play some mind games with you if you display any doubt; stammer or display a lack confidence! Appearances [the pomp and majesty] of these pseudo Courts, is totally for your benefit and is intended to invoke fear and intimidation! If you show fear or intimidation, you get a pony ride!

NOTE: I've seen and heard of Judges and Prosecutors interfering with a defendant's response, which made the defendant, become confused and he was subsequently committed into a mental hospital for a psychiatric evaluation. The Judge and Prosecutor successfully twisted what the defendant was trying to say and then the Judge Ordered a mental evaluation.

Understand that the County Attorney will be forced to pay the Cost of Court out of his own pocket, if the case is discharged, so he isn't going to give up that easily and the Judge; Clerk and County Attorney, stand to make a pretty penny off of your conviction and incarceration! So don't screw it up...

If the County Attorney begins to act too cocky with you, you can take the wind out of his sails by asking him to produce the 1040 for this case? If he denies the need to do such a thing, inform him that you will be taking care of that for him ASAP [as soon as possible]! He may move for a discharge at that point because you are a little too dangerous or smart! The last thing that Prosecutor wants is the IRS examining his files for the last seven years because he makes money on every conviction but he doesn't pay TAXES on them as a Rule! He usually only declares the salary he receives.

Also: Should you accidentally find yourself in a mental hospital; the Psychiatrist who is assigned or appointed to evaluate you is just as corrupt as the Judge; Clerk and County Attorney and he will falsify all of your responses to him, just so that you are recommitted back into the mental facility with a review in six months! So lie to him and deny that you ever made such remarks! Of course, if you accept the criminal charges against your Birth Certificate, then you will instantly be deemed SANE!

Sorry that I had to be the one to tell you this but this is how corrupt many of my fellow Judges truly are and it should explain why my conscience caused me to retire early! Before I learned what was really going on; I believed that my duties and performance were entirely Constitutional. I was lied too also!

3) CITATIONS:

The CITATION process can be handled much easier; through the mail. When a Police Officer issues you a CITATION, he is actually requesting you to CONTRACT with him! He is alleging that you violated a corporate regulation in writing, which you have accepted by signing and thus requires you to respond.

The Police Officer is instructed to explain that your signature is merely an acknowledgment that you received a copy of the CITATION but in actuality, your signature is notification to the Court and Judge that you have accepted or CONSENTED to this offer to CONTRACT, which also grants the Judge CONSENT; PERSONAM and SUBJECT MATTER jurisdiction over you and the case! You can cancel that CONTRACT however by rescinding your CONSENT. The Federal Truth in Lending Act provides that any party to a CONTRACT may rescind his CONSENT, within three business days of entering into such a CONTRACT. So across the face of the CITATION you should print or type in large print, the following words:

I DO NOT ACCEPT THIS OFFER TO CONTRACT
and
I DO NOT CONSENT TO THESE PROCEEDINGS.

Use blue ink [for admiralty] or purple ink [for royalty]. Admiralty is the Court and Royalty represents your Sovereignty. Either way is appropriate. Sign your signature underneath in blue or purple ink and in front of a Notary and under your signature type: Without prejudice, UCC 1-308. This is another way to declare that you may not be held responsible for this Contract pursuant to the Uniform Commercial Code.

Serve Cancelled Citation back on the Clerk / Court, along with a Certificate of Service, by Certified Mail, Return Receipt Requested.

This kills the CITATION; removes your CONSENT and removes the JURISDICTION of the Court, all at the same time. It really is that simple!

NOTE: A Certificate of Service is a letter that first identifies the Citation and then defines how and when you returned the document to the Court and is signed. If not denied, it becomes a truth in commerce by Tacit Procuration.

Remember to keep a copy of everything, in case the Clerk attempts to trash your response, which certainly will not happen with a Certificate of Service or if it is mailed back by the Notary. The Notary is actually a Deputy Secretary of State and is more powerful than the Court Clerk!

Public Notaries originate from the time of the Egyptian and Roman Scribes who were the purveyors of certified documents, which are sworn affidavits. Certified documents and sworn affidavits are truth in commerce. [e.g.] Birth Certificates are certified documents on bonded paper. The word bonded is derived from bondage as in slavery, which makes all of us Bond Slaves to whoever retains custody of our original Birth Certificates. I bet you believed that the Emancipation Proclamation freed the slaves and it did for a short time and then the Birth Certificate and the 14th Amendment enslaved us all!

4) SUMMONS and LAWSUITS:

The SUMMONS process, whether it is defined a Civil or Criminal Action, is once again an offer to CONTRACT, despite what words are used to command your appearance or response. It too can be cancelled just by following the same procedure as the CITATION process above. A million dollar lawsuit is no different than a CITATION and both can be cancelled! Hard to believe, isn't it? Does your lawyer know about this? You bet he does but he is not permitted to embarrass the Court and besides, Court is where he makes his money!

NOTE: How many of you have ever attempted to avoid Jury Duty? All you had to do was cancel the SUMMONS [OFFER to CONTRACT]; Notarize it and mail it back to the Jury Commissioner. Don't worry, they won't bother you because you are obviously too smart and may influence their Jury! The Jury [controls] the Court and not the Prosecutor and Judge and if you know that, they lose and the defendant wins, which is why they prefer only the dumbed down candidates to serve on a Jury.

There are a few matters or issues that are next to impossible to circumvent or quash because of the depth of corruption within these pseudo Courts, such as child custody and the division of property resulting from a divorce. The Birth State claims the custody of your children pursuant to the Birth Certificate and records them under the Department of Transportation as a State owned Vessel!

A marriage is a CONTRACT and all that is required is a PRE-NUPIAL AGREEMENT to complete the marriage but if you are sufficiently indoctrinated to believe that a Judge or Mayor or a Minister or Priest, must join you in holy matrimony and you subsequently applied for a LICENSE; now you both have married the STATE as well! Now the State is entitled to its fair share of the division of your marital property should the marriage not work out or should you die [called probate]! Some people might say that a divorce should be included on this list of impossible issues but then they don't know what I know!

5) DIVORCE:

An Action in Divorce is a request to break the LICENSED MARRIAGE CONTRACT. If you desire a divorce and your spouse refuses to consent to a divorce, no State Judge will grant you a Divorce Decree because the Judge has not been granted the CONSENT of both parties! There is a way around this however, which your lawyer will never admit to because he cannot make any money from giving you truthful or sound advice!

NOTE: Puerto Rico is a United States Territory acquired from Spain and it still operates under Spanish Law. This was never changed by the Corporate United States when Puerto Rico became a US Territory, so first you need to fly to Puerto Rico.

Once in Puerto Rico, you can establish residency by simply opening a Post Office Box for a period of three days. Just after opening the Post Office Box, hire a local Paralegal to prepare an Action in Divorce for you. The Paralegal will file the divorce petition immediately, which is generally a certified form document and it will be heard by a Puerto Rican Judge within three days.

Under Spanish law, your spouse is not required to be served the divorce petition; only the divorce decree. Five days after the Decree, your former spouse will receive the divorce decree in the mail, written entirely in Spanish, which cannot be contested and must be honored by all US Federal and State Courts!

NOTE: Immediately after the Puerto Rican Judge declares you divorced, if you choose, you can marry again by Contract or by License. Both are legitimate, but no one will ever tell you that!

The division of marital property and custody of children is a much more complicated issue but at least the divorce cannot be utilized as leverage against you to divide up your property, less than proportionately, which is exactly why American Judges will not bifurcate the issues involved in a divorce. [e.g] Divorce; division of property; custody; support and alimony. The hope is that your desire to obtain a divorce is worth more to you than anything else you own, now or in the future!

6) FORECLOSURE:

If you are involved in a FORECLOSURE or you are thinking about filing for BANKRUPTCY protection to buy you more time, instead of trying to defeat the corrupt Bank and your Creditors in a State or Federal Court, where the cards are certainly stacked against you, plan to file for BANKRUPTCY and do it this way, too insure that you come out on top!

All BANKRUPTCY FORMS are printable; can be obtained on line and they can be completed in longhand with an ink pen. The Forms to use are: B-1 through and including B-8. You only need to prepare and file the first five or six pages to obtain a Case Number and then you must sit through a Credit Counselling session, which can be done all in a day. When you are completely finished with preparing your petition, you should have filed about 58 pages in total and the filing fee is around $280.00.

Here's the reason for using the Bankruptcy Courts:
List all your debts on one schedule and when it comes to listing your assets include your BIRTH CERTIFICATE and its CUSIP NO. The value of the Mutual Fund Investment for your Birth Certificate can also be found on line using the Cusip Number under Fidelity Investments. You will discover that it is worth multi-millions but you must have the CUSIP NO. on your asset schedule or the Birth Certificate will be discharged as frivolous by the JUDGE or the TRUSTEE.

The Bankruptcy Judge will then appoint a LAWYER TRUSTEE to dissolve the Mutual Fund Investment; pay off your debts and the balance must be paid to you! This procedure usually attracts the attention of the (DOJ) Department of Justice because they don't want the LAWYER TRUSTEE to screw up and short change the Vatican; the Federal Reserve and the Corporate United States and so they tend to warn or threaten the LAWYER TRUSTEE to be very careful!

Most of these Mutual Fund Investments usually involve a group of between 10 to 25 Birth Certificates and so only a fraction of that Mutual Fund belongs to you! The Bankruptcy Judge will not certify the final disposition until the LAWYER TRUSTEE can prove his math and every aspect of his work because the Judge inherits responsibility for the Trustee's errors, if he made any!

After the first LAWYER TRUSTEE resigns, you can probably cut a deal with the DOJ or you can proceed on with the same Bankruptcy proceeding and the newly appointed LAWYER TRUSTEE! Now isn't that easier and better than attacking or defending yourself against the Bank and a bunch of greedy Creditors; knowing full well that the cards are stacked against you because of the Vatican and the Federal Reserve System?

While you are in Bankruptcy, you are protected. No one can proceed against you for any debts or foreclosure, as long as you have a bond or sufficient assets; the Birth Certificate guarantees that aspect and while in Bankruptcy, you won't have to pay on any of those past debts!

Your debts will eventually be discharged and the balance of the Trust Fund is to go into your pocket! It's a WIN, WIN situation any way your shake it and the Vatican; Government and Bank loose the Trust Fund assets they planned to steal from you all along!

NOTE: There is a process to follow to determine your CUSIP NO [or] you can ask a Stock Broker friend to help you [or] hire a Broker on the side to assist you. There are people in the Patriot movement who also know how to apply the formula, which converts your Birth Registration Number and or Social Security Number into a Cusip Number. I paid to have mine done and discovered that I am worth about 167 million. It's all FIAT money but as long as it can be spent, who cares?

I hope that this entire expose' has enlightened and elevated your personal knowledge and will benefit you now and in the future.

Pax vobiscum (Peace be with you).

Judge Dale.

A SIMULATED WORLD

You will notice that for some reason our current society is obsessed with simulating nature. This is driven by the countless products on offer by the corporations that create new technology, 3-D movies on TV and the big screen, virtual reality and countless computer games containing deeply encoded subliminal information to affect our behaviour. Our television tries to reproduce real life by displaying a picture that is so close to perfect that we cannot tell the difference. Toys we buy of dolls and bears help us accept and love synthetic carbon copies of the real live animals. Our football fields and gardens are clad with plastic grass, swimming pools are lined with plastic or simulated rocks, Blue Ray and High Definition screens create clear images that look real, but are not. Computer games and the internet allow us to create avatars, which themselves are simulated characters.

But these simulated copies are not us – they are not human. Pharmaceuticals create synthetic remedies that are based on nature's ideas, but are not natural. We are falling into a 'simulated reality black-hole' and instead of rejecting it, we are begging for it. This is all done in the attempt to detach us from our humanness, to reduce our human emotion and to accept inhumane activity in our lives.

How often do we see couples at a dinner table busy on their cell phones texting others, instead of talking to each other. Teenagers seem to be the worst examples of this. We are sucking it up, falling into the technology trap and can't wait for the next new model of i-Phone so we can text the person that is sitting right next to us. We need to stay vigilant against this quiet onslaught, stay close to nature, take long walks on the beach, hike in the mountains, sit by the fire and listen to the sounds of nature around us, to stay connected. Without our own efforts to retain our humanness and connectedness to mother nature, we will be stripped of our connection without even realising it.

LAW ENFORCEMENT – ARMY – AIR FORCE – NAVY – POLICE

The 'force of law' is a simulated force, not a natural force. All these sectors of our society and any other enforcement agency that deals with aspects of 'security' are mere instruments to enforce the rules that enslave the people. The word 'force' is inextricably linked to these activities – like police force and defence force. The majority of the people join these groups because they believe that they will be doing something good for their country or community. Fighting crime and corruption, keeping people safe and allowing people to be free – fighting for democracy. These are all misguided perceptions that we have been indoctrinated with and these ideals will fade very quickly once the people in these sectors realise they work for a corporation to uphold the laws of a corporation – not the people.

Their loyalty will shift rapidly towards the people once they discover that our countries are corporations that keep their people enslaved as property and stock options that are traded on global stock markets.

They will be filled with anger and feel betrayed when they realise that they have acted with force against their brothers and sisters while pledging their loyalty to a corporation called the UNITED STATES OF AMERICA or any other, with an objective to keep people under control and limit their freedom at all costs with laws that are unjust and inhumane. They have been subtly moved from being peace officers protecting the common law, into revenue generating policy officers that uphold the policy of their profit-driven corporation.

In the UBUNTU Contributionist communities, nobody will be forced to do anything. People will choose to live in a community based on its location, or the people, or the climate, or some other reason. Nobody will be forced to live anywhere or do anything other than their contribution to the community they live in. As outlined in great detail, these contributions will mostly be linked to the people's Labour of Love and can never be interpreted as forced labour. People will not be bound to their community the way they are forced to do so today because of economic restraints, or a job that keeps them in a part of the world they dislike. Anyone can move to any other community at any time.

The mining industry in South Africa caused unimaginable damage to community life in many rural areas and the neighbouring countries between the 1950s and 1980s, when they began importing cheap labour for the mines, displacing the male family heads, tearing families apart, creating long lasting damage to such communities. All because of money and the promise of a better life. These better lives never materialised – they only brought long lasting misery and devastation to most of these communities.

This was and still is, slave labour disguised by the cloak of capitalism – nothing more. Today people do this voluntarily when mothers or fathers take a job in a distant city and are forced to work there for an extended period, while leaving their families behind in some other location. Anyone who is forced to live in a specific place because of a job or the fear of not being able to survive otherwise, is clearly a slave to the system and the company they work for.

The words 'force' and 'security' will become alien to our society very quickly in a world without money, greed, gluttony, envy, pride, lust, sloth and crime. There will be very little to enforce in UBUNTU communities, unlike today. We will deal very differently with people who do not conform to the guidelines and morals of our communities because nobody is forced to live anywhere, especially if they do not agree with the activities, morals or lifestyle of that community.

There will be new laws created by the people of each community themselves – there will be a completely different legal system far removed from the inhumane complex laws of today. The Council of Elders will be the body that deals with all such issues in the community. People who continually disrupt the peace and tranquillity of their community may simply be asked to leave the community. The council will have the authority to do this, based on the will of the people. Dispensing punishment for breaking the laws will be up to each community and the laws and guidelines they agreed to as a community. These measures will range from the benign to the extreme, and can be changed on a daily basis.

Let me use an extreme example that many of us can relate to at present. If I enter a town with the intent to steal, rape and kill, I will most likely not commit such acts in a town where they will hang me, or chop my head off in public, or simply throw me into a crocodile infested lake. I will choose a town where their laws are not so extreme. This is unlikely to happen in UBUNTU communities because there is no need to steal, but I also believe that extreme freedom requires extreme measures to protect such freedom – and only time will tell how communities deal with extreme criminal or inhumane behaviour.

There will be very little need to enforce anything in a world where everyone does what they love to do; where everyone has everything they need; and problems are dealt with daily for the benefit of the people and the entire community. This kind of lawful society is alien to us today.

So what will happen to the police, army and other security forces?

They will change dramatically and will probably morph into support groups to help serve communities in times of disaster like fires, or flooding, or earthquakes, hurricanes or other disasters that are unpredictable and unavoidable. They will make up the emergency services and other groups of such nature that are unavailable today because there never seems to be enough money to sustain them. Every community will establish their own emergency and support services filled with highly skilled individuals who do it for the love of it, just like everyone else does what they do because they love it and they chose to do it.

WEAPONS OF WAR – GUNS & FIREARMS

The armies that were created to protect us are now used against us when we rise up against the government corporations that enslave us. The weapons they use are the products of secret military research projects where highly advanced technology is being used to create such weapons of war and mass destruction. There are many deadly weapons and unheard of technologies that have been developed by the Industrial Military Complex.

The HAARP installation in Alaska is probably the most infamous of such weapons but there are many more that we do not know about. That is why they are called "secret projects" by our governments. Why our governments should keep secrets from the people that they are supposed to serve has remained one of the greatest mysteries for millennia. Such weapons and technologies have been used in wars like the Gulf war, where microwave frequency based technology was used to make thousands of Iraqi soldiers suddenly surrender for no reason at all.

It is used among soldiers and other employees of secretive government departments in subconscious programming of assassins that are called 'sleepers'. The people are activated to perform a specific task, most often via a phone call, by hearing a few strategic words or a sound frequency that makes them go into a hypnotic state and perform a predetermined act, of which they have no memory at all after the event. The movie "The Manchurian Candidate" is a good example of this.

We have to stop thinking of weapons in the conventional sense, as guns and bombs and tanks and planes. Even chemical weapons are old-hat these days. Most of the new weapons are based on frequency technology. Either LASER, SASER, or other ways of generating invisible energy that affects or disintegrates matter.

This technology is also used to manipulate weather, create holographic deception, protective shields around objects like some of the stealth aircraft, and even shields that can make things invisible. Pretty much all the special effects we have seen on Star Trek or Star Wars have been possible for a long time. This stuff is so advanced that the average person will simply deny its existence out of sheer ignorance. And so, this hidden technology makes it easier for the government corporations to keep us enslaved without any backlash from the masses.

But in a society where new technology and free energy is run-of-the-mill daily creation, ordinary communities will also have access to such highly advanced technology and LASER and SASER weapons. This will be an immediate deterrent to anyone trying to harm them. It's the levelling of the playing fields where everyone will have access to the same advanced technology and no one will have any reason to feel inferior or superior because of this levelling effect. The bottom line is that every community will probably have some kind of tool or technology to defend themselves very effectively if absolutely necessary.

But this kind of thinking is based on our current conditioned ways of responding to problems, as products of our competition driven society. Such thinking will have no place in a money-free world.

TOP SECRET

It is astounding how we have been conditioned by the media and movies to accept concepts like, secret missions, and secret departments, and secret agents. So much so, that many of us believe that such activity is necessary to keep people and our countries safe. Movies like *James Bond* keep exposing us to slick characters that have a "license to kill" because they are "on her majesty's secret mission." Why should her majesty need to have a secret mission and be allowed to kill, if we are not?

And if you still think that those are mere fictional characters in movies than you have been thoroughly deceived. Global espionage and murder has been part of the game for thousands of years. It is always about the control and the money. In a free and open society where people control their own communities and destiny, where the Council of Elders implements the will of the people on a daily basis, there can be and will be no need for secrecy. It will be impossible to keep any kind of secret from the people, by anyone. There will be no need for the kind of behaviour we have become accustomed to in a capitalist world driven by money.

FARMING AND AGRICULTURE

Let us make the farmers the heroes of our country and give them everything they need to produce every kind of food imaginable for the people – so that no one shall be hungry.

Ref: Michael Tellinger 2005.

Farming is one of the most exciting areas of change in the new UBUNTU community, because it provides an immediate solution for the biggest problem we have – hunger and lack of nourishment for our people. Because food is the fundamental thing we need to survive, together with water, it will most likely become the model which is applied to all the other sectors of society as we implement Contributionism.

According to a report by the United Nations in 2011, one third of the world food production is dumped and left to rot. Not because there is no one who would eat it, but because people do not have money to buy the food. This is a blatant crime against all of humanity.

Our rural towns and farming communities are filled with farmers and other skilled people who can grow anything with ease. People with real green fingers that can turn a desert into a forest in a few years. All they need, are the tools, materials and support of the community and we should be producing so much food that we could feed the rest of the solar system. And this is exactly what we must to do in the UBUNTU Contributionism communities. Produce food and other products not only for ourselves, but for others who may not be able to do so.

But to achieve this, farmers must be seen and treated as the heroes of our country and given all the support they need on every possible level. Fuel, tools, machinery and other equipment that many farmers cannot afford.

Furthermore, they must be supported by the research laboratories that will provide them with other scientific tools and treatments and seeds that are not genetically modified, allowing our farmers to grow healthy organic food and livestock. Utilise water that has been energised through the active processes of mother Earth OR energised by those who know how to achieve this.

Scientists and researchers know that crops and animals grow at several times the normal rate under specific natural conditions, and with basic nutrients or sound and light manipulation. These techniques have been slowly eradicated by multinational corporations like Monsanto who want to control the global food supply. They have replaced natural techniques with dangerous genetically modified components to achieve large and beautiful looking crops. Such control gives them the opportunity to induce disease in people and animals, in turn upholding the drug and medical corporations, who will quickly provide the treatments for our induced diseases from GMO foods. This is part of the "problem-reaction-solution" plan for humanity.

Growing food is a beautiful and a simple task for those who know how. There are millions of wannabe farmers around the world who do not have the opportunities to get involved in farming. Those who want to farm must be inducted by master farmers and become masters themselves. We will use the many experts in natural and organic farming techniques, as well as the specialists in the field of bio-mimicry to enhance the quality and quantity of all farming and agricultural produce. These experts will also be used to train new farmers so that we can diversify the entire agricultural sector to areas that were previously thought to be financially not viable. There are solutions for every possible problem, and we will implement them.

- **The people shall produce what they need;**
- **NOT what the bankers or politicians or corporations allow them to produce.**

Let's face it, we cannot eat money and we cannot eat gold – and in a land where the economy has collapsed, the man with a vegetable garden, a cow and a chicken is king.

Thousands of farms are being stolen from farmers on a daily basis by the unlawful activity of the banks. In South Africa, just like the rest of the world, the objective of Monsanto is very clear – to take control of the global food supply, and they are succeeding at a rapid rate. Once they control the food, they control the people. Their activities must be declared unlawful and their laboratories and other facilities should be put to use by the scientists within our communities to provide valuable resources for the entire farming and agricultural sector.

Farmers are under constant threat to conform to genetically modified seeds, fertilisers and farming practice, or face possible bankruptcy and losing their farms. This is happening at such an alarming rate that if we do not stop this, Monsanto and the banks will own all the productive farm land across South Africa and the world within the next few years. The consequences will be devastating.

This is where the strength of united UBUNTU communities will start making a difference by producing natural, organic, healthy crops from 'Eden' seeds. We can neutralise the devastating effects of Monsanto in a short time.

We must use the skills of existing experts in treating pests and disease in crops and livestock using alternative techniques. Many such methods have been used with virtually 100% success rates, without poisoning the land, the food or the animals. These advanced scientific techniques are well known to some but vigorously opposed by the current leadership in favour of the poisons and other harmful treatments of our food and animals. These proposed alternative techniques also cross over into the health and pharmaceutical sector, which we will discuss in greater detail under that section.

Arguably the most powerful asset a farmer can own and use are "effective micro-organisms" or EM. They rehabilitate poor soil with an extraordinary genius that only nature can provide. EM is such a powerful pro-biotic that it can be used to purify large tracts of polluted water, but sensitive enough to be drunk by babies. The only 'problem' with EM is that it can be brewed naturally without any corporate interference and therefore it cannot be controlled for profit by the corporations. EM is high on the list of "wonder-products" that must be used immediately for soil and water purification.

People are prevented from growing certain natural plants that have been part of ancient African (traditional) culture for thousands of years. Governments that declare certain plants unlawful or illegal, is like saying that God makes mistakes and that there are problems with his creation and it is up to the government to fix the mistakes. Numerous plants and herbs have been made illegal by governments to protect the drug industry. Hemp is just one small example. The cultivation of Hemp will solve many problems in several industries virtually overnight. This includes the eradication of nuclear fallout. For this reason Hemp is the second wonder-product that tops the list of must-have assets for an UBUNTU community.

Traditional healers will be encouraged and supported to grow any kind of plant or herb that they need for their traditional healing. Specialised farmers will be trained in the skills to help grow such natural plants and remedies for the traditional healers so that this can be returned to the honourable service that it once provided. We will fully honour and support the Sangomas and Shaman who uphold ancient African wisdom and tradition without fear of exploitation from any 'authority'.

The production of herbs for aromatic oils will be maximised to use in all kinds of treatments currently frowned upon by the medical and pharmaceutical mafia, who close down any possible opposition with a promise of a cure.

In the UBUNTU Contribution System, one in every ten people will most likely be involved in the farming and agriculture sector in some way. These skills and the love for mother Earth must be taught to all our children from the earliest age – because if you truly love mother Earth, you will never allow anyone to harm her.

Farmers from all walks of life, from every community, will be the real heroes who produce every kind of food imaginable in so much abundance that we simply cannot imagine it today.

If we can feed our neighbours and teach them to do what we do, we will very quickly alleviate many socio-economic problems in every part of the world, and we will replace misery and neediness with abundance and cooperation on all levels. We will create countries and communities where people love and respect each other, and do not harm or betray each other because they are homeless, desperate or hungry.

Just like in every area of society, we must consult the experts – and not the politicians – to provide the solutions and solve the problems. To solve the food and agriculture crisis is obviously a task for those who know everything there is to know about farming and the associated sectors.

And so, the farming and agricultural sector will have a huge impact on many other sectors of our society like scientific research; training in all related areas of farming and agriculture; medicine, transport and delivery; packaging; storage; etc.

Today, the main obstacle to providing food for our people are the bankers and ignorant politicians, who in most instances are just gullible people who believe they are doing good, who have allowed the banks to operate their unlawful empires in our countries and so manipulate and destroy our people.

Let us support the farmer every step of the way and make every community a farming community, living in harmony with Mother Earth, producing abundance for all.

FARMING – PLAN OF ACTION:

These are merely suggestions of what every community should initiate as the first small steps in their transition to becoming UBUNTU communities. This is a living document that will be modified by the communities as they identify new needs and develop more appropriate solutions.

1) Appoint a Council of Elders.
2) Reach an agreement with the farmers in the community who want to participate by offering their land for the benefit of the community.
3) Reach an agreement with the land owners who may not be farmers to utilise land and factories standing vacant.
4) Identify the UBUNTU members and those from the community who want to contribute their time and skills to work on the farms and factories – 3 hours per week only.
5) Raise the funds from the community from monthly contributions to provide all the tools, materials, seeds, fuel, and other.
6) The farmers provide their knowledge in farming and training of the people who work on the farms for free – as part of their contribution.
7) The farmers retain 33% of the harvest – community receives 66% of the harvest.
8) Most farmers will be happy with this arrangement – since they have no layout or costs and still retain as much as they would normally generate on their own, or more in some cases.
9) The farmers can do what they want with their share and sell it on the open market to generate cash for survival in the transitional phase.
10) The community will distribute the 66% to their members – only to

those who participate and those who made financial contribution. This is after all Contributionism. Those who contribute their time will benefit immensely.

11) The rest of the produce is sold at very low prices to the rest of the community – those who do not contribute – so that they also feel an immediate benefit.

12) Set up a farmers market to outsiders and neighbouring towns. Sell the excess produce at slightly higher prices to everyone outside the community – but still considerably cheaper than what they can buy in their own towns or supermarkets.

13) This will create an immediate attraction to all surrounding towns and a need for them to adopt the same model for themselves.

14) The funds that get generated go back to producing more, and constantly expanding productions to other foods and products.

15) Expand this formula into other areas of industry like wood and metal products; building materials; arts and crafts, and more.

16) Use the same 33% - 66% principle of sharing with artisans in other sectors of industry.

17) Plant fruit trees and nut trees in large numbers in all parks, schools, along the streets and roads to provide an ongoing supply of food in times of crisis.

18) Every household should be given fruit and nut trees to plant.

This is the basic model that can be implemented and grown organically in every town. The key component will be to appoint a Council of Elders as soon as possible in every community. This will prevent any bickering and disagreements among active members in the initial phases – which must be expected because of our conditioning by capitalism and ego that seems to permeate every part of our lives today.

Farmers will benefit from the financial and labour assistance from the community, while the community benefits from the expertise and products. It must be a complete cooperation on all levels to be successful and forms a critical part of the early transition stage to full UBUNTU Contributionism.

The objective is to grow three times as much food as is required by the people of each town. This will also provide a large education and training programme to millions of people in all of the many associated sectors. Training and knowledge that is easily acquired by working with experts in the field, not sitting in classrooms reading 'approved' textbooks.

CITY DWELLERS – PARTICIPATION IN UBUNTU

We have to find a way to include those who live in cities, who cannot contribute 3 hours per week on community farms or other community activity. This is one of the challenges that in itself provides some exciting opportunities – just like every area of the UBUNTU Contributionism model, as soon as we start to think about it.

There are millions of people who have successful careers in cities, who cannot just give it all up to move to the country. These people have many specialised skills and talents that will become critical in times to come – but in the initial stages it will be impossible to utilise such a diversity of talents – even though such individuals have been offering their skills to the UBUNTU movement already.

The community talent exchange, which was outlined earlier will be a perfect match for large numbers of city dwellers with diverse skills to serve each other without money. Furthermore, to benefit from the UBUNTU farming projects, city dwellers can make monthly or regular contribution in cash, to help establish more UBUNTU farming and other industries. These funds will be pooled and used to continuously expand the abundance of goods produced.

The initial focus will be on water supply and food production, since these are the critical cornerstones for survival, and because this is the area of life where humanity is very vulnerable. Our food and water have become unaffordable and unsafe.

One of the models proposed is to create UBUNTU Warehouses – in every city – that are stocked with the remainder of produce and goods from the growing UBUNTU communities around the country. All contributing members in the cities can benefit from the labour of UBUNTU communities everywhere. This is merely an interim solution to help city dwellers to become part of this transitional period and this structure can easily be managed with a smart card system for members and the community talent exchange.

Remember that many farmers are facing bankruptcy and farm repossessions. Many farmers desperately need help to remain productive. These financial contributions can help the farmers to participate and survive in the face of real challenges. Special UBUNTU farms can be activated by the contributions from city dwellers to supply the urban warehouses with food and other produce. This action can save thousands of farms, reactivate many more, and continue creating new UBUNTU farms delivering a continuous stream of produce to UBUNTU members, providing affordable food and other goods.

Conversion of existing farms into UBUNTU farms is a vital first step. Farmers who are currently struggling to make ends meet, will allow communities to be established on certain parts of their farms. Having such a community on the property will not only make the property extremely difficult to sell on auction by the banks and thus protect the farmer/owner, but over time it will become the foundation for a whole new way of thinking and living for that farmer and his family.

Because the human spirit is strong and endlessly creative, the people stuck in larger cities will come up with their own plans to turn their suburbs into UBUNTU communities. I trust that this will happen at an unpredictable rate, but once the first few suburbs are sharing and benefiting from their united efforts to provide for each other, other suburbs will follow at an exponential rate. This is what makes the Contributionism model so exciting – it has no boundaries and creates true unity and abundance for all.

This is not a pipe dream. The town of Sedgwick, in Maine, USA has recently declared "food sovereignty" – and there are many others around America and the rest of world that are doing the same. http://www.foodrenegade.com/maine-town-declares-food-sovereignty/.

Russians who were inspired by the Ringing Cedars book series have set up communities containing 1-hectare family domains and have become major contributors to the annual Russian agricultural production. We have to initiate a planting culture among our people and especially the children. In South Africa this has been done by www.plantingseason.co.za – an initiative that aims to inspire 1 million South Africans to grow their own food.

It is all about 'seed communities'. Whether they are in small towns or in city suburbs. We have to start somewhere. So do not be afraid to talk to others and share your knowledge, and start something. Plant the first seeds of UBUNTU in your community – do not be afraid and lead the way.

MINIMUM AND MAXIMUM LAND REQUIREMENT FOR TOWNS

CIRCULAR COMMUNITIES & POPULATION

Plato said that the circle is a perfect shape. It is also evident in sacred geometry where circles and spheres are the primordial shapes. This is why ancient cultures who lived in harmony with nature built round structures and not rectangular structures.

The UBUNTU model for towns and entire communities is based on these principles. As the small towns develop into UBUNTU communities, they will acquire land for all their needs. Each town will acquire the minimum land area required to provide for the needs of the people and to produce all the food for the community. This will be calculated by the farmers and town planners, based on the population, and endorsed by the Council of Elders in each community.

Everything produced by the community will be done in the space occupied by the community – not on outstretched farms and industrial areas that are separated from the people. There will be no need for such wasted space and the transporting of goods from distant isolated farms. As the community grows it will occupy more land based on the needs of the people – not on the greed of individuals.

This is all possible because land ownership does not exist in UBUNTU communities. Everyone has what they need and land is allocated to everyone for all the diverse activities of the community. Farming, manufacturing, sports, recreation, arts, culture, engineering, research, and all other human endeavours.

But this poses a potential problem that communities could grow into huge cities, just like today. There is however the consideration that population growth will diminish dramatically in UBUNTU communities – statistics clearly show that when people are happy and content, they breed a lot slower than when they are impoverished and desperate. There are many countries with negative population growth rates today, and I expect this to become the case in UBUNTU Contributionist communities.

Children are often seen as a retirement policy in poor communities, to look after the parents when they get older. This is obviously a major contributor to population explosion and will not play any role in UBUNTU communities.

We should nevertheless consider an optimum size and population for towns and communities. What is the optimum number of people in a specific community to make it as functional as possible? Is it ten thousand people? Or fifty thousand people? What do we do when the town gets a little too big for comfort? These considerations can only be made once a community is fully functional and makes such decisions for the people, by the people.

CREATING NEW COMMUNITIES – FOLLOWING THE LAWS OF NATURE

The circular plan for communities is critical. It allows us to grow and create new communities without encroaching on others. When a town reaches a certain size, the people will automatically do what human cells do – they divide, multiply, and create new self sustained cells in our bodies that exist in harmony with all the other cells in our bodies. With its own nucleus, DNA and internal structures that makes it a unique cell – a new community of cells.

There are all kinds of cells in our bodies that perform different functions all for the benefit of the whole body. They do not compete with each other. They cooperate and contribute their tiny little functions to ensure the survival of the whole body. There are brain cell, liver cells, heart cell, muscle cells, blood cells, and billions more that make up the various organs, that in turn work together for the benefit of the whole body. However, because communities are so flexible, they can fragment and re-fragment naturally, which will probably happen in dense urban areas. Sub communities and sub-sub communities can be structured but how this will operate cannot ever be standardised. It is based purely on geographic and cultural principals specific to each community.

The cells in our bodies do not encroach on other cells, but when they do that, we call them cancerous cells and our body automatically starts to get rid of such cancerous cells. Circular communities will always provide space for expansion. Furthermore, there will always be space to move between communities on neutral land for travellers, transport and other needs, never having to encroach on any community. Rectangular communities will not allow such freedom.

LIVING OUTSIDE OF COMMUNITIES – SINGLE FAMILY FARMS/UNITS AND LONE RANGERS

One of the frequently asked questions is: *"What if I want to live alone on my farm, far away from everyone. I don't want to be forced to live in any community."*

Once again this is where we instantly recognise the "self correcting" aspects of the Contributionism model. Keep in mind that there is no land ownership under UBUNTU – only land usage by those that contribute to the greatest benefit of all in the community. Therefore the community will only occupy as much land as it needs to achieve this.

Also keep in mind that *community* is not just a noun – it is also a verb. Even if you live alone with your family, that is still a form of community and at some stage, you would have to connect with other human beings. This too is a form of community.

If you are a community of one – or a family of four – or twelve – you will only occupy as much land as you need to provide abundance for your family community. Therefore, we will not see farmers in the middle of nowhere with 500 cows. There is no market for their cows – unless they are doing it for a community nearby, because looking after 500 cows takes a lot of work. You will not see farmers with large tracts of land harvesting thousands of tonnes of maize because there is no one to eat all that maize and the nearby town has its own programme to feed the people of the town.

So, people who choose to live on their own will have a beautiful life and they will only have to look after themselves and their family – with no additional stress of worrying how to earn money. Even though they live separated from the community, they may still be providing a service to their closest community, like spinning wool or making special cheese, or making salt. And therefore they will be counted as members of the community and in return will have access to all the benefits of the community.

But if they choose to be completely separated, sooner or later the lone ranger family will need something from the nearby town and once again we see the simple principles of Contributionism apply. For the lone ranger to get something from the town, he will have to contribute some of his time towards any of the community projects of that town.

There is very little that the lone ranger will be able to offer the town that they don't already have. The most obvious thing that they do not have is his LOL contribution for the greater benefit of the town. This kind of exchange will smooth itself out very quickly and the Council of Elders will play an important role in assuring that everyone is treated fairly in these exchanges.

It is also highly unlikely that the children of the lone ranger will feel the same way he does. They will be inspired to visit other communities, to learn and to grow with them. As such, the essence of Contributionism will proliferate.

There may be some form of barter between small farmsteads, but this will be entirely up to the individuals who decide upon such exchanges. No one is forced to do anything at any time against their will. In reality it would be silly for anyone to exchange anything they have – because whatever they have will be something practical and useful – unlike the crap that we accumulate today.

So, instead of exchanging things, the ranger may as well just contribute his LOL in the town for 3 hours of the week and get access to whatever he may need, like that saddle for his horse, that he could not make himself, or the building materials for his new barn, that he also cannot produce on his own.

ENERGY – ELECTRICITY

Energy is probably the most fiercely guarded sector of industry, by those who control its generation and supply. The continued supply of electricity has become one of the key areas of concern for every single human being alive. Electricity is not the only form of energy. It is the 'type' of energy that was chosen for us around the year 1900, by those with money and power, to use this form of energy for enslaving the global population. While there was an obvious option of FREE energy presented to the bankers, they chose the one we still use today, because its supply could be controlled and it could be measured for consumption.

At the same time these bankers under the leadership of JP Morgan, ensured that all traces of the alternative, radiant and un-measurable free energy systems were wiped from human memory. Once this was in place they could control the supply of electricity and they could meter it so that they could charge the people for its usage and control the price.

Shortly after constructing the famous Tesla Tower, or Wardenclyffe Tower, at Shoreham, Long Island in New York state, in 1901, Nikola Tesla gave the world FREE, non-lethal, radiant energy that connected the world without wires, allowing free telecommunication around the world and powering every imaginable device. The radiant energy from the tower could power from cars to lights, to machines to aeroplanes and ships.

Tesla had this to say about his gift of free energy to the world. "It is to be noted that the phenomenon here involved in the transmission of electrical energy is one of *true conduction* and is not to be confounded with the phenomena of *electrical radiation*, which have heretofore been observed, and which, from the very nature and mode of propagation, would render practically impossible the transmission of any appreciable amount of energy to such distances as are of practical importance."

Unfortunately, Tesla's funder was JP Morgan, one of the most powerful bankers in the world.

Above: Tesla Tower, or Wardenclyffe Tower, at Shoreham, Long Island in New York. Above Right: Nikola Tesla

After realising that his funding gave birth to free energy from which he could not profit, Morgan pulled his funding to Tesla and was undoubtedly behind the destruction of the tower by the US Federal Government in 1917, to ensure that any reminder of free energy would be wiped from human memory. It is important to note that in 1913, JP Morgan was also one of the founders of the unlawful privately owned Federal Reserve Bank in the USA and the owner of JP Morgan Bank. The Morgan family remain one of the three most powerful banking families in the world today, together with the Rothschilds and the Rockefellers.

Scientists know that the universe is an infinite source of energy – there is free energy everywhere around us – converting from one form to another. So why are we paying for it?

There are many scientists with all the energy solutions we can imagine, ready for us to embrace these new forms of energy, but it is the will of the people that is necessary to start the process of change. The old regime and old energy will not change without our action. Inventors of new and free energy have been threatened, bribed, tortured and killed to prevent free energy from landing in the hands of the people.

We have to understand how important this simple step is, in emancipating humanity from enslavement. Once we can provide the energy we need for all aspects of our lives, from cooking, heating, water, transport, industry, and many more applications, it will be very difficult to control people. In fact, I believe that the release of free energy to the people of the world will cause a global awakening and result in a rapid rise of consciousness among humanity. Energy in its many forms used today is a deadly stranglehold on each and every one of us, affecting us in ways we don't even recognise any more.

All the food we eat; all the clothes we wear; the products we buy; the cars we drive; the technology we use; the baths we have... need energy to be produced in some form or another. Free energy will lead to the emancipation of people everywhere – from the deepest jungles to city high-rises, overnight.

TRANSITION AND THE SEARCH FOR FREE ENERGY

Our aim is to find sustainable free energy solutions as soon as possible and start the implementation without any delay. The universe of the Divine Creator responds to action – so let us act and bring in the change that we want.

Let us expand the search for alternative and FREE energy by giving all the inventors and scientists – whether private, or part of existing institutions, all the help and support they need to deliver free energy to the people.

Explore the many existing leads into free and alternative energy; solar; hydro; tidal; wind; geothermal; gas; magnetic and other. Many such devices and technology already exists and our scientist and inventors will very quickly develop real and lasting energy solutions when given the opportunity.

DECENTRALISE THE ENERGY SUPPLY

The existing global energy grid is simply a tool to control the people – it is one of the most powerful grids of control. If the grid goes down, most of us are affected immediately. But the grid cannot fail – if there is no grid. Our communities will not be in the cold or darkness if they control their own energy supply. All energy supply must immediately be decentralised. Every city, town, and community must take collective action to provide new solutions for themselves, with the help and advice of scientists – not politicians. We must use every possible option to provide immediate to long-term solutions.

These will be largely dictated by the location of the community. For example, rivers and oceans are great energy generators and very soon we will stop burning coal to generate our energy.

Remember that all the existing cables and transformers and the whole network was paid for by us, the people. Therefore we need to take control of the grid in our towns and connect them to our own new source of energy supply.

IMMEDIATE SOLUTIONS AVAILABLE

- Every river will be utilised to generate hydro power for nearby towns and villages. These are simple concepts that can be applied immediately. Hydro turbines have become very advanced and a few turbine placed in rivers at strategic points will not be visible, nor create any kind of environmental pollution, while providing uninterrupted power to the towns. The cost of such energy, once installed, is so low that it can be called free.

- All coastal towns and cities can be powered by using the inexhaustible energy in the waves of the ocean, without creating any waste or pollution. Turbines and other devices that generate energy by water moving in both/all directions can be installed very quickly and stop the burning of coal and polluting our planet. Once these systems are in place, the cost of electricity will be virtually free.

- Sustainable gas can provide a major solution to the energy crisis. All sewage plants to be converted into **methane gas** (natural gas) producing centres – providing methane gas to the people of the area. Chemical engineers know how to enhance the methane generating process without great cost to the community. Let us use our own waste for our own benefit. Gas can provide heat, light, cooking, baking, hot water, refrigeration – almost all of our energy needs. Pig farms and dairies should also be used for generating methane from pig and cow dung that generates large amounts of methane gas. There are simple adaptations of this kind of gas generation that can be used on rural farms that are far away from other centres.

- Many inventors have demonstrated **perpetual motion generators, magnetic and other devices** that create large amounts of energy. Some have been silenced and some have even been killed to prevent their inventions from reaching the people. We will actively seek out these inventors and allow them to share their inventions with the people of South Africa and the rest of the world.

- This includes the use of **sound and frequency as a source of energy**. Only the truly informed scientists will be aware of this technology that has been demonstrated and has existed since 1888 with the inventions of John Keely, with his Musical Dynasphere, and later, by Nikola Tesla.

- There is a frequency of **sound that boils water** – this is possibly the most important discovery of the past 100 years demonstrated by New Zealand inventor Peter Davey as far back as 1940. Davey died in 2011, taking the knowledge to his grave. A dedicated group of scientists will discover this very quickly and will liberate the world. We encourage every researcher with access to the right tools to find the frequency that boils water. This frequency can boil the water in the power plants instead of burning coal.

- Sound frequencies also create a cooling effect and can be used for refrigeration and cooling of all kinds. It is known as thermo-acoustics.

(Some guidance to discovering the frequency to boil water – Please measure the harmonic resonant frequency of boiling water, and then create a vibrating device that acts or behaves like a tuning fork, and creates a standing wave of such a frequency. This should boil water instantly as opposed to the heat generated from the friction between molecules that takes a long time to boil, as we know from conventional electric kettles. There may also be a role played by the angles and relative frequencies of the hydrogen atoms in relation to the oxygen atom at boiling point. The actual angle of the bonds may hold the secret to the frequency.)

- **Radio frequencies** between 20 – 90 mega-hertz make salt water burn at around 1500 deg Celsius, as demonstrated by John Kanzius from Akron, Ohio, before he died. This can be utilised as a major energy solution in some sectors.

All nuclear reactors will be shut down and dismantled with immediate effect.

This is unpredictable technology that many leading scientists have warned us about – we do not understand it and we cannot control it. It is far more explosive than children playing with fire. It has the potential to destroy all of humanity and has caused unimaginable damage in the past and will do so again unless it is deactivated.

NOTE: There will be many more incredible inventions and discoveries once we give our scientists the freedom to find the solutions and we look forward with great anticipation to these breakthroughs.

John Keely, seated, with his musical Dynasphere, circa 1888.

THE CURRENT STATE OF AFFAIRS IN ELECTRICITY

ESKOM is the energy provider to the people of South Africa. It is seen by most people as a government owned enterprise with its primary objective being to provide affordable electricity to the people.

ESKOM generates approximately 95% of the electricity used in South Africa and approximately 45% of the electricity used in greater Africa. To achieve this ESKOM uses mostly coal, which it gets from various coal mines in South Africa.

The problem is that these coal mines are mostly owned by international corporations that are raping the land, destroying our beautiful country and selling the coal to ESKOM at international market related prices, making unimaginable profits for their international owners.

South Africa is the fourth largest exporter of coal in the world – coal that belongs to the people. But the people see no benefit at all, either from the coal or the energy it generates. Instead, the coal is sold to ESKOM and other countries generating huge profits for the international shareholders.

The GOVERNMENT OF THE REPUBLIC OF SOUTH AFRICA, which is a corporation registered on the US Securities & Exchange Commission, is the sole shareholder of ESKOM. The shareholder representative is the Minister of Public Enterprises. At first glance it seems as if the government is taking responsibility for the people and looking after the people's needs. But unfortunately this is not the case.

The word 'public' suggests that all such enterprises should benefit the public. This is also not the case. Most of these government enterprises are all tied in with private multinational corporations, that are dependent upon the South African public working in the these corporations and become trapped and reliant on the bad salaries they receive for their sweat and blood.

Furthermore, THE REPUBLIC OF SOUTH AFRICA and THE GOVERNMENT OF THE REPUBLIC OF SOUTH AFRICA are both registered as corporations as pointed out before. This means that the government is profiteering from the hard work of the people in South Africa, secretly trading and selling shares in corporations like ESKOM, that it is the sole owner of. It means that the labour and efforts of the people is being traded on the international stock markets by invisible shareholders all over the world.

In 2011 ESKOM posted a profit of 13.2 Billion Rand (about 1.7 billion US dollars) according to their website. The directors and CEO were paid many millions for keeping the scam alive and successfully pulling the wool over the eyes of the trusting people.

OUR RIGHTS TO FREE ENERGY

This level of deceit is almost unthinkable to any normal person on the street. It is a complete betrayal of all our rights and the highest form of deception that can be perpetrated by the leaders against their own people.

Since its inception in the early 1900s, all of the installations and infrastructure of ESKOM have been paid for many times over by the tax revenue of the people and the profits made from the rich mineral mining industries.

These minerals that have been mined and sold while making unimaginable profit for their international owners, belong to the people of South Africa, and therefore by rights, everything that forms part of ESKOM belongs to the people.

So why are we still paying so much for electricity if we have already paid for everything that is owned by ESKOM many times over? Shouldn't our governments be working on improving our lives as our duly elected servants, rather than allowing more and more corporations to make our lives more difficult every year?

Some facts that each of us needs to know and share with others:

This applies to all power generating corporations in all countries.

1) All of ESKOM's installations; infrastructure and technology belongs to the people because it has been paid for many times over by the government on behalf of the people. Either with tax-payers money, or revenue earned from selling the minerals in the ground that also belong to the people.

2) Any business deals that have been made by ESKOM with international investors, funders, partners or shareholders of any kind or any nature, are unlawful and should not be legally binding because they were done deceitfully, behind the backs of the people, without full disclosure of the grossly negative implications to the people.

3) All the deals and agreements made by ESKOM have not been for the benefit of the people but rather for the government corporation, benefiting the shareholders and investors around the world. Most of these investors are the same powerful bankers that have taken control of all other aspect of society. Every funding deal made by ESKOM only means more debt for the South African people without any benefits at all.

4) In all such deals, the hardworking, trusting and ignorant people of South Africa were basically sold into slavery, to pay exorbitant prices for electricity and to make huge profits for the invisible shareholders.

5) If ESKOM belongs to the people, it should provide extremely cheap, if not free, electricity to the people, because that is what the people need and want. The government should comply with its role as the servant of the people.

6) If the coal in the ground belongs to the people, why are we paying for it to make electricity?

7) There has been no effort made by ESKOM to find alternative and reusable sources of energy to provide cheap or free energy to South Africans.

8) In 2010 ESKOM allocated 368 Billion Rand ($36 billion) to the upgrading of their own facilities instead of providing cheaper electricity and finding alternative solutions to benefit the people.

9) This huge amount of funding, using the people as collateral, was generated to allow ESKOM to build new facilities and install

appropriate control measures to be able to charge the people for electricity in the future.

10) By using these funds, ESKOM could have provided every single household in South Africa with the most advanced solar energy system worth around R30,000 (thirty thousand). This would have catered for all the needs of a substantial household. The only thing needed would be continued maintenance for which the people could be responsible and could be covered by a very small and proportional monthly fee.

11) In essence this could have lead to the decentralisation of energy supply, allowing communities to take control of their own needs in electricity.

12) Every true scientist and researcher knows that there has always been, and that there is a growing number of new, green, renewable, reusable and even FREE perpetual-motion energy solutions available. We will find them and release them to the people.

13) Now, ask yourself – who is funding ESKOM and all the other electricity supply giants around the world? The same powerful bankers that destroyed Tesla's free energy and have kept his knowledge under lock and key ever since.

14) And so, since 1923 and the official establishment of ESKOM, it has been doing everything possible to cover up any development in free energy, to ensure that they continue creating huge profits for their shareholders or those invisible individuals who profiteer from the sweat and blood of the South African people.

ENERGY – PETROLEUM

The petroleum industry is the other highly guarded part of the energy sector. Oil companies have guarded their empire vigorously for over 100 years and will not allow anyone to upset their global control.

Most people have heard of someone somewhere who developed a car that runs on water, or ethanol, or hydrogen; or gas, or compressed air, or oxygen, or some other ingenious devices like magnetic motors. But astonishingly, all these amazing discoveries by thousands of great minds have mysteriously disappeared, never to be seen again. Why is that?

Because petroleum and oil is not just about running cars – our entire global industry and economy is almost completely based on oil today. It makes up the active ingredient in most synthetic materials like rubber and plastics, that are major components of almost everything we manufacture and consume as a species.

The amusing thing is that we have made almost no real progress in technology since the very first car engine was made. The so-called technological advancements are mere deceptions that keep us going around in circles believing that we are presented with new technology. Every year new cars are released with new shiny metal covers, but the engines still run on the basic principles of steam train technology.

This is always a major point of contention with the Formula One racing enthusiasts, but the fact remains – all our cars are still propelled by combustion technology that drives pistons or some other mechanical device, that in turn makes the wheels spin around and around. We are like hamsters caught up in the merry-go-round of being baffled by pseudo technology. We are being drip-fed little bits of technology every year, claiming to be the latest and the best and the newest technology available.

The same can be said for all other areas of technology, in the fields of electronics and even space exploration. The concept of planned obsolescence is built into everything that we buy today so that it will have to be replaced in the not too distant future. In other words – all technological products are made to break after a short period of usage.

This is how it has been planned and orchestrated by the petroleum giants and other global corporations. It has been suggested that SONY is not exactly a Japanese company, but is in effect the acronym for Standard Oil New York – SONY, which is a Rockefeller company. While it is not always easy to verify such reports it would not surprise me at all. I hope this is starting to make sense.

It must be made clear that we are not in this situation because there are no other alternatives – NO – there are many alternatives that have been presented by scientists and inventors over time. We are in this predicament by the design of the same small number of powerful families who control global economies and mould them around their own production plans and continued control over the human race. Over the past 200 years these giant corporations have manipulated the behaviour of the entire global population so that they benefit from every aspect of human endeavour. Their actions contribute to one of the most devastating aspects of global pollution in all of human history.

If we are to survive as a species, we have to put an end to this destruction of our beautiful planet immediately and offer the world one of the many green and renewable alternatives that exist.

You can imagine that a simple discovery like a car that runs on water will almost immediately cripple the oil giants – they will go to any extreme to prevent this from happening.

I have had a number of invertors tell me about their own personal experiences and how their lives and families have been threatened because of the research on alternatives to petroleum. Once again it is up to the will of the people to make this happen and open the doors to the brave inventors who have all the solutions we need. Cars that run on water, is a reality – not a fairytale.

Today there is cross-ownership and other agreements between car manufacturers and petroleum companies so that the car manufacturers do not manufacture cars that run on water or some other device and put the oil companies out of business.

One such example is that of scientist and inventor Otis Carr, who in the 60s approached the major car manufacturers in the USA, offering them cars that float with anti-gravity technology without using any oil. According to Ralph Ring, who was an associate of Carr in their laboratory, the response from the motor executive was "if you put them up there, we will shoot them down".

There are many detractors who claim that Carr was a con artist, but this is exactly the clever disinformation smear tactics that are used by these corporations to remove any level of credibility from those who pose any threat.

This has been done very successfully to a long list of inventors over the past 120 years, like John Keely; Nikola Tesla; Royal Raymond Rife; Rene Caisse, Max Gerson, Harry Hoxsey, John Searle and many more.

All they need to do is create a little bit of doubt in the minds of the public, and suggest that the inventor is either possibly crazy, a con artist, or paedophile, or simply insist that their inventions do not really work, and very quickly such disinformation permeates into society, creating doubt in the minds of people while undermining the original achievements.

SASOL, a South African company, is the world leader in solid-to-liquid & gas-to-liquid fuel manufacturing. The history of Sasol began in 1927 when a White Paper was tabled in Parliament to investigate the establishment of a South African oil-from-coal industry.

Since 1950, SASOL has developed world-leading technology for the conversion of low grade coal into a variety of fuels, products and chemicals. Today its operational footprint extends to more than 20 countries and exports to over 100. Sasol is one of the top five publicly listed companies in South Africa and is quoted on the JSE and the NYSE, making unimaginable wealth for its shareholders, at the expense of the South African people.

Principal Subsidiaries: Sasol Oil (Pty) Ltd.; Sasol Technology (Pty) Ltd.; Sasol Chemical Industries Ltd.-Operations Division; Sasol Mining (Pty) Ltd.; Sasol Synthetic Fuels (Pty) Ltd.; Sasol Petroleum International (Pty) Ltd.

Principal Divisions: Sasol Alpha Olefins; Sasol Fertilizers; Sasol Fibres; Sasol Fuel Oil; Sasol Solvents; Sasol Carbo-Tar; Sasol Ammonia; Sasol Akrylo; Sasol Minchem; Sasol Mining Explosives (SMX); Sasol Gas; Sasol Engineering Division; Sasol Amsul; Sasol Synfuels International (Pty) Limited.

UBUNTU PLAN OF ACTION - PETROLEUM

1) SASOL with all its technology and facilities was developed and paid for by South African tax payers' money, and therefore should belong to the people.
2) It is a crime against the people of South Africa to have sold all this technology to private shareholders and create a multinational corporation that exploits the labour of the South African people with no benefit to the people while creating unimaginable wealth for the international owners.
3) SASOL uses coal and gas from the ground that belongs to the people – so why are we paying for the petrol and products created from this gas and coal?
4) SASOL exports the fuel and a long list of other products, which are manufactured from resources that belong to the people, to over 100 countries in the world – and yet we cannot afford the petrol in our own country.
5) All the oil or gas that is pumped from the ground or any coastal areas of South Africa belongs to the people – why are we paying for it?
6) In the interim phase, while we are exploring alternative fuels, SASOL will provide virtually free petrol and all other by-products to

the people of South Africa.

7) All exports of SASOL will be terminated immediately, so that we can ease the mining of coal to make the fuel.
8) SASOL will provide all the farmers with all the fuel they need for free.
9) SASOL is to provide all the fuel necessary for all public transport for free.

We must support new ideas presented by inventors and scientists, as outlandish as they may seem, to create new alternatives.

HEALTH – HOSPITALS – PHARMACEUTICS

Healing should be a beautiful and spiritual experience done by people who resonate deeply with being human and caring for others. While many people who go into this sector of life start out with noble thoughts, they soon get worn down by the ugly aspects of its control. Most of us are familiar with the symbols on the ambulances and hospitals of the world. We see them almost every day of our lives, and yet we never question where these weird symbols have their origins. They are no longer just a simple red cross, which has its own esoteric origins with the Knights Hospitaller and Knights Templar, but today our medical centres are identified by a strange six-pointed cross with a caduceus, or a winged serpent at the centre of it. The caduceus is well recognised symbol associated with Hermes and Mercury in Greek and Roman religions.

The Templar cross – that became part of the Swiss flag – a country associated with banking and money as were the Templars. Used as a symbol for hospitals and medical aid still used by the Red Cross today.

The newly adopted six-pointed cross used by the medical industry – with a serpent twisted around the staff. Now on most ambulances, hospitals and medical clothing.

Above: The ancient caduceus symbol, recognised all over the world – has been the symbol associated with alchemy, medical practice and secret societies for millennia. Notice the pine cone at the top of the staff – as reference to the pineal gland in the human brain. The caduceus is deeply encoded with knowledge of the laws of nature and the manipulation thereof, with reference to the enslavement of the human race. Carvings like these are found on thousands of buildings all over the world – hiding their secrets in plain sight of the unsuspecting humans. These are examples from buildings in Livorno, Italy and The Bronx, New York City.

Above: The Maltese Cross – proudly displayed at the centre of St John ambulance service. This form of the cross was used by the Knights Hospitaller, also known as the Order of St John. But the symbolism, which often includes an eagle, is carried into more surprising logos, linked to governments and empires for millennia – including Anatolia, Rome, Germany and the USA.

But the origins of the caduceus can be traced much further back in time to the Sumerians. It is often referred to as the "winged serpent" or the "feathered serpent" and remains one of the oldest symbols known to us. It is repeatedly associated it with the creation of the human race by the gods in ancient times, which includes African, American, European and Asian cultures. In the Sumerian culture the caduceus is linked to the deity knows as ENKI, who was the medical mastermind behind the creation of the human race, with knowledge of DNA, genetic cloning, and curiously a higher level of consciousness. According to Zulu shaman, Sanusi Credo Mutwa, this creator of the human race is know in Africa as ENKAI.

It is obvious that this symbol is not used accidentally by the health services but forms part of the esoteric knowledge held by the royal bloodlines for thousands of years. And so they continue hiding their knowledge in plain sight of the ignorant and zombified humans.

Our hospitals are not place of healing, but places of controlling people's misery, while they pay every step of the way. Remember, it is all about absolute control of the human race, on every level.

It is obvious for all to see that the global health sector is in a deepening crisis. This is not only evident in South Africa. Our public hospitals are a disgrace and an insult to the people they are supposed to serve. This is not what the people want, not what they voted for, not what we deserve, and not what we pay tax for.

Our hospitals are understaffed, badly equipped and a sad reflection of the commitment to delivery by our servants, the government. Ordinary people cannot get professional treatment or care at most of our hospitals. Sometimes they have to wait for days in the corridors, bleeding, and at times even dying while waiting to be treated.

The health of our society and our people starts with a new understanding about what disease really is and how all disease can not only be treated but also cured. It may come as a surprise to some, that the cure for all disease has been discovered many times by great minds of the past and present. Legends of curing all disease go back to the Egyptians with their mystery schools and secret healing chambers for the royalty.

One of the most famous cases in recent times is the story of Royal Raymond Rife, who in 1931 was credited with being the man who found the cure for all disease.

After studying at Johns Hopkins, Rife developed technology which is still widely used in the fields of optics, electronics, radiochemistry, biochemistry, ballistics, and aviation.

He received 14 major awards and honours and was given an honorary Doctorate by the University of Heidelberg for his work. Rife's inventions include a heterodyning ultraviolet microscope, a micro-dissector, and a micro-manipulator. He was arguably one of the most gifted, versatile, scientific minds in human history.

By 1920, Rife had finished building the world's first virus microscope. By 1933, he had perfected that technology and had constructed the highly complex Universal Microscope, which had nearly 6,000 different parts and was capable of magnifying objects 60,000 times their normal size. With this incredible microscope he became the first human to actually see a living virus. Until quite recently the Universal Microscope was the only one able to observe living viruses.

Modern electron microscopes instantly kill everything beneath them, viewing only the mummified remains and debris. What the Rife microscope could see, is the bustling activity of living viruses as they change form to accommodate changes in their environment, replicate rapidly in response to carcinogens, and transform normal cells into tumour cells.

Rife painstakingly identified the prime resonant frequency of each microbe, or what he called the individual spectroscopic signature. No two species of molecule have the same electromagnetic oscillations or energetic signature. Resonance amplifies light in the same way that two ocean waves intensify each other when they merge.

The result of using a resonant wavelength is that micro-organisms which are invisible in white light suddenly become identifiable by a brilliant flash of light when they are exposed to the colour frequency that resonates with their own distinct spectroscopic signature. Rife was thus able to see these otherwise invisible organisms and watch them actively invade tissue cultures. Rife's discovery enabled him to view organisms that no one else has seen before with ordinary microscopes, without killing them. A feat which today's electron microscopes cannot duplicate.

Royal Rife had identified the human cancer virus and successfully transformed normal cells into tumour cells, all by modulating the frequency they were exposed to.

Rife worked with top scientists and doctors of his day, who confirmed or endorsed various areas of his work. They included: E.C. Rosenow, Sr. (longtime Chief of Bacteriology, Mayo Clinic); Arthur Kendall (Director, Northwestern Medical School); Dr. George Dock (internationally-renowned); Alvin Foord (famous pathologist); Rufus Klein-Schmidt (President of USC); R.T. Hamer (Superintendent, Paradise Valley Sanitarium; Dr. Milbank Johnson (Director of the Southern California AMA); Whalen Morrison (Chief Surgeon, Santa Fe Railway); George Fischer (Children's Hospital, N.Y.); Edward Kopps (Metabolic Clinic, La Jolla); Karl Meyer (Hooper Foundation, S.F.); M. Zite (Chicago University) and many others.

By increasing the intensity of the prime resonant frequency to which the microbes were exposed, they first distorted and eventually disintegrated from structural stresses. Rife called this frequency 'the mortal oscillatory rate,' or 'MOR', which did no harm to the surrounding tissues in any way.

This principle can be illustrated by using an intense musical note to shatter a wine glass. Because everything else has a different resonant frequency, nothing but the glass is destroyed. It took Rife many years of research until he discovered the frequencies which specifically destroyed herpes, polio, spinal meningitis, tetanus, influenza, and an immense number of other dangerous organisms. Today, there are many inventors around the world that have emulated Rife's success to various degrees. But they are persecuted, threatened and silenced, by the pharmaceutical giants, just like Rife was. I know of at least two such people in South Africa alone.

In 1934, the University of Southern California appointed a Special Medical Research Committee to bring terminal cancer patients from Pasadena County Hospital to Rife's San Diego laboratory and clinic for treatment. The team included doctors and pathologists assigned to examine the patients after 90 days of treatment, if they were still alive.

After the 90 days, the Committee concluded that 86.5% of the patients had been completely cured. Rife adjusted the frequencies of his treatment and the remaining 13.5% of the patients were cured within the next four weeks. Rife produced a 100% recovery rate among terminally ill cancer patients – with non-intrusive, non toxic, frequencies that destroyed only the targeted disease.

On 20 November 1931, forty-four of the nation's most respected medical authorities honoured Royal Rife with a banquet billed as "The End To All Diseases" at the Pasadena estate of Dr. Milbank Johnson. But by 1939, almost all of these distinguished doctors and scientists were denying that they had ever met Rife.

Morris Fishbein was a truly nasty piece of work. By 1934 he had acquired the entire stock of the American Medical Association, and made Royal Rife an offer he couldn't refuse. Unfortunately for Rife, he refused not realising the depths to which Fishbein would stoop to destroy him.

Some other names in healing and curing all kinds of disease including cancer, were Rene Caisse, Max Gerson and Harry Hoxsey. Some years earlier, the same Fishbein made an offer to Harry Hoxsey for control of his herbal cancer remedy. Fishbein's associates would receive all profits for nine years and Hoxey would receive nothing. Then, if they were satisfied that it worked, Hoxsey would begin to receive 10% of the profits. Hoxsey declined and decided that he would rather continue to make all the profits himself. Fishbein used his powerful political connections to have Hoxsey arrested 125 times in a period of 16 months. The charges were mostly based on practicing without a license and were always thrown out of court, but the harassment eventually drove Hoxsey insane.

But Fishbein must have realised that this strategy would not work on Rife, mainly because Rife could not be arrested, like Hoxsey, for practising without a license. The last thing in the world that the pharmaceutical industry needed was a public trial about a painless therapy that cured 100% of terminally ill cancer patients, cost nothing, and only used a little bit of electricity. It could give people the idea that they didn't need drugs.

And so the onslaught began. The first incident was the gradual pilfering of components, photographs, film, and written records from Rife's lab. The culprit was never caught. While Rife struggled to reproduce his missing data, at a time when photocopies and computers did not exist, someone vandalised his precious microscopes. Several pieces of the 5,682-piece Universal Microscope were stolen.

Earlier, a convenient fire had destroyed the multi-million dollar Burnett Lab in New Jersey, just as the scientists there were preparing to announce confirmation of Rife's work, and to cap it all, the police illegally confiscated the remainder of Rife's fifty years of research.

In 1939, agents of a family that controlled the drug industry, assisted Philip Hoyland in a frivolous lawsuit against his own partners in the Beam Ray Corporation. This was the only company manufacturing Rife's frequency instruments. Hoyland lost the case but his assisted legal assault had the desired effect. The company was bankrupted by legal expenses and the commercial production of Rife's frequency instruments ceased completely. This is just one of many examples how the courts, the laws and money, have been used to destroy great human discoveries.

All of Rife's information had to be wiped from public memory and replaced with doubt and speculation about some quack who made impossible claims. It was not an option for the drug corporations to have a universal cure for all disease floating about. Doctors who tried to defend Rife lost their grants for their foundations and their hospital privileges.

The cancer industry is a lucrative business for the drug companies raking in on average $300,000 per treatment of a single cancer patient. Rife got in their way and paid the price. But the industry needed to clean the slate completely.

Arthur Kendall, the Director of the Northwestern School of Medicine who worked with Rife on the cancer virus, accepted almost a quarter of a million dollars to suddenly 'retire' to Mexico. That was an exorbitant amount of money during the Depression.

Dr. George Dock, another prominent figure who collaborated with Rife, was silenced with an enormous grant, along with the highest honours the American Medical Association could bestow. Everyone who had any connection to Rife, with the exception of Dr. Couche and Dr. Milbank Johnson, gave up Rife's work and went back to prescribing drugs.

To finish the job, the various medical journals, which are supported almost entirely by drug company revenues and controlled by the AMA, refused to publish any papers, by anyone, about Rife's therapy. This has resulted in at least two generations of medical students practicing today without ever once hearing of Rife's achievements in the treatment of disease.

And so the onslaught on humanity through cancer began in earnest. This is a blatant crime against humanity that eclipses all the mass murders and is more equivalent to a full scale war. By 1960, the casualties from this tiny virus exceeded the carnage of all the wars the USA ever fought. In 1989, it was estimated that 40% of humans will experience cancer at some time in their lives.

The global cancer foundations are filled with people who believe they are doing good work, for a good cause, and helping people. Little do they know that the majority of these are funded by the same corporations who spread the disease and keep cures out of sight. These foundations rake in hundreds of millions of dollars that achieve very little. All they do is keep giving people false hope, while the cures for cancer and many other diseases have been around for a long time. In fact, 'foundations' in the USA now exist for almost every kind of ailment and disease imaginable. It has become so obvious, to those with eyes to see, that these foundations are set up and designed for the benefit of the pharmaceutical companies.

At one stage there were around 176,500 cancer drugs submitted for approval. Any one that showed 'favourable' results in only one-sixth of one percent of the cases being studied, could be licensed. Some of these drugs had a mortality rate of 14-17%. When death came from the drug, not the cancer, the case was recorded as a 'complete' or 'partial remission' because the patient didn't actually die from the cancer. In reality, it was a race to see which would kill the patient first: the drug or the disease.

Royal Raymond Rife, the man who gave us the cure for all disease, died in 1971 from a combination of valium and alcohol at the age of 83. Rife's work is a validation of our coming to grips with the laws of nature and the harmonic resonant principles that hold the entire universe together. The same principles that form the foundation of UBUNTU Contributionism. When organisms or people harmonise in unity, they grow in abundance. When they are in disharmony or conflict, they disintegrate and perish.

This is substantiation that, just like in the petroleum industry, those who make such discoveries are silenced, bribed or even killed to prevent their discoveries reaching the people on a mass scale. The major drug companies have become the distributors of death – NOT cures. Most of the so-called medicines we are prescribed are dangerous drugs with severe side-effects and yet our 'authorities' find it acceptable to unleash such drugs on humanity while they imprison people who grow benign plants and heal themselves with God's natural gifts to humanity.

Ref: <u>www.rense.com</u>

Once you start to discover the incredible deceit and cover-ups of the pharmaceutical industry, it is almost too shocking to believe. I urge you to stay strong and focused because the revelations in this sector are some of the most evil deeds that anyone could have conjured up. It amounts to nothing less than a total onslaught on humanity by the drug companies, supported every step of the way by our leaders. Their actions are gross crimes against humanity and the architects need to be exposed.

In five years at WITS Medical School in Johannesburg, I never once heard the word "medicine". What they do teach us is all about drugs – the action, use and administration of drugs. But once the dangerous drugs leave the labs in which they are synthesised they become known as medicines – so that the common people on the street don't accidentally confuse them with those other really bad drugs that have been outlawed by our leaders.

There are countless published researchers that graphically expose the atrocities committed by the medical fraternity to keep poisoning our bodies. Our minds are also poisoned, with psychotropic drugs, when people are conveniently diagnosed with so-called psychiatric problems. Several documentaries show how the entire psychiatric drug industry was an artificially created sector, which has no scientific basis but is vigorously imposed on unsuspecting and trusting humans.

Other researchers and documentaries like *"Run From The Cure"* show the success rate in curing all kinds of diseases, especially cancer, by using natural plants like cannabis. Our corporate governments and their watchdog agencies are doing everything possible to prevent humans from healing themselves.

It is very simple – drug companies have no interest in curing people, because if they did, they would go out of business. And the drug business is probably the most lucrative business on this planet. The drug companies profiteer and rake in trillions of dollars from keeping people sick and re-selling them drugs over and over again. It is a simple formula that works better every year and most of us ordinary people believe that they are doing the best they can to find cures for our diseases.

The treatment of cancer alone is a billion dollar industry for these corporations and they will not allow a cure to get in their way. There are thousands of doctors, traditional healers and alternative healers who work on the fringes of the medical industry, successfully treating and curing people every day.

These heroes of our society are treating cancer, aids, tuberculosis, diabetes, and many other so-called incurable diseases, while our servant, the government, is doing everything in its power to stop them from doing so. The mainstream media hardly ever reports on these success stories accurately, but rather reduces these brilliant healers to backroom quacks who are playing with people's lives. This is just a lack of education on the part of our journalists who unwittingly promote the disinformation agenda of the elite.

Traditional healers have been marginalised and prevented from healing people by new laws and regulations that restrict their access to certain herbs and natural treatments. Every self-respecting doctor will tell you about the health benefits of marijuana (THC). It is a natural herb that is one of the most effective cures for many diseases, including, and especially, cancer. But marijuana is constantly turned into an evil drug by the so-called authorities, while legal drugs, cigarettes and alcohol, kill millions of people every year. It is estimated that more people die every year from the side-effects of legal medicine, than people who die of cancer.

The incredible success that has been demonstrated with vibrational and frequency healing, as well as stem cell treatments, have been covered up and kept out of reach of the people. The agenda is simple – keep the people sick and their minds poisoned. Many natural plants and herbs that have been used by healers for thousands of years are systematically made illegal by our governments.

Over the past 80 years, drug companies did the following: They began to identify the active ingredients in plants and herbs that have been used as natural cures for thousands of years. Then they extracted these active ingredients and began to create them synthetically in their laboratories, while at the same time making sure that the original plants were made unavailable or even banned. Then they patented the active ingredient under a new name, giving them virtually complete control of that sector of treatment – then they shelve the treatment well out of sight of the public, ensuring that nobody is allowed to release anything similar because of their patent. Great strategy that has worked extremely effectively.

As mentioned earlier, this is the strategy of "simulating nature." It is all about the ability to create a synthetic version of the natural substance so that it can be patented and commercialised. It's all about the money and the control. They will go to any length to shelve natural products in favour of other natural products that are more profitable. For example, *stevia* is a completely natural product that only requires about 5% of a teaspoon to provide the equivalent sweetness of two teaspoons of sugar. Although sugar may be a natural extract of many plants, it is often referred to as "white death" by alternative healers and has many unreported side-effects that are desirable to the pharmaceutical companies.

Our food is being manipulated on every conceivable level, way beyond our wildest imagination, to create disease among humanity. This has been going on for many decades with the rise of the pharmaceutical monsters. This merry-go-round keeps many of us diseased and in the loop of dependency on the system. Once you are sucked into it, and you live on prescribed drugs, it is very difficult to get out.

Furthermore, it is a fact that we are being poisoned on a daily basis by virtually everything we consume, that is provided by the mass food and drug companies that fill the shelves in the supermarkets. The preservatives, flavourants, colourants, sweeteners, stabilisers, thickening agents, and many other secret ingredients that are given strange names like E211(sodium benzoate) and so on, are mostly toxic to our bodies. The hormones in our beef and chicken have a long list of lasting negative effects on humans. This is just one example of published research about sodium benzoate – which is present in virtually all processed and packaged foods and drinks.

Sodium Benzoate – As an example
Peter Piper, a professor of molecular biology and biotechnology at the University of Sheffield, tested the impact of sodium benzoate on living yeast cells in his laboratory. What he found was that the benzoate was damaging an important area of DNA in the "power station" of cells known as the mitochondria. These chemicals have the ability to cause

severe damage to DNA in the mitochondria to the point that they totally inactivate it – they knock it out altogether.

The mitochondria in your cells consume the oxygen to give you energy and if you damage it, as happens in a number of diseased states, the cell starts to malfunction very seriously. "There is a whole array of diseases that are now being tied to damage of this part of DNA - Parkinson's and a number of neuro-degenerative diseases, but above all the whole process of ageing" said Prof. Piper.

Sodium benzoate forms a chemical known as benzene when in the presence of vitamin C. Benzene is a known carcinogen (cancer causing substance), which is, among other things, used as a solvent in various plastics, synthetic rubber and dyes. Our air may contain low levels of benzene from tobacco smoke, wood smoke, automobile service stations, the transfer of gasoline, exhaust fumes from motor vehicles, along with industrial emissions.

The major health effects of benzene are damage to the bone marrow, and a decrease in red blood cells leading to anaemia. It targets the liver, kidney, lung, heart, brain, and causes damage to DNA, which is known to contribute to neurodegenerative diseases like Parkinson's, and more generally, is likely to speed up the entire aging process. Benzene is known to lead to cancer in both animals and humans.

It seems that our entire human environment is being poisoned with the intention to keep humans sick and age rapidly – before they can reach enlightenment or find the wisdom to realise what is being done to us.

The poisoning continues. A study at Harvard University has shown that Fluoride is a neurotoxin that causes severe I.Q. depression. It does NOT prevent cavities nor create stronger teeth in any way. This was one of the greatest deceptions unleashed on humanity. There are many websites that go into great detail about all the toxins in our water, food and air. Fluoride has a well documented calcifying effect on our pineal gland, which is nested in the centre of our brain. This tiny gland has the internal structures identical to our eyes, without the lens but with rods and cones to receive information from a wide spectrum of light frequencies – just like our eyes do. The ancients referred to it as our "third eye". What did they know that we don't – and why have our authorities been feeding us with fluoride to calcify our "third eye"?

The pineal gland is the organ in our body that should connect us to everything in creation around us – like a radar or sonar transmitter/ receiver. Similar to what whales and dolphins use. In other words, the pineal gland should give us ESP – Extra Sensory ability. This is obviously not an option for those who are attempting to control humanity because people with ESP cannot be controlled. This manipulation can be traced back thousands of years to the Sumerians and Egyptians using images of pine cones and the Eye of Horus to hide their occult knowledge in plain sight.

Just like Michelangelo and da Vinci encoded their art with secret knowledge, or the Illuminati placed the New World Order pyramid on the US dollar bill, so do ancient Sumerian seals and carvings contain occult knowledge. Many examples of these seals show bearded men and winged bird-headed beings manipulating the tree of life (DNA) while holding a 'pine cone' in their hands. This strange obsession with the pine cone is also transmitted to the staff of Mercury, Hermes, the Caduceus symbol, and even the pope's staff has a pine cone at the top end. The Egyptians simply created the all seeing Eye of Horus as the symbol for their secret.

Above: Bearded and winged men and a winged bird-headed beings, hold pine cones while manipulating what has been described as the tree of life or human DNA.

Above: The deeply encoded USA one dollar bill – proudly displaying the all seeing eye, the pyramid of enslavement and the launch of the New World Order in 1776.

Above: The staff of the pope and the courtyard of the Vatican Museum proudly display a pine cone.

Above: The Eye of Horus is actually a symbol for the pineal gland in the centre of the human brain.

Aspartame, that is offered as a sweetener in most restaurants and virtually all low-fat foods, is a powerful neurotoxin with much research and evidence to support this. Yet it has become one of the most widely used poisons in sugar-free soft drinks slowly poisoning our minds and killing our ability to think clearly. The government bodies like the FDA in the USA, and MCC in South Africa, are well aware of this and yet they do nothing about it. They should be charged with cognitive complicity, together with the pharmaceutical giants, to harm the people of the world. But which court will convict them? Overwhelming evidence shows that vaccines are not really cures for flu and chicken pox, but rather voluntary injections of genetically engineered drug cocktails that trigger a variety of diseases at various points in our lives. We have become the lambs that walk to our own slaughter by accepting vaccines in our naive ignorance. This is why our governments have made it compulsory to vaccinate our children and why children will not be admitted to school unless they have been vaccinated.

Monsanto's genetically modified foods and the fertilisers and chemicals they force our farmers to use have been causing a growing number of related health problems. Lab tests with rats that were fed only GM maize have shown uncontrollable cancerous tumours. It is now very clear that humanity is under attack by unscrupulous giant corporations involved in keeping us sick – while keeping the giant pharmaceutical corporations in control of our health.

As unthinkable as this may be to most of us, it is a simple plan implemented by the controlling families, and it has worked very well for a long time. The sad thing is that the people who work for these companies are just ordinary people, trying to stay alive and hold down a job so that they can take care of their families – and so the spiral of enslavement and entrapment continues as many people still defend these corporations in their ignorance. Please inform yourself – because ignorance will get us nowhere, making us believe that we are free.

UBUNTU PLAN OF ACTION – FOR HEALING CENTRES

1) Every community, town or village will have the most sophisticated hospital, trauma unit, emergency facility, treatment and healing centre imaginable. We call these 'healing centres' because we do actually expect to heal and cure people instead of just sustaining them and curing the symptoms.

2) Every existing hospital or clinic will be upgraded to meet these requirements and the needs of the people as soon as humanly possible.

3) These Healing Centres will be large enough to service their community with ease, and never run the risk of being unable to meet the demand of their community.

4) Healing Centres will be designed and adapted differently from our current hospitals to create the necessary environments that promote healing in every way.

5) The Healing Centres will be well staffed with healers from diverse backgrounds to promote the growth of new and alternative healing and not just the currently accepted methods.

6) Healing will be holistic, including food, plants and healing

therapies. All 'patients' will be taught health practice while being treated in the Healing Centres.

7) The Healing Centres will also be used as training centres, where those interested in healing will learn hands-on from master healers in every field.

8) Birthing Centres will be established in every community and treated as separate from Healing Centres. Because giving birth is not a disease.

9) Let us declare all questionable activities by the drug companies unlawful with immediate effect.

10) Appoint a new independent group of medical scientists and researchers, supported with the most advanced equipment and technology, to investigate all existing drugs whether legal or illegal, and give the people a new scientific perspective on the positive or negative effects of these substances.

11) We will promote the work of traditional healers and alternative healers who have been marginalised and belittled by the medical and drug industry for their own financial benefit.

12) All traditional healers, and alternative healers, Sangomas and Shaman, will be given all the respect and support they deserve in their service to the people.

13) Provide all the necessary support for the cultivation and production of plants and herbs to support the traditional healers, homeopaths and others.

14) Every Healing Centre will have a research laboratory attached to it where our brilliant scientists can do ongoing research into diverse areas of healing.

15) Any new discovery will be shared with the people of South Africa and the world immediately and will not be kept as a secret to benefit only a few.

16) We will vigorously support extensive research into vibrational and frequency healing made famous by Royal Raymond Rife and others.

17) We will vigorously support the development and use of Stem Cell treatment – because our research has shown that stem cell treatment has already been successfully used in curing virtually all disease, including the re-growing of organs and even severed limbs. This has been one of the best kept secrets of the drug cartels.

18) Communities will have the freedom to determine what they need

in the area of healing, based on their own experience, and agreed to by the Council of Elders in each community. These decisions will be activated immediately giving the people of the community all the tools necessary to deliver, build or grow whatever the community has decided. Whether it is in the healing sector or any other.

Important Information & Research:

Here are a few statements that will hopefully make you realise how evil the activity of the drug industry has been. Please do more of your own research.

- The pharmaceutical and medical industries – the very industries we entrust with our health routinely suppress information about drug-free, non medical alternative treatments that cure disease. http://www.faithdrops.mu/page/home
- HIV is an ethnic weapon developed by secret government projects in the USA. Dr Macdonald says he has a cure which he showed President Zuma. http://www.faithdrops.mu/page/the_invention_of_aids
- Mercury Fillings cause disease: http://www.faithdrops.mu/page/mercury
- Fluoride is being added to our water and toothpaste. This is a neurotoxic chemical that adversely affects our Pineal Gland and more. http://www.faithdrops.mu/page/neurotoxic_chemical
- How they treat cancer and their success: http://www.faithdrops.mu/page/cancer_what_to_do
- Aspartame – A deadly neurotoxin. Dr. Mercola educates people on the dangers, side effects, and health problems linked to Aspartame, an artificial sweetener also known as NutraSweet and Splenda. www.drmercola.com
- Researcher David Rietz points out in his must-read article that there are at least 91 symptoms of aspartame poisoning. The following are documented symptoms caused by aspartame ingestion as compiled by the FDA. It is astounding that the FDA classifies 'death' as a symptom.:
Abdominal pain, anxiety attacks, arthritis-like pain, asthmatic reactions, bloating, blood sugar control problems, brain cancer (pre-approval studies in animals), breathing difficulties, burning eyes or throat, burning urination, chest pains, chronic cough,

chronic fatigue, confusion, death, depression, diarrhoea, dizziness,
excessive thirst or hunger, fatigue, feel unreal, flushing of face, hair
loss (baldness) or thinning of hair, headaches/migraines, hearing
loss, heart palpitations, hives (urticaria), hypertension (high blood
pressure), impotency and sexual problems, inability to concentrate,
infection susceptibility, insomnia, irritability, itching, joint pains,
laryngitis, marked personality changes, memory loss, menstrual
problems or changes, muscle spasms, nausea or vomiting,
numbness or tingling of extremities, other allergic-like reactions,
panic attacks, phobias, poor memory, rapid heartbeat, rashes,
seizures and convulsions, slurring of speech, swallowing pain,
tachycardia, tremors, tinnitus, vertigo, vision loss, and weight gain.
http://www.gene.ch/gentech/1998/Jul-Sep/msg00010.html

- Vaccines are part of the problem-reaction-solution plan for humanity. First they create the virus or organism in a laboratory; then they expose entire communities or groups of soldiers in combat to it; then they miraculously present the cure in a vaccine. Vaccines are death cocktails that contain genetically modified substances which trigger disease in humans throughout our lives. So think very carefully before you vaccinate your children. For a quick glance at the unsavoury content in some of the most famous vaccines see this website. http://www.informedchoice.info/cocktail. html

- Hepatitis B vaccine – linked to Infant Sudden Death syndrome. http://articles.mercola.com/sites/articles/archive/2011/05/19/ us-government-concedes-hep-b-vaccine-causes-systemic-lupus-erythematosus.aspx

MINING AND MINERALS

The mining and minerals sector in South Africa, and around the world, is probably the most sensitive sector to contemplate. It will raise many deep emotions within people from all walks of life because of our long and proud history of mining, that goes back many thousands of years, to the great kingdom of Monomotapa, and even further back in time. South Africa is one of the wealthiest countries in the world, producing virtually all the precious metals on Earth in large quantities. And yet our people live in poverty, hunger and many are homeless. Nineteen years after our so-called liberation, there is more poverty, more hunger and more homelessness than ever before. It is very clear that something is desperately wrong with this picture. The people may have been given their political freedom – but we have been denied our economic freedom.

This immense wealth of the land has been stolen from the people by our government and a handful of international corporations that have laid claim to the minerals and have been given the rights to take our precious gold and platinum and coal and diamonds and anything else they can lay their hands on. The people of the land have been reduced to mere slaves, while the corporations make unimaginable wealth for invisible foreign shareholders.

Our government – the so-called "servant of the people" – has allowed these greedy corporations to do as they please. Their greed has no boundaries and they are slowly turning our beautiful country into a mining wasteland. The coal mining companies are probably the worst culprits because the scars they leave behind on this planet are so visible. The areas that surround the coal mines and power stations have become so polluted and so disturbed, it will take a long time to rehabilitate them to their former natural beauty. The mine owners are certainly not going to do that.

All of this is done in the name of greed and profit for the very few. The tragic and inhumane massacre of striking mine workers at Marikana, South Africa stands as a chilling reminder that our government holds the rights of corporations above the rights of human beings – the honest hardworking people whom the government is supposed to serve.

African elders and the custodians of ancient knowledge around the world believe that the Earth is sacred and that we are the custodians of this sacred planet. It is our duty to protect all living things, to honour the sanctity of life and to live in harmony with mother Earth. We have to live in a symbiotic co-existence if we are to sustain humanity and thrive with abundance while maintaining a balance of all life on Earth. Only then will we ensure the continued abundance for all future generations.

But we cannot do so while we are denied the right to our land and the natural wealth and beauty of our country. Before we can start to protect our sacred land we need to remind ourselves of our inalienable rights and we have to re-claim that which belongs to all the people. I use the word "belong" not in the sense of ownership, but rather custodianship, to care for and protect our countries against all forms of exploitation.

- We are born free on the land that we live
- The country belongs to its people – the custodians
- The land and all in it and on it belongs to its people
- The rivers, mountains, sky, seas and coastline belong to the people
- We must honour mother Earth and protect her against harm

These DO NOT belong to the politicians, the government, or any corporation that has unlawfully laid claim to it. The private government corporation has stolen the country from its people. We, the people, need to take it back!

To top this all, all the minerals in South Africa are paid for by the privately owned South African Reserve Bank, with worthless pieces of paper that contain some fancy logos on them. Then SARB sells it on the global markets and we are forced to buy it from them with the money we earn from our sweat and blood.

NATIONALISATION

The word 'nationalisation' sends shivers up many people's spines, thinking of the so-called "communist threat" that the people of the west were indoctrinated with. I need to stress the difference between "nationalisation" and "ownership by the people".

"Nationalisation" means owned and controlled by the government. But because the government is just another corporation, this policy is just a clever deception to confuse the people and is used as a means to steal the country and all its resources from the people.

"Ownership by the people" means the people themselves benefit from all the natural wealth of the country and they themselves hold the deciding power as to how to use the resources and wealth for the benefit of all – and not the benefit of the government, which is clearly not working for the people.

UBUNTU PLAN OF ACTION – FOR MINING

1) Every mine in South Africa becomes the property of the people with immediate effect. (Not the property of the government – that would be called nationalisation.)
2) A national **Council Of Elders** will be appointed by the people of South Africa, consisting of the most trusted and respected individuals, to look after the interests of the people in this regard – this council will have absolute control to implement the will of the people – not the will of the corrupt government or politicians who

are controlled by powerful multinational corporations.

3) The Council can be replaced at any time by the will of the people.

4) All foreign shareholding and ownership in all mines, or any directly related companies will be cancelled immediately.

5) This includes the smelting plants, production plants of all metals, alloys, steel and so forth.

6) A comprehensive program to expand the refining and manufacturing industry will be implemented immediately. There is no need for us to export anything for the sake of re-importing it in a refined form. This has been a devious convoluted system to create wealth for the governments and corporations on both sides of the import-export fence.

7) All exports of minerals, coal, iron ore, diamonds, or any other resource that comes from our ground, or is mined in any way, will be stopped immediately.

8) Exports will be strictly controlled by the Council of Elders on behalf of the people – all the income will go into community projects to develop fully sustainable communities and promote decentralisation.

9) South Africa will produce only as much of these commodities as is required by the people of South Africa for the various industrial sectors of our own society and other needs that may arise as the process of transformation takes place.

10) Every sector of manufacturing will be fully supported and provided with whatever materials it needs to manufacture according to the needs of the people. Whatever the people need, the people will get.

11) The Council of Elders will determine what needs to be implemented based on the will and needs of the people. The people will remain in full control of this process and be fully informed of the exact status of all mining activities.

12) We will do whatever is necessary, or desired by the people, to create abundance on all levels of society. This means that new opportunities and new activities will constantly arise and will be implemented on a regular basis in areas that were previously deemed financially not viable.

13) We will not continue to enrich foreign shareholders and allow our precious commodities to be stolen from us and traded on the global stock markets at the expense of our people, who are being used as slaves and cheap labour.

14) The new interim money system or currency adopted by the

people will be linked to the mineral wealth of South Africa. Not necessarily the finished polished product, but the potential that lies in the ground. This will make the SA currency the strongest currency in the world with immediate effect – because all the other major currencies are FIAT currencies with absolutely no intrinsic value – other than the confidence of its people.

15) This will be a temporary interim phase while communities begin to restructure and gravitate towards not using or needing any money at all.

16) The people will decide how to proceed and how to develop the mining sector into the future so that it provides a real tangible benefit for the people in every sector of our society and in every community. Always keeping in mind the damage to the planet and environment associated with mining and delivering solutions to such problems.

17) This will open up new exciting eras of research and development by our brilliant scientists, engineers and inventors for the greater benefit of all the people.

FORESTRY

CURRENT SITUATION

The forestry sector in South Africa is a huge multinational industry that exports its products to over 100 countries around the world. The forestry companies are unquestionably the largest land users in South Africa. The plantations of SAPPI, MONDI and other smaller forestry companies cover more than a million hectares of land throughout South Africa.

Land that lawfully belongs to the people, but has somehow landed up in the hands of giant multinational corporations. They claim that this is either by title, which means ownership, or by lease. The question is: how exactly was this sale and title deed structured? Where did the money come from originally to buy all this land? And who had the authority to sell the land that belongs to the people to these companies in the first place?

These companies produce a huge amount of wood, paper, cellulose and other products, most of which are exported for the benefit of the international shareholders, while most of our people cannot afford the wood or paper that is produced. The people get absolutely no benefit from the use of our land while most of the plantations remain restricted areas to ordinary people.

SAPPI has over 35 million tons of timber plantations, while the people cannot afford the wood to build homes. SAPPI boast that they make enough paper every day to go around the equator four times. It is the leading producer in the world of fine paper for glossy magazines, annual reports and other high end products, raking in billions in profits for the shareholders, while our children cannot afford simple writing books to take to school.

Mondi claim to own 307,000 hectares of plantations and manage one of the largest Forestry Stewardship FSC™-certified plantation units in the world. The internationally recognised FSC™ accreditation means that the company's plantations are managed in a responsible and sustainable manner. These are all very nicely constructed statements by corporations, but it holds no benefit at all for the people of our country who have been deprived of their land.

On a daily basis homeless people without anywhere to live are being evicted from vacant government land while these corporations are given all the protection they require. This is a perfect example how our legal system is not written to bring justice to the people, but rather to protect the needs of corporations. The rights of the corporation are placed above the rights of human beings. This has become blatantly clear and one of the great tragedies in South Africa and the rest of the world.

The one thing that all these trees need is a vast amount of water. Mainly because the majority of trees planted by the forestry corporations are exotic trees like pine, blue gum (eucalyptus), and wattle. And so the trees in all of these plantations that cover over a million hectares use up unthinkable amounts of water on a daily basis, while millions of people across our land are denied access to water by our servants, the government.

Does this sound like a fair dispensation to you?

Many environmentalists have repeatedly shown how bad these massive monoculture plantations are for the ecosystems and propose that there are much better ways to grow trees and wood in harmony with nature while enhancing the growth of trees for human consumption.

For all the large tracts of land that forestry occupies, the entire forestry sector only employs about 20,000 people in South Africa. This is completely out of balance with the amount of land they use. The bottom line is that this situation needs to be corrected.

UBUNTU PLAN OF ACTION – FORESTRY

1) Forestry is an exciting sector of society that needs to generate huge benefit for the people of the world everywhere.

2) I stress the word **benefit,** and NOT profit – and NOT benefits to corporations and their international shareholders at the expense of the people.

3) Since the land belongs to the people, all forestry activity must be for the benefit of the people and only the people.

4) Forestry should be one of the great providers of work/activity (Labour of Love) to the people in many diverse sectors of society including environmental management, wood, paper, food, clothing, and more.

5) Forestry will probably involve more than 200,000 people in South Africa, constantly managing and planning for the current and future needs of the people.

6) Forestry must provide all the wood required by the people in the building of homes, furniture and other activities and other products on a large scale.

7) Every town or community will be provided with as much wood as it needs for the activity in the community and the continued development of that community.

8) Wood will be used on a much larger scale by the people because it will be freely provided to the people, because trees are renewable – trees grow – they are not manufactured or mined from the ground. It is a living and renewable resource.

9) This will result in new products being made from wood while today it is not affordable or economically viable.

10) Artists, craftsmen, artisans, builders, designers, architects and more, will use wood on a much larger scale.

11) People everywhere will be encouraged to use wood as opposed to other synthetic materials that are not eco-friendly.

12) New sustainable and eco-friendly alternatives will be explored for the manufacturing of paper. Hemp is just one obvious alternative.

13) This sector will provide all the paper and other paper-based products needed by the people.

14) Just like wood, the paper and related products will be monitored and manufactured based on the needs of the people and every aspect of our society.

15) Because communities will no longer be based on the creation of profit but rather the provision for the needs of the people, it will

be much easier to predict how much wood each community will require for their continued activity.

16) There will be a close relationship between each community and the foresters that provide them with the wood and timber they need.

17) The needs of the people will be assessed and long-term plans must be maintained to provide all the needs by means of new sustainable and eco-friendly methods.

18) Scientists will constantly develop new and more practical solutions to meet the needs of the people – not the needs of corporations.

19) Forestry must become environmentally friendly and ecologically sustainable.

20) New solutions will be found by our scientists for the pollution caused by the paper mills and associated industries because money will not stand in the way of progress.

21) Solutions are simple, but in today's money based economy, solutions are mostly not financially viable – therefore we go on polluting our world.

22) Ecological experts will constantly monitor and improve the management of the forestry sector to keep up with the needs of the people.

23) The aim of this sector is to provide for the people and the development of our country and not create profits for foreign shareholders at the expense of the people.

24) There will be no exporting of any wood or paper or other products associated with forestry – unless all the needs of the people have been met.

25) Any income or benefits generated from exporting of forestry related products will belong to the people.

26) In general – as we move away from a money driven society – towards a people driven society where money has no value, the concept of exporting our natural resources will make no sense at all. In fact it would be a crime against the people to try to sell, export or deprive the people of what belongs to them.

27) The expression JOBS; WORK; CAREER; etc, will be redefined in this, and other sectors.

28) In the UBUNTU community there are no jobs, or work, or careers. We call it **Labour Of Love** – since the people choose to do what they are good at or passionate about – they use their God-given talents or acquired skills for the greater benefit of all of the people in the community. Everybody becomes a contributor for the greater

good. And this is why communities will thrive – because there is absolutely no need for money and money can no longer be used as a hurdle to human progress.

FISHERIES

The fishing towns and villages have been severely affected by government policies that have prevented thousands of fisherman from fishing and providing for their families. The current policies have destroyed the lives of hundreds of thousands of people. Fishermen along our coastline are being fined and arrested for trying to make a living to keep their families alive.

These inhumane policies have opened the doors to international fishing corporations that deplete our coastlines of fish and destroy the ecosystem. This does not benefit the people of South Africa in any way. They export our fish while making billions of dollars profit for international shareholders, while our people go hungry or are put in jail for trying to survive off the sea.

These current policies protect the rights of the corporations and destroy the lives of honest, hard working human beings. Once again this indicates that the rights of international corporations are protected vigorously while the rights of human beings are desecrated. Our Bill of Rights is not worth the paper it is written on.

This unlawful and unconstitutional activity must be stopped and reversed immediately. Our fisherman and marine experts will play an equally important role, alongside the farmers, to provide food for the people in abundance and beyond our wildest imagination. This is very simple to achieve by those who know how – not the politicians.

The fishermen will be seen as the heroes of the land because they provide a crucially important part of our diet while protecting and maintaining our beautiful coastline.

UBUNTU PLAN OF ACTION – FISHERIES

1) Every coastal town, city and village will play a crucial role in the fisheries sector.
2) This will include other fish farms and fish breeding areas, like trout and bass farms, and others, that are not necessarily on the coast.

3) This activity will include fishing, research, conservation, breeding, packaging, shipping and other activities that will become necessary as this sector becomes reactivated and new needs are identified by the fishing communities and the people they supply.

4) The people will receive all the technical support required and all the tools and expertise necessary to allow this sector to grow rapidly and deliver according to the needs of the people – not the needs of international shareholders.

5) This is a wonderful calling for marine biologists, scientists, researchers, breeders, conservationists and more, to follow their passion and maximise the success of the fisheries and related sectors.

6) Implement an immediate ban on all foreign trawlers or fishing boats of any kind within the coastal waters of South Africa, while restoring our ecosystem and providing food for the people.

7) The coastal towns will be encouraged to diversify and start to produce all kinds of marine and fresh water produce that was previously not financially viable. Since money is not going to be a hurdle to progress, everything will be possible.

8) We must support the upgrading of existing research facilities with the latest technology available, and create new facilities, wherever there is a need.

9) This will include the upgrading and expanding of aquariums and other marine aquatic centres, for the purposes of rehabilitation, healing, education, research and more.

10) Our coastal towns and villages will provide sea food for the people in abundance and beyond our wildest imagination.

TRANSPORT AND TRAVEL

This section contains our plan of action for **Road, Rail, Air and Sea** transportation and travel. It is one of the key activation initiatives for the creation of new opportunities for everyone across a wide spectrum of talents and provides for the following:

1) Work for millions of people – work in the short term transitional period when money is still part of our society. This will rapidly morph into a myriad of LOLs as people find their personal niches and passions.

2) Activation and stimulation of existing and new industry in all sectors
3) Decentralisation of overpopulated cities
4) Rapid development of rural towns and villages
5) Delivery of all necessary goods across the land
6) Large scale material production – building and other
7) Development of new sustainable industries in rural towns
8) Establishment of necessary farming and agriculture in rural areas
9) Training and educating of people in a diverse number of skills
10) Development of new technology and how we travel during this process
11) Creating abundance and sustainability across our country.

Under the UBUNTU Contribution System, we expect a rapid advancement in new technology, free energy, materials and all aspects of industry. This will be the drive behind how communities adapt and change. It will affect how people live, where they live, what they do and how they contribute to their own community as well as the larger community of the entire country.

These new developments will dramatically change the way we travel and the tools we use to transport goods and people. In this light, it is difficult to predict how this sector will change – but we do expect it to change dramatically and very quickly once the chains of financial restraint are removed, allowing us to deliver new and free energy, and innovative solutions on all levels of society.

For example: Today people have to travel for hours, catch busses, trains, taxis and sit in traffic for many hours each day, to get to their jobs and then home again, just to earn some money to pay their bills. This is clearly a complete waste of productive time. But once people can choose to live in a community of their choice, where they contribute their natural talents or acquired skills for the benefit of that community, there will be no peak traffic – or very little traffic on the roads, compared to the madness of today.

This simple change in our behaviour will dramatically change the way we build and use roads, the way we travel and how we transport goods. It is probable that other forms of transport will be developed with new technology to make all of that much easier and quicker.

But we will not have a magical transition in a flash. During the initial transitional phase, the existing railway system will play a crucial role in all of these activities, as we move from a money driven society to a human driven society.

The proposals in this sector are therefore based on the use of the current tools and technology at our disposal – which can be rapidly adapted for the needs of the people as we are presented with new solutions from our brilliant scientists, engineers, researchers and inventors.

The word 'transport" is very confusing and forms part of the words and laws that enslave us, as shown in the Law section. All such words are related to the *Maritime Law* that forms the basis of all our current legal system. Please see more detailed information on this subject under ***Laws And Words That Enslave Us.***

The word "transport" suggests that while we travel around our country or neighbourhood, we cross borders or "ports" as in 'ports of entry' and 'exits'. The evidence can be seen at Airports – where we pay airport duties and taxes. WHY?

New toll-gates have sprung up on many of our roads that prevent the people from travelling without paying a toll – as if we were crossing ports or borders. WHY?

ROADS

All roads in our country are on the land that belongs to the people. Our servant, the government, has sold these roads to private multinational corporations that now extort money from the people while they travel. Our rights to travel on these roads have been restricted dramatically. The secondary roads have been so neglected that they are almost unusable, forcing us to use the privately controlled toll-roads. This is pure highway robbery in modern times and it is a gross violation of our rights and a betrayal of the people, preventing us from travelling freely in our land.

Nobody should have to pay to travel, drive, walk or use our roads, no matter where they are. Any form of taxing, charging, or tolling is unlawful and not in the greater public interest – it is therefore unconstitutional and must be abolished immediately.

The UBUNTU model proposes a massive public works project across South Africa that will possibly involve as many as one million people, to re-think; re-plan and upgrade all our roads across South Africa. All the participants, from the engineers to the labourers, will be given all the tools and latest technology possible to make this as smooth and easy as can be.

This will be part of a major move towards instituting UBUNTU as a principle of society across the land. Professionals and trainees from the many towns that lie along the roads will participate in this giant project creating a network of activity across our country. Every aspect of the project will be local, resulting in a widespread increase of skills and training.

All this activity will be integrated into the various needs of towns and communities everywhere, which will include town planning, public areas, sport and recreation, and all other activities in our communities.

The engineers and architects and town planners will be required to apply all their knowledge of sacred geometry, or the laws of nature, to enhance the natural flow of energy in all areas. This has been part of ancient and eastern philosophy for thousands of years and all the great architects and artists of the past incorporated sacred geometry into their works because they understood its effect on those who are exposed to it.

Everything we do in the UBUNTU communities should subscribe to these basic principles because of the positive effects it has on the people who live in such environments. This applies to every sector of society. Farming, engineering, construction, town planning, water purification, science and everything else in our lives.

HEALING WHILE REBUILDING

We have been separated from Mother Earth through the massive modernisation frenzy at the expense of our physical and mental health. All true healers and scientists are aware of the fact that everything in creation functions on the basic principles of harmonic resonance and coherence.

In other words, the entire universe vibrates in harmony – that is what keeps galaxies and solar systems and atoms together. If we are not in harmony with our Earth, we are in 'dis-ease' and become sick. I needed to highlight this again in this section, because it crosses over into every human activity and affects our lives in everything we do. Unfortunately our society does not follow these principles and therefore we find ourselves in dis-ease with our environment.

The channelling of water in spirals that energises the water is just a small example. Energised water has almost super powers in its ability to heal and invigorate our bodies and enhance the growth of corps and livestock.

Researchers have shown how raw sewage water can be purified and energised by simply allowing it flow along specific spirals over a few hundred metres. No chemicals or poisons required. We have been denied this simple knowledge that follows the laws of nature, because of the greed of corporations and government.

We need to reconnect with Mother Earth in everything we do. This is part of the healing and the awakening of humanity. Our roadworks projects will be just one of the many sectors to play a key role in this beautiful transformation process.

RAILWAYS

South Africa once had a very efficient railroad system that was used by people all over the country. This has been completely destroyed by our servants, the government. Every town and village has a railroad running through it or near it and yet very few towns have an active railway connection between them, serving the people. Hundreds of old railway stations lie in ruin and more are deserted every year, while they could be providing a desperately needed service to the people across our country.

At first glance it seems as if our railways are not functioning at all, but this is not the case. The trains are running all the time, twenty four hours a day, crossing our land and crossing our borders into our neighbouring countries – not to serve the people, but rather to serve the giant corporations – coal, ore, petroleum, cars, forestry, and other industries.

Tax payers money is used to provide transportation for the corporations while the people are left stranded. This is not acceptable.

The UBUNTU way, will initiate a large scale project to reactivate and upgrade the once mighty railroad network of South Africa. All the old railway stations will be rebuilt and upgraded; deserted railroads will be restored, and every town and village will have an active railway system to serve the people.

This will become one of the key driving mechanisms to give millions of people work to do, learn new skills, and fill everyone with the belief that we can control our own destiny and provide true and lasting prosperity and abundance for all the people.

WATER TRANSPORT – OCEANS, RIVERS & OTHER WATERWAYS

Every coastal town and city will play an important role in the reactivation and transformation of our country. This will include provision of energy; fisheries and fish farming; conservation of coastlines and marine life; upgrading and maintenance of ports and harbours; and even import and export of our goods – which will change dramatically as we enter an UBUNTU way of life – driven by people and their passion and not driven by money.

Every port and harbour will be upgraded and redesigned to serve the needs of the people and not the needs of international corporations at the expense of the people.

Every coastal town, city and village will have its own port or harbour, based on the needs and activity of that community. It will be up to each community to plan and decide what is necessary. This will require skills and the participation of many people to upgrade and maintain. Those who love to live by the ocean will see this as a great opportunity to relocate from overpopulated cities to the tranquillity of coastal living. It is obvious that this movement of people will significantly activate the building, housing and town planning sectors everywhere, providing many new opportunities for people in all walks of life.

Existing boat and water transport vessels will be upgraded and adapted to provide specific functions necessary for serving the people across the land and the immediate communities. Every fisherman and boat owner will be encouraged to get involved in the many aspects of transport and travel along our coastline, rivers and other waterways.

This will in many ways be a whole new initiative and a massive expansion to the travelling options and lifestyle we have today. It will require innovative thinking, massive construction, building and training, providing an exciting opportunity for many people with a variety of skills.

Our coastlines, rivers and waterways should provide an exciting new way to travel and transport goods that are not options today because of costs and availability. Anyone, anywhere along the coast, will be able to catch a boat or transport goods to any other coastal town.

AIRPORTS, AIR TRAVEL & TRANSPORT
South African Airways and all other government controlled airlines; the airports and all related facilities have been paid for by the people. Therefore, the airplanes, the airports and all related facilities that are under government control belong to the people.

Any agreement signed by the government with multinational

corporations to control or manage these facilities on behalf of the people, at the expense of the people, is unlawful and was done without the knowledge of the people. There is no benefit to the people from such agreements that are in existence today.

The entire air transport and travel sector will be restructured to be of benefit to the people everywhere. Every pilot and owner of aircraft will be encouraged to become part of the solution and add their skills to this sector.

Airports and air transport will be important components to change the way people travel and transport goods. We will use the new technology, that will emerge from the freeing up of scientists, to develop new kind of aircraft as soon as it becomes possible. But at the same time we will encourage the use of all functional aircraft that are standing in hangars around South Africa (or any other country) to be upgraded and made operational to benefit the people.

There are many such craft, most of which are not operating merely because of the cost of repair. The UBUNTU plan will allocate every resource available without the restraint of funds, to the repairing and upgrading of every possible aircraft in the land. There is a sense of excitement in flying in older propeller driven craft that many people have not experienced and would love to experience. Just because there is new jet technology available does not mean we have to discard the older tools. As long as they serve the people or provide a role in remembering the past, such tool must be utilised. This will apply to the rail and motor vehicle industries as well.

Since South Africa is a major petroleum producer through SASOL, the fuel used by the airlines and all other airplanes in SA will be provided by SASOL very cheaply – if not free to some sectors.

PLAN OF ACTION FOR TRAVEL & TRANSPORT
Massive Public Works Projects Across The Land
The UBUNTU plan is to initiate a large scale national project to reactivate the entire road system, railways, ports and harbours, airports and air travel for the benefit of the people and not for the benefit of private corporations that claim to manage them on behalf of the people.

This could involve well over 4 million people across South Africa, and probably over 40 million people in the USA, with a diverse variety of skills. It will involve training and the supply of huge quantities of materials.

This will be the foundation of the liberation of the people from financial tyranny. It is the seed that will produce sustainable prosperity on many levels and in every sector of our lives. These projects will propel us rapidly towards an UBUNTU society that does not depend on money and greed, but rather on cooperation of the people – doing the best for everyone in their communities and for the entire country as a whole.

All the old railway stations will be rebuilt and upgraded; deserted railroads will be restored, and every town and village will have an active railway system to serve the people. Old steam locomotives will be refurbished and displayed or used for recreational and sentimental purposes. We will restore and upgrade the once mighty railroad network of South Africa.

We see the railways as the main transport medium of the near and interim future. It will also benefit the industrial sector, which in turn will benefit the people. Once we start this process of change for the benefit of the people, there is no stopping this machine of prosperity.

Every community will have the opportunity to get involved in the planning, designing and implementing the railway system in their community, as well as the roads, ports, airports, and all related activities. It will also provide a large number of opportunities for those who are passionate about these industries to get involved on all levels in every city, town and community.

It provides an opportunity for the decentralisation of the overpopulated metro areas, as people will be able to choose a town or community to settle in, while becoming involved in the roads, rail, ports and air travel public works with its many exciting activities.

Furthermore, these projects will require skills, materials and training that will spread out across our entire country, reaching every little village. It will be accompanied by the establishment of many associated industries, that are almost impossible to predict. Many new sectors will develop based on the need to provide the tools, technology and expertise to achieve this.

Every community will develop various facilities to be able to provide the necessary building materials for the projects. This will include steel works; metal works; stone works; cement; bricks, sand; saw mills; woodwork; other natural sustainable materials and more.

INTEGRATION AND TRAINING
Training of people in all the various skills in these areas will be an

important aspect in the activation of the projects and their continued success. All this activity will also provide the local town developers and planners, architects and builders with the materials necessary to plan and upgrade the town layout, with all its facilities, for the greatest benefit of the people.

This will include housing, sport and recreation, art and culture, local industry, agriculture, energy supply and anything else that all the towns need to be self sufficient in all its requirements, as far as possible. The objective is always to provide immediate benefits to the people and to produce three times as much, as is required by the community. This allows the UBUNTU Contribution principle to kick in and start providing for others and not just for ourselves.

Many of the people involved in the transport sector, such as the large taxi industry, will be involved in this transition process and will be given all the support they need to integrate and convert to other aspects of the giant support network around the roads, railways, harbours and airports. No one will be left out or neglected in the process – it has to be a comprehensive and inclusive process to benefit all the people everywhere – based on cooperation and not competition.

Remember that this activity is not about making a fortune of money for a small group of people at the expense of the majority, as it has always been in the past, but rather as a transitional phase in which we all move towards the principles of UBUNTU – where we use less and less money, because most of our needs will be provided and everyone has everything they need, all of the time, because that's how it works.

Money will no longer be a hurdle to progress, or used as a tool to create scarcity. The model and the solution is basic and simple – do not allow those who do not understand this to complicate it and sow confusion. The farmers provide the food, the engineers build the bridges, the teachers teach, the scientists provide the scientific solutions, the bakers bake, the painters paint, and so on. There is a place for everyone and everyone has everything they need all of the time without any worry about having to earn money.

COMMUNICATIONS AND BROADCASTING

Telecommunication and broadcasting is a crucial aspect of our lives and our society. It should be freely available to the people.

"The airwaves belong to the universe – not to governments or private corporations."

Until recently, TELKOM was the only fixed-line telecommunications company in South Africa. All the technology and installation that allows TELKOM to bring telephone wires to our homes was paid for by the tax payers many times over. Once the lines are installed, there is very little expense to keep them working. If the people paid for all of this, why are we paying to make telephone calls? It is our system and we should have the benefit to use it for free or almost free in the least.

NEOTEL is a privately owned company, that was recently given the right to operate as a newcomer to the fixed-line telecommunication monopoly. The problem with this is that NEOTEL now has the rights to use the fixed line infrastructure that was paid for by the people, which belongs to the people.

It is insane to imagine that the people would pay for something and then allow a private company to take ownership of our installations so that they can charge us for making phone calls. This is just another indication of how we are being deceived and financially abused by our leaders who are supposed to serve us.

CELLULAR COMMUNICATION

Cell phone companies use microwave frequencies, or 'air waves' to carry the signal without any wires. These signals and frequencies are transmitted by transmitters scattered all over our country and sometimes they are supported by satellite links.

Cell phone companies are multinational corporations that are amongst the most profitable companies in the world. This can be seen by the number of sporting events they sponsor. In many ways, these cellular corporations have become huge banks that collect insane amounts of money, crossing borders without anyone questioning their activities. They have virtually no cost of delivery once the towers are up and able to transmit. And yet they are raking in billions from the hard working and poor people of the world.

All these corporations are literally making money, out of THIN AIR and extorting money from the people to fund their global domination initiatives. The airwaves and frequencies are part of the electromagnetic spectrum that makes up the entire universe. It is unthinkable that someone can lay claim to it – something that was created by the divine creator of all.

But somehow our servant, the government, has laid claim to these frequencies and they have given exclusive rights to private cellular corporations to use these air waves to extort unimaginable amounts of money from the people.

The airwaves and frequencies belong to the people. They do not belong to the government or any other corporation that has unlawfully laid claim to them. All this activity by the government and the cell phone companies is unlawful and unconstitutional and is in direct conflict with the will of the people.

Research has shown that the microwave frequencies used in cellular phones are extremely harmful to human beings. Our governments have gone to great lengths to keep this information covered up. We will appoint the most knowledgeable scientists and researchers to provide the people with our own information and act accordingly.

It has also been shown that these frequencies are used as carriers to transmit a variety of frequencies that manipulate our minds, thoughts and more. As farfetched as this sounds at first, there has been much evidence presented by researchers all over the world claiming that this is a very real threat to humans everywhere. In his TV show 'Conspiracy Theory', Jessy Ventura exposed only the tip of the iceberg in the use of such technology as a tool of mind control, and even torture, by the USA government.

We need to realise that this onslaught against humanity is all about absolute control over the people. As it stands now, those who control the money, control the world. If we remove their tool of control, they have no more power over the people.

BROADCASTING – RADIO – TELEVISION – INTERNET – OTHER MEDIA

Here are some quotes by the elite regarding the control and use of the global media.

"Not every item of news should be published. Rather must those who control news policies endeavor to make every item of news serve a certain purpose."
Joseph Paul Goebbels - Nazi Propaganda Minister

"We are grateful to the Washington Post, the New York Times, Time

Magazine, and other great publications whose directors have attended our meetings and respected their promises of discretion for almost forty years. It would have been impossible for us to develop our plan for the world if we had been subject to the bright lights of publicity during these years. But, the world is now more sophisticated and prepared to march towards a world government. The supernational sovereignty of an intellectual elite and world bankers is surely preferable to the national auto-determination practiced in past centuries."
David Rockefeller - C.F.R and Trilateral Commission Founder

"It is not enough for journalists to see themselves as mere messengers without understanding the hidden agendas of the message and myths that surround it."
John Pilger

"We [the Zionists] have it all under such control that no one - no one or no-body can [reach] people unless it is done through 'our' media control. We have it sewed up!"
Harold Wallace Rosenthal - from the Harold Wallace Rosenthal Interview 1976

"In March, 1915, the J.P. Morgan interests, the steel, shipbuilding, and powder interest, and their subsidiary organizations, got together 12 men high up in the newspaper world and employed them to select the most influential newspapers in the United States and sufficient number of them to control generally the policy of the daily press... They found it was only necessary to purchase the control of 25 of the greatest papers."
U.S. Congressman Oscar Callaway, 1917
"The world can therefore seize the opportunity [Persian Gulf crisis] to fulfil the long-held promise of a New World Order where diverse nations are drawn together in common cause to achieve the universal aspirations of mankind."
George Herbert Walker Bush

The broadcasting/media sector is equally monopolised and controlled all over the world by a small group. In South Africa, it is in the hands of the SABC, Multichoice, Primedia and a few more. The government has stolen these rights from the people and granted them to a handful of corporations. The government continues to dictate who may start a broadcasting business, and who may not. This is the same all over the world.

The global mainstream media is controlled by the same small number of powerful people who control the supply of money. They use the news as a medium of indoctrination, continuously promoting the agenda of the banking and political elite. This is why the issuing of broadcasting permits is highly restricted and controlled.

Global news has become the most powerful tool used to make people believe what they want us to believe – in most cases it is completely contrary to the truth. Please be objective about this. In the entire world of great minds in science, technology, discovery, archaeology, wildlife, plant life, space exploration, new inventions and an infinite spectrum of activity – how is it possible that when you turn on the news, all the major networks are covering exactly the same events and have no real news to share, other than to promote fear amongst the people?

All we ever see is violence, crime, war, politics, business reports and economics. We see politicians making endless promises that never materialise, telling us that we have to "tighten our belts". We see long debates by arrogant economists about money markets going up and down, and indicators, and financial predictions, all numbing our minds and making us think that this is all very important stuff and an inextricable part of life. Slowly but surely, the global media have convinced people that money makes the world go round. Well, nothing could be further from the truth. The sun comes up every day and the world goes around all on its own. People make the world go round with their creativity, scientific minds and infinite ability to love. Money does the opposite.

While there may be a number of new private radio and TV stations in South Africa that seem to represent some of the people, the government has made it very difficult to enter this market and will not issue national TV and Radio broadcasting rights to just anyone. It is virtually impossible for a normal person off the street to start a broadcasting business.

We should have hundreds of private stations allowing people of every town or culture to express their views and interact with the rest of the people in our country and beyond.

As in every other sector of our society, our servants, the government, have stolen all our rights and granted them to a small number of multinational corporations at the expense of the people, who are continually financially abused by these corporations. All this activity is unconstitutional, unlawful and will be redressed with immediate effect.

SATELLITE INSTALLATIONS
There are several advanced satellite installations scattered around South Africa that have become highly secretive places with restricted access to the public, such as the radio telescopes at Hartebeeshoek. Why is it that the people who pay for these installations and technology do not really know what these are being used for and are denied access? We the people should have access to information about every government and military installation and be informed as to what such sites are being used for.

UBUNTU PLAN OF ACTION – COMMUNICATION & BROADCASTING
1) All old legislation and laws that govern this sector will be abolished and will be replaced by new guidelines that benefit the people and not corporations or uphold secretive activity by the government.
2) All foreign shareholding and ownership in all telecommunication companies, including cellular phone companies, will be cancelled with immediate effect.
3) All cell phone companies will be given the opportunity to change their operating models to start providing virtually free cell phone communication to the people.
4) All communication done via fixed line providers and their infrastructure will be made freely available to all the people. A small monthly fee may be charged for maintenance and upgrades if it is necessary.
5) During the transition phase to UBUNTU communities, the employees of the communications companies, just like all other sectors, will be paid directly by the newly established People's Bank, that will replace the privately owned South African Reserve Bank..
6) This will free up many of the people who work for these companies – in the accounts departments, for example - to follow their passion to do what they choose to do, as their contribution to the community, and move to a town or city of their choice –

not restrained by financial considerations. This is after all the model of UBUNTU – people following their passions, creating abundance by doing so.

7) Anyone, anywhere, will be allowed to launch new cellular communication technology as long as they comply with the new laws written by the people.

8) A new cellular phone provider of the people will be launched using existing infrastructure. This will incorporate the latest and most advanced technology possible, which is not harmful to the people.

9) This new service will be free to the people everywhere, in essence making it impossible for any of the existing cell phone operators to continue exploiting our people.

10) We, the people, will promote and support ongoing research to constantly improve the technology in these areas and make it available and safe to use by the people as quickly as possible.

11) The internet will be made stable in South Africa so that it cannot be sabotaged by international internet providers who do not agree with our new approach.

12) All internet communication will be provided freely to everyone – in schools, public places and private homes.

13) Every school and every student will have access to the internet freely.

14) The internet will become a prominent medium to broadcast information to the people freely.

15) Everyone will have the right to start a radio or TV station anywhere in South Africa as long as it complies with the new laws written by the people.

16) Existing TV and radio monopolies in South Africa will have to adapt to the new way to remain competitive in their service to the people.

17) All sponsorships of TV and radio programmes, which include sport, will no longer be necessary.

18) Sporting and cultural activities will be broadcast on a much wider basis – covering as many events as the people want to see - not restricted by financial constraints or sponsorships.

19) The concept of advertising will change dramatically. The people will not tolerate the promotion of brands or services that are exploitative. Because everything will be free – capitalistic companies will not have any reason to advertise, but rather

restructure their products to benefit the people. Advertising will morph into something new that will most likely be seen as a platform to release new information to people.

20) Planned obsolescence will be eradicated very quickly as people stop using tools and technology that breaks down or has to be replaced.

21) Independent news channels will most likely become information platforms that cover real news, discoveries, activities and inventions, inspiring people – instead of the propaganda by the global news giants who control the flow of disinformation to keep us ignorant.

22) All the new radio and TV stations will require new programmes and live broadcasting of events, news channels and community interest. This will provide many new opportunities for thousands of people who want to be involved in radio and TV broadcasting and the production of content for all these sectors. Broadcasting is a hungry beast.

23) This will include the movie sector that will become a contributor to the broadcasting. The production of movies will change dramatically as people's interests change and we develop new passions, while discarding the obsessions of the past. For example, violence in films will most likely disappear immediately as this will no longer be part of our new reality.

24) All satellite installations and sites including telescopes will be accessible to the people and the people will be informed what such installations are being used for all of the time.

25) Any devious activity that may be potentially harmful to the people; or any activity that is not for the benefit of the people, conducted at these sites will be stopped immediately.

26) All the satellite installations will be constantly upgraded with new technology so that they can keep providing a better service to the people.

27) The communication and broadcast sector, together with the movie sector, will truly become a medium of sharing knowledge and information by the people – for the people – helping them to achieve abundance on all levels of our society everywhere.

PRINT MEDIA

Every town village and city will be able to publish and print their own local news on a regular basis as decided by the people. National newspapers and magazines of special interests will be encouraged and paid for by the People's Bank in the interim phase. Eventually these will simply become aspects of every community that people do as their LOL for the benefit of their community and country. This will provide an exciting platform for many new writers, photographers and other artistic people to contribute. National monopolies will be allowed to continue but will most likely have to conform to promoting truth and real information, instead of government and banking agendas, as nobody will be interested in reading such drivel, and because they will no longer be part of our reality. All printed media materials will be bio-degradable, recyclable and non toxic.

FINANCIAL SECTOR AND BANKING

This includes every corporation that is in any way connected to money, the creation of money, the storage of money, the printing of money, banks, accounting firms, insurance companies, and others that have probably escaped our attention because of their clever disguise.

The entire banking system and the industry that supports it is based on an unlawful, exploitative and corrupt foundation. It is the greatest act of criminal deception ever perpetrated against humanity. The banks break the law with no remorse every day without any kind of legal backlash, destroying the lives of millions of trusting people.

Together with the legal/justice sector, the financial sector needs a complete overhaul so that it truly serves the people and not the shareholders of the banks or the multinational corporations that are using it as a tool of control over the people.

The misery and hardship caused by the financial industry is almost unimaginable. So much so, that every year many people kill their families and commit suicide as a result of the unlawful activity of banks. This makes their actions utterly unacceptable in a moral society that upholds human rights above all.

Although our philosophy is that we do not need money to thrive as the human race and that we can reach much greater heights of success as a society without money, it will take some time and several key steps to move closer to such a final destination. So what do we do about the financial industry? How do we begin to change things in the short term and long term?

An immediate restructuring of the financial sector is paramount to stop the bleeding.

We have to look at successful examples in the world where similar activity has succeeded and provided immediate relief for the people. The people's uprising against the government, the banks and the central bank in Iceland in 2010, is a perfect model for us to follow.

Few countries blew up more spectacularly than Iceland in the 2008 financial crisis. The local stock market plunged 90 percent; unemployment rose nine-fold; inflation shot to more than 18 percent; and the country's biggest banks all failed. This was not a post-Lehman Brothers recession, it was a full blown depression.

According to the president Ólafur Ragnar Grímsson, "the government bailed out the people and imprisoned the banksters, opposite to what America and the rest of Europe did." Unlike the rest of the western world, Iceland went after the people who caused the crisis – the bankers who created the problems as they did all over the world. What Iceland did is not just emotionally satisfying, it should be held up as an example to every country. While Iceland is recovering, the rest of the western world, which bailed out the bankers and left the general population to pay for the bankers' crimes, is not.

To keep it simple, the people caused the resignation of the government, appointed a new government; they prosecuted and jailed the banksters; they wrote off more than 50 billion of unlawful mortgage loans and vehicle finance loans, and in so doing freed the people from the exploitative and fraudulent activity of the banksters. Then, they redenominated foreign currency debt into devalued krona, effectively giving creditors a big haircut. In June 2010, the nation's Supreme Court gave debtors another break by declaring bank loans that were indexed to foreign currencies illegal. Because the Icelandic krona plunged 80 percent during the crisis, the cost of repaying foreign debt more than doubled. This ruling allowed consumers to repay the banks as if the loans were in Icelandic krona. Today, Iceland has arguably the strongest economy per capita, linked to the Euro-zone.

Do not be baffled by the complicated language of the economists, bankers and the lawyers that protect them. They use such language to inflate their egos and to confuse others into thinking that it is too complicated for the common people and that only very highly trained financial people can deal with such matters of importance. This is a blatant lie and a clear manipulation to keep the majority of ordinary people in the dark so they don't question what the bankers are doing.

Nothing is complicated – everything is simple and if they cannot explain it to the people, it needs to change so that the people can understand it and are able to make sense of it and change it so that the system benefits the people. But the chances of that happening are zero. What most people simply cannot believe is the sheer size of the fraud committed by the banksters. The global banking fraud has a monetary value dozens of times the GDP of the entire planet.

To fully understand our unshakable opposition to the banks and the entire financial sector, you need to fully grasp how money is created; who owns the banks; how the supply of money works and how the handful of banking families control this global empire that controls the entire planet.

To make this easier to grasp, here is a list of facts about the global banking cartel.

FACTS ABOUT THE GLOBAL BANKING MACHINE

1) All the major banks in the world are owned and controlled by the banking families.
2) They control the entire process of the creation, the printing, and supply of money around the world.
3) The three biggest names in this cartel are the Rothschilds; Rockefellers and Morgans, and they ultimately own or control all the banks in the world, together with a small number of other powerful banking families, like Carnegie, Harriman, Schiff, and Warburg.
4) Collectively they have become known as the "banksters" by those who became aware of their devious activity.
5) All the major central banks of the world, including the Reserve Bank of South Africa, just like the Federal Reserve Bank in the USA, are privately owned corporations with complete control of the financial markets.

6) These privately owned central banks have been given the right to dictate the financial policy to the people of each country. This is simply unimaginable and unacceptable in any conscious community.

7) These banking families and central banks are a law unto themselves and do not have to answer to anyone. For example, section 33 of the South African Reserve Bank Act allows them to keep their actions secret.

8) The global financial system created around the supply of money is so convoluted and complex that only a few people truly understand it. This is always used as an excuse to exclude the involvement of ordinary people.

9) The deeply complex legal system is used in the same way to manipulate and support this structure, denying the ordinary person access to lawful justice.

10) Lawful justice cannot exist under the situation where the country is a corporation; the president appoints the judges, therefore the judges work for the corporation and have to uphold the wellbeing of the corporation – not the people. Therefore the courts are mere enforcers of the banking policy.

11) Banks officially do not work with money. They work with Bills of Exchange, Negotiable Instruments and Promissory Notes.

12) The word 'money' does not even have a definition in the Bank Act of South Africa, and neither is the word 'payment' defined.

13) All the major money of the world is 'FIAT' money – this basically means that it has no intrinsic value AND it is not supported by any precious metals like gold or silver, as it was a long time ago. FIAT money is created by banks, out of thin air, when you take out a "loan." There is actually no real loan – nothing physical is exchanged – this is the equivalent of counterfeiting. South Africa's money supply has quadrupled in the past decade, and yet this increase supply has not seen a parallel increase in gold, silver or other real commodity reserves.

14) This means that the paper/plastic money we use is completely worthless. They are just fancy pieces of paper with some fancy logos printed on them with no value at all. The 'value' is derived purely from the masses of people who have confidence in their currency and keep using it as a method of exchange.

15) For example, very few people know that a payment / commission

/ legal bribe is paid to the South African government every time a worn note or coin is returned to the SA Reserve bank. This payment is called *seigniorage* and allows our government to profit from the exploitation of the people by the paper/plastic money controlled by the Reserve Bank, and ultimately the Bank For International Settlements from whom our Reserve Bank receives their orders.

16) Yet it is illegal to destroy these worthless pieces of paper, and people who introduce alternative pieces of paper, or copy these pieces of paper are jailed for infringement of its copyright.

17) The only reason our money has any value, is because we give it value – our perception of value is the only value it has. If the people lose faith in their money, the money will collapse, because nothing supports it. In fact the word 'credit' comes from the Latin *credere* which means "to believe." Evidence of this is found almost every time a central bank governor opens their mouth. You will hear the word "confidence" uttered over and over and over again because the prime directive of a central bank governor is to *maintain confidence in banking at all costs.* Erosion in confidence leads to the collapse of the system. This is precisely why they placed Nelson Mandela's face on the new South African notes – to instil and renew confidence in our money, while completely desecrating Mandela's commitment to freedom.

18) Banks create money out of "THIN AIR" by simply creating debits and credit on the accounting computer system. This is called the Matching Principle and is governed by the Generally Accepted Accounting Principles (GAAP).

19) A "loan" is not a loan in the ordinary sense of the word, it is an instruction that you, the customer signs, in the process creating a promissory note, which you "submit" to the bank authority, giving the bank permission to issue one of their promissory notes in return. Their promissory note (which comes in the form of a computer generated bank statement) is designed to look like a loan. So, their promise back to you (in exchange for your promise to them) is the loan you are receiving. So, in essence, you instructed the bank to make money out of thin air. Because you are none the wiser, you agree to the exploitative terms and conditions outlined in the agreement which, of course, the courts will enforce in the bank's favour.

20) Banks do not have money of their own to lend you as most people

believe. No money existed in the system before the so called "loan" was granted to you.

21) Banks create money on the signatures of their clients and the so-called contracts and loans signed by their customers. These contracts are sold in a process called securitisation to third parties, who in turn sell it on the global stock markets. This is a highly secretive and well guarded technique in which they profiteer and create undue enrichment. Then they bundle such loans and sell them back to the people via pensions funds and insurance policies. Are you confused yet? You should be – many lawyers and most judges do not understand this, and this is why we had to study this ourselves, to be able to defend ourselves in the courts against those lawyers, who defend the banksters and understand it extremely well. The people have to know.

22) By selling your signature or 'promissory note' or mortgage bond contract, the banks lose all legal rights to any property that they financed. In legal terms this is called losing *'locus standi'*.

23) When the bank securitises a loan, they get paid the full capital amount of the loan, plus interest, up front. This means that your loan has actually been pre-settled by a third party who is insured in case you default, while you have no idea that this is going on behind the scenes.

24) The banks break contract law by claiming to lend what they do not possess – money. They only create money, in most cases cyber-money, after you have signed all the documents and they sold your promissory note to the third party who then on-sells it, sometimes many times, to other parties, by trading it on the global stock markets. This is why securitisation is a ponzi/pyramid scheme that everyone must become aware of. It is also known as "shadow banking" which is easy to research online.

25) They do not disclose any of this to their customers, keeping us in the dark. You may believed that they actually loaned you real money. That is a lie. They never loaned you anything of any value and therefore there was never "equal consideration" where both you and the bank stands to lose something. This flies in the face of basic contract law, never mind common morality and integrity among people. But then banks are not people – they are legal fiction corporations.

26) You created all the value with your own *mind* and it was your signature that caused the release of money from the third party

buyer, which the bank received on your behalf – except they never informed you of that, did they?

27) The banks act as intermediaries, like estate agents, because they do not lend us THEIR money. Since they do not lend us anything, but only obtain it on the strength of our signatures, from a third party, any interest they charge is pure extortion and fraud. Disclosure must take place for a valid agreement to occur.

28) The money in South Africa is printed by the South African Mint – also a private company that simply profiteers from the hard work of our people. However, recently this has been outsourced to Sweden, which was a disaster, causing huge embarrassment for the Reserve Bank, after several billion Rands worth of notes were printed incorrectly with the wrong dimensions and had to be destroyed. But don't panic – It's just paper with some fancy logos.

29) The Reserve Bank, which is a private company, is in charge of printed money, which it sells or loans to the banks at a fraction of the face value of the bank notes.

30) When the banks return the used bank notes to the Reserve Bank, they get paid almost the entire full face value of those bank notes, creating enrichment out of thin air for themselves, by creating money out of thin air from shuffling paper.

31) Banks practice what is called "Fractional Reserve Banking". This means that they only have to retain a small percentage of any deposit and can lend out the rest many times over to the public, creating a spiral of debt on money that does not even exist.

32) For example: For every $100 you deposit, the bank lends out about $900 of imaginary fictitious money to their clients. The real fraud is that they charge compound interest on this non-existent money. This is blatant fraud and anyone else would be jailed for a long time for doing this.

33) Interest is charged up front. Interest is considered to be "real money" by the bank, and this imaginary money is used to make more loans, out of thin air, against that interest, that did not exist in the first place.

34) As it stands today, there is not enough money in the world to pay off all the debt in the world, because of interest. This is exactly the situation the banksters wanted to create. A situation that gives them complete control over property and other assets that can be repossessed by the banks, only to re-sell it to another naive person who will most likely end up in the same debt situation.

35) All this activity is continually supported by the legal system and the ignorant judges who just perpetuate the fraud in the face of clear evidence. But not all judges are ignorant. Many are on the payroll of the banks and are vigilant in upholding the fraudulent scam against unsuspecting people who believe judges to be high on the list of humans with integrity.

36) In some countries, hard working people are jailed for not being able to repay their debt. This is a blatant crime against humanity for which the bankers should be jailed and the judges should be answerable to the people they serve. But then, they don't serve the people, they serve the corporation that employs them – THE REPUBLIC OF SOUTH AFRICA and other corporations that masquerade as countries. And therefore most judges uphold the rights of corporations, not people.

37) The printed notes we call money are really instruments of debt and should be illegal. Money as we know it today can only be issued as debt. It has been said that about 40% of the debt of the USA is fictitious / counterfeit debt, owed to the Federal Reserve Bank, who initially created it out of nothing and then charged interest on that debt. All the income tax collected in the US is used to pay off just the interest portion of the debt to the Federal Reserve Bank owners.

This is just a small taste of the convoluted web of deception that has been created to keep us ignorant and completely enslaved to the global control of the banksters.

There is no reason why we, the people, cannot create our own new form of money as an alternative to the banks' tools of enslavement and use this new money as an interim tool to stabilise the economic crisis. A lawful kind of money that serves the people.

UBUNTU PLAN OF ACTION – FINANCE & BANKING

1) We follow the example of Iceland – prosecute the bankers and the lawyers who defended them knowing that they are committing crimes against humanity.

2) Prosecute the judges who handed down unlawful judgements in favour of banks, against honest people who were defrauded by the banks. The judges did not serve justice, did not apply their minds, and they failed the people and should be prosecuted for the unimaginable hardship they have caused millions of people.

3) Create a new PEOPLE'S EXCHANGE/BANK whose loyalty lies with the people and not international shareholders of private corporations called banks. This must be seen as a short-term step towards working without any form of money at all. As we begin to realise that money is provided for all our needs, as and when we need it, to build or develop everything the people need, we will soon realise that the money is not needed at all. And that we can just get on with building and developing and inventing, without the money getting in the way.

4) Link our new currency to gold or silver to give it real value – this will make the Rand the strongest currency in the world overnight. This underpinning can be a theoretical one, based on the rich mineral deposits – not actual gold in a vault somewhere. We need to stop raping the Earth for financial gain immediately.

5) Close all commercial banks and the Reserve Bank and let their directors and shareholders be **personally** responsible for the debt they created on the backs of trusting human beings. In other words, they created it, they can have it.

6) Convert the existing bank branches into outlets of the People's Exchange.

7) The current employees of the banks can remain, but as employees of the new People's Exchange, that is owned by the people and serves the people.

8) Write off all existing home mortgage loans, vehicle finance loans; credit card loans and any other bank loans of this nature that were created by securitisation and other banking trickery like fractional reserve banking. (Remember that all the so called money they loaned to us, has already been paid to the banks through the process of securitisation, by selling our signatures on the global stock markets – so in essence there is no debt in any case.)

9) All private and public security structures acting for the banks and corporations will be immediately disbanded. Ironically this included just about every military and police force in existence today.

10) Create alternative currencies for different towns to protect them against exploitation in the initial transition phase, by those with loads of money and malicious intent. The greed factor will take a while to subside amongst humanity as we move towards a moneyless system.

11) All property financed today is already paid for on the strength

of our signatures and there should be NO debt. That is the magnificent deception that the bankers have created to keep driving us into more and more debt with exorbitant compounded interest.

12) As crazy as this may sound to some, nobody loses other than the greedy bankers who profiteer from us.

This plan of action will continue to grow and correct itself just like every other sector of society under the Contributionism system. I am of the opinion that any system that is controlled by the people, with the intention to benefit all the people in true transparency is infinitely better than the fraudulent inhumane financial system of today.

INDUSTRY & MANUFACTURING

In Livermore, northern California, a light bulb was switched on in 1901. It continues to burn bright today. We used to build things that lasted forever. Today we build stuff to last a season.

Imagine living in a world where everything imaginable is obtained, designed, measured, planned, manufactured, implemented, built, planted, cooked, sculpted, painted or provided by the people, for the people. This is the world of UBUNTU Contributionism – No hurdles to progress.

There are simply no restrictions on what people can do. Whatever people are capable of, the people shall do for the benefit of their community – never for the benefit of individuals alone at the expense of others. This obviously does not refer to personal interests or hobbies or arts and culture that people participate in, but rather activities that require involvement of people to produce something for the community.

This unbridled way of thinking will create unimaginable industries and manufacturing that we can only dream of today. Many existing sectors of industry will dissolve, especially those that cause pollution or have any kind of negative impact on the ecosystem, to be replaced by new ways of doing things.

There will most likely be rapid decentralisation of all industry, moving into close proximity to towns and villages, as these communities begin to take control of their own destiny, providing as much as they can for their people. Such industry will not only include the supply of daily foods, but will also extend into more diverse and specialised manufacturing like building materials, wooden products, metal workshops, ceramics, fabrics, shoemaking, and so on.

We will see the establishment of specialised communities that form around the production of raw materials which are needed across the board by manufacturers in other communities. Like iron, alloys, metals, silica, new-age plastics, and many other materials that are not financially viable today.

The towns that have sprung up around existing mines that produce platinum, gold, iron, steel, and other heavy industry, will themselves become key communities in the continued supply of such raw materials. These were originally established closer to the source of raw material and should remain there until new technology has provided alternatives.

Remember that under the UBUNTU system, items will be built to last as long as possible, greatly reducing the pressure placed on our resources. This is contrary to the planned obsolescence that our current corporate structure thrives on. Therefore the demand for these materials will diminish dramatically, also because of our new approach towards consumption. There will be no export for profit of our minerals or raw materials – we will only produce what is needed by the people and the diverse activities in our own communities.

The way we package things today is utterly wasteful and will also change rapidly. Everything comes in a box, or bag or some kind of wrapping that is removed and discarded. Most packaging is designed with the primary aim to advertise the content. The food industry is especially guilty of unimaginable waste – where people discard the wrapping within seconds of receiving the item. Almost everything in our world has become disposable, landing up in a landfill.

We will see an explosion of new technology and materials that will provide many new alternatives in the field of manufacturing. The way we use such materials will change dramatically. But initially the major industry will continue to provide the raw materials to a growing number of secondary manufacturers that make more specified items; who supply the makers of even more specialised items; and so on.

Think of all the components that go into making a car and it becomes evident how many different manufacturing steps there are. Now think of what goes into building trains; roads; helicopters; computers; lights; radios; speakers; books; reading glasses; fridges; heaters; spanners; door handles; drills; wheelbarrows; lawnmowers; pencils; printer; phones; etc, etc.

Every manufacturer gets what they need from those who

manufacture the components – who get their materials from those who make those materials; and so on. This will all require accurate and skilful management. The managing of the supply chain will therefore be a critical part of our new UBUNTU communities and offer many people the opportunity to get involved in this sector.

If a new factory is needed, it will be designed by the best architects to the best specification possible; built by the best engineers; using the best available building materials; to deliver the best quality products imaginable; that will last for as long as possible. The priority for the UBUNTU movement is to return all community enterprises back to the community with utmost urgency. Corporations cannot and will not be allowed to continue to usurp community industries, leaving them dry, barren and forcing people to buy back their own products at a premium.

We may see the development of specialised communities that are more focused on certain aspects of life. Some will be more reclusive like Buddhist ashrams; some will be more sports oriented; some may focus on arts and culture; technology and computer geek-type communities, and so on. Only our imagination can create limits. It is so exhilarating to imagine how life will change when the debilitating burden of survival is removed from our lives. But I may be completely wrong in my assumptions and we may see a completely different accumulation of people based on diverse interests. Our current social habits, of people hanging out with others who have similar interests, may simply be a subconscious reaction to fear of the unknown.

All our subconscious problems that influence our behaviour will change dramatically once money is removed from the system and replaced by complete freedom. Very few of us, if any, have had the benefit of this kind of freedom. Whatever happens, or how it unfolds will be the realisation of a rapidly rising unity consciousness that embraces everything in creation. We are the catalysts of this change.

LIVING IN HARMONY WITH NATURE & MOTHER EARTH

RECYCLE – RENEW – ECO-FRIENDLY – NON-TOXIC – BIODEGRADABLE
Everything we do in our new world and our new utopian lives must be in complete harmony with mother Earth. Any new synthetic materials

we develop must be completely biodegradable and renewable. This is not difficult to achieve if left to the experts and those who are passionate about this subject. The new and free technology that will be shared with everyone will allow us to create all kinds of new materials that we can only dream of today.

Everything we use or create must be recyclable – or if for some reason it cannot be recycled, we should probably not be using it. But if we absolutely have to have something for our survival that is not recyclable, we must ensure that it can be converted to something else that is of use to the community. It will be very difficult to convince a people in a free society to manufacture something that is harmful to them or their environment.

This will apply to all sectors of our society – packaging, food, agriculture, industry, technology, construction, education, healthcare, and all the others. For this reason it becomes evident that UBUNTU Contributionist communities will automatically and rapidly move towards living in harmony with our planet. Any other behaviour is simply in conflict with the laws of nature, not acceptable to a highly conscious society. It would be like trying to swim without water.

In short, living in an UBUNTU community means living in perfect harmony with nature and mother Earth.

STRUCTURE OF COMMUNITIES

As outlined earlier, our communities will grow like the cells in our bodies, circular in shape, dividing and supporting each other every step of the way to ensure the health of the entire community. Some communities will grow larger, consisting of more cells, just like the larger organs in our bodies, while some will remain small and quaint. But they all work in unity and cooperation, performing crucial tasks that are unique and appreciated by the rest of the community. Never in competition or conflict. So let this be a great lesson to us all that only out of unity can we achieve infinite diversity and abundance on all levels of human endeavour.

UBUNTU communities will be filled with some of the most breathtaking designs and architecture, that is reserved only for the rich and powerful in a capitalistic society. Thousands of people pay thousands of dollars to go on exclusive safaris in Africa every year where they stay in luxurious camps that most of us will never be able to afford. Everyone will be able to live in such 7-star luxury constructed from the best and most natural materials that some of the most exclusive resorts in the world are built from. The New Earth Project, which is closely associated with the UBUNTU movement has already started showing us the way of what is possible. Eco-friendly homes with free energy, and all the necessary components to create a harmonious living environment for all. http://www.new-earth-project. org/

Above: An artist's impression of harmonious living without stress and the need for urban jungles. But every community will have its own designs, structures and layout based on the needs and desires of the people.

Above: Spectacular workmanship and design that only few can afford today, will be available to everyone, everywhere. Below left: Everyone can feel as if they are on a permanent 5-star safari, living in lodges like Londolozi in South Africa. Below right: Earthships are great examples of natural building styles for harmonious living.

THE POWER OF WORDS AND LANGUAGE

Unbeknown to us, our language is an almost infinitely powerful tool of enslavement well beyond our wildest imagination. We have already covered the laws and words that enslave us and the principles of 'legalese' language that has a completely different meaning to what we believe, but the way we use our language today is very cleverly designed to keep us in a kind of hypnotic spell.

We can use the example in the heading of the next chapter; "words and slogans that enchant us". To enchant someone is to put them in under some kind of magical spell. The ancient mysterious practice of voodoo is a form of enchantment in many ways. While many of us today are lead to believe that it is all a bunch of nonsense made up by fiction writers, they would be utterly mistaken.

We have already covered the fact that frequency technology has been used to control people's minds and make them do things that they normally would not do. Soldiers and ordinary people are turned into assassins that are activated by a voice or a sound frequency to perform an act that they have no memory of after the event. The key word here is 'frequency'.

Words and sounds that can make people become assassins, are merely frequencies that are used as weapons to cause an effect. This is where we find the link between ancient wizardry, witchcraft, magic spells, and voodoo; and modern technology used by our military. Experiments in German supermarkets with subliminal frequencies hidden in background music, caused shoppers to choose specific items rather than others.

And so we come to realise that our language, the words we utter and the phrases we use are truly powerful tools that can be used to our benefit or our detriment, but most of us just don't know about it.

The sounds that make up the letters of our alphabet have mysterious origins. Every letter has a sound/frequency associated with it. Those sounds/frequencies have an effect on the physical world we live in.

This is why wizards can cast spells by chanting a specific sequence of words or phrases or spells to cause an effect. As crazy as this may sound to some people today, this is all part of the long periods of disinformation we have been exposed to – using our own language and words to achieve this. Not only are many works of art, created by the great masters of the past, encoded with advanced knowledge of the laws of nature and sacred geometry, but the great written works by Shakespeare are equally encoded with subliminal information that truly boggles the mind.

Electrical engineer, Willem de Swart in Johannesburg, South Africa, has uncovered many of these examples of encoded information, but his major contribution comes in the decoding of Hollywood blockbuster movies. Please see his website www. secretnumbers.org for mind blowing information on this subject. It is curious that Hollywood blockbusters are encoded with advanced knowledge – but to what purpose? Is it to enchant us, to cast a spell over us or to help us wake up from our ignorant hypnotic state?

It seems that the encoded information is actually aimed at helping humanity wake up from a deep unconscious hypnotic state of mind, into higher levels of consciousness and begin to recognise our place in the universe as highly conscious beings with infinite ability – to create with our minds and thoughts. That is what some of the great teachers of past and present have been trying to tell us – "we can move mountains" with our minds. Conversely it is also the very thing that enslaves us.

All this strange activity with encoded messages in art, literature and movies, becomes even more mysterious when we analyse the name Hollywood. It was essential for wizards to use the wood from a Holly tree – in other words, "holly wood" to cast their spells.

One of the greatest examples of encoded messages in books and movies is in the famous work of L. Frank Baum, who wrote *The Wonderful Wizard of Oz* in 1900, which later became an iconic movie of the early Hollywood era. Clearly Baum knew exactly what he was writing and we should examine his ancestry to see how he fits into the bigger scheme of things.

The story tells us about a yellow brick road, or road paved with bars of gold, that leads to the Great Wizard who is hidden from sight behind a veil of secrecy, from where he controls the gold, ounce by ounce. The measuring unit for gold is ounce, or oz.

The character known as the Scarecrow is really just a representation of our Straw Man. That fictitious ALL CAPS legal fiction, or a PERSON – that is created for each one of us by our corporate governments at birth. All the Straw Man wanted from the Wizard of Oz was a brain, because a legal fiction is just a piece of paper, so it cannot have a brain. Unfortunately the Straw Man could not get what he wanted, but in place of a brain he was given a Certificate – a Birth Certificate for a new legal creation. He was proud of his new legal status with all the other legalisms he was granted. He became the true epitome of the brainless sack of straw who was given a Certificate in place of a brain to figure out the lies and deceptions that enslave him.

The Tin Man represents the people as they slave away to pay their taxes. TIN represents *Taxpayer Identification Number.* The poor Tin Man just stands there mindlessly doing his work until his body literally freezes up and stops functioning. We are the living breathing human beings, believing that we are Tin Men, working ourselves to death for the unlawful governments. He represents the heartless and emotionless legal fiction, or creature robotically carrying out his daily task as if he was already dead. His master keeps him cold on the outside and heartless on the inside in order to control his human emotions and connection with others. This is why Tin Man wanted a heart from the Wizard, but he did not get one. He got a placebo made of velvet filled with sawdust, disguised as a heart.

The cowardly Lion wanted courage from the Wizard because he was always too frightened to stand up for himself, but he was a bully and a big mouth when it came to picking on those smaller than him. Just like those in positions of authority act as if they have great courage, but they really have none at all. The cowardly Lion always buckled and whimpered when anyone of any size or confidence challenged him. And therefore he wanted courage from the Wizard, but he was awarded a medal of official recognition instead. Now, regardless of how much of a coward he still was, his official status made him a bully with officially recognized authority.

He is just like the bankers' lawyers who hide behind the law and attorneys who hide behind the Middle Courts of the Temple Bar.

The trip through the field of poppies is truly fascinating. It probably highlights the fact they were legal fictions, not real people, and that is why drugs had no effect on them. *The Wonderful Wizard of Oz* was written at the turn of the century, and yet the author had a premonition America was going to be drugged. Just like the 'War on Drugs' is a false flag operation created by the USA government, the Crown has been playing the drug cartel game for centuries. The history of Hong Kong and the Opium Wars is a reminder of what these unscrupulous secret societies are capable of. The Crown has had valuable experience conquering all of China with drugs, and so the rest of the world would follow.

But it was the little insignificant dog called Toto, who finally exposed the Wizard for what he really was. In Latin, *Toto* means "in total, all together", commonly used in courts and legal documents by lawyers. As small as he was, Toto was not scared of the Great Wizard's pompous theatrics. The smoke, flames and shadowy images were designed to frighten people into doing as the Great Wizard of Oz commanded. Toto simply snuck around, looked behind the curtain – corporate veil of the banks and courts – and saw it was a scam. His persistent barking alerted all the others who finally paid attention and came to see what all the fuss was about.

To their surprise they found just an ordinary person, with no special powers, controlling the levers that created the illusion of the Great Wizard with self appointed authority. The corporate veil of deception that hides the legal fiction and its fraudulent courts was lifted. The Wizard was exposed for all to see.

There are many people in the world barking just like Toto about the global corporate and banking scam. It is only a matter of time before the people realise how they have been manipulated, abused and lied to. So let us remind ourselves that we have the power to change all this, as Glinda the good witch told Dorothy, "you've always had the power... you've had it all along"...to find eternal happiness and a utopian life free from abuse and slavery.

Humanity has become obsessed with movies that are projected images activated by light on a silver screen – movies are therefore a projected reality – not real. The actors are called 'stars' that shine brightly in the lives of ordinary people. Real stars like our Sun radiate light – and life on Earth has been energised by the light from our star, the Sun.

There is therefore a very strong resemblance between the projected reality of movies and the so-called reality we experience as human beings. It may just be this relationship that highlights our true origins as immortal souls that are infinitely connected to the creator of all, acting out this projected reality on this planet called Earth.

It is also important to note that this is why we are taught to 'spell' words while learning to read. Subconsciously we are working with tools that are used to weave spells and have the potential to change our reality. This 'spelling' of words and the strategic use of words is immaculately exposed by Judge David Wynn Miller in his research.

In 1988 he discovered the mathematical interface for language and introduced the world to his study of QUANTUM-LANGUAGE-PARSE-SYNTAX-GRAMMAR, with which he explains how and why our language was bastardized over the last 8,500 years.

David teaches us that the way we use words in our language today is completely unproductive. Our words have been stripped of their frequency or energy to have a positive effect. The root of the deception lies in the language we use and how we use it. There are those among us that know this and are masters of using this tool against an unconscious humanity. He explains the numeric structure of words and sentences and how these can either have a powerful effect on others or be completely benign. Basically, David is explaining the basics of wizardry. You can learn more about this amazing breakthrough research on his website at www.davidwynnmiller.com

There seems to be a fascinating tug-of-war between certain sectors of the media. Some are doing their best to keep us dumbed-down, like the news and reality shows, while the Hollywood 'blockbuster' movies are feeding us subliminal information which allows us to 'bust' out of our subconscious 'block' of universal knowledge and raise our collective consciousness.

WORDS AND SLOGANS THAT ENCHANT US AND KEEP US IN A SPELL

Let us explore some key words and slogans used on a daily basis to keep us in a hypnotic state of being. We accept such words without ever questioning their meaning or intent to influence our reality.

Most of these words and expressions are a product of capitalistic society and are inextricably linked to our continued enslavement. We hear most of these expressions many times a day, keeping the matrix alive in our subconscious reality. By simply opening our minds and recognising the activity around us for what it is and why it is happening, we get a true sense of how everything operates against the natural flow of energy – especially human energy. Below are words and phrases but also things people do and expressions we use that take on a whole new meaning when we simply open our hearts, and think as human beings.

COMPETITION IS GOOD

Competition is not good – it leads to separation, division and conflict. It leads to the suppression of knowledge and it drives the divide and conquer principle. Cooperation is what we should strive for. Through cooperation we will achieve infinite abundance, knowledge and breakthrough on all levels.

ECONOMY & ECONOMIC GROWTH

Is based on the principle of scarcity – to economise – the fear of not having enough for everyone – having to save for the future – its foundation is money – that stuff we don't need or want if we want to thrive in abundance. Economic growth makes us believe that if the economy does not grow, humans will not prosper. It is linked to famine and depression, which is always linked to the availability of money – never the ability of people to create and provide – which is infinite. Free humans can never experience an economic slowdown. The word economy is completely alien in UBUNTU communities where everything is produced and created by the people at will – not governed by the supply of money.

FINANCIAL STABILITY

Makes us believe that without money we cannot be stable – we become unstable and unfit for society. It makes most of us equate a lack of money with poverty – because of the 'economy' that keeps us in a state of scarcity. A society without money is not poor – it is free and filled with abundance on all levels of human endeavour. Money and finance does not stabilise our lives, it controls our lives. Without money, we are unstable – we cannot be controlled.

POVERTY

This is a construct of capitalism and is used as a fear tactic. A world without money does not make people poor, it makes them free from slavery. Poverty cannot exist in an UBUNTU community – a world without money, where everyone has what they need and do what they love – where everything is available to everyone at all times – where the people build and create whatever they need, to achieve abundance for everyone.

FREEDOM & LIBERTY

How can we talk about freedom when we have been enslaved for thousands of years – we have no real concept of what freedom really is as an enslaved species. We are however constantly reminded that we must stand up for our freedom and liberty. Those who believe they are free are deceiving the rest of humanity into a similar sense of ignorant belief. Patriotism is promoted by governments and is becoming a deep division in families where some become soldiers who help to invade other countries in the name of liberty, while others become vocal about the abuse of liberty and freedom, and are accused of being un-patriotic. Remember, liberty is NOT freedom! Liberties are benefits that are granted by a higher authority to someone who has sworn allegiance to them. Liberties can be withdrawn or altered at any time because the assumption is that each person has agreed to obey that higher authority.

SECURITY

Makes us feel safe – but safe from what? Safe from others that are trying to harm us? Subconsciously security creates division, anxiety and suspicion because it suggests that there are constant threats to our property and our lives from others around us. Security also just happens to be the word used by banks and finance companies for the instruments that they trade with. When a bank informs you that they are recording your call *for your security*, they are actually recording your call to *confirm that you are a security / tradable commodity and that you are bonded to them.* Before you laugh out loud, spend time thinking about this.

EDUCATION

Is constantly confused with wisdom. People do not have to be educated in the current system to be wise. Some of the wisest people in the world have never seen a school. We are lead to believe that without education we will amount to nothing – end up homeless and hungry – that we will not be able to find a job – it's all about preparing people to become slaves with jobs working for corporations. A very powerful tool to keep us in fear of failure because we have not been educated.

CAREERS & JOBS

This is what we do for most of our lives as ignorant slaves, once we have been sufficiently brainwashed through EDUCATION and have landed a JOB that we do for most of our lives – at which point it is called a CAREER. The system rewards you with a golden watch because you were such a good slave, not questioning the system and devoted your life to supporting the system that enslaved you. We ask our children "what are you going to become?" As if they are nothing, and they have to perform some weird ritual to "become" something – unconsciously planting the seeds of inferiority in their young minds. We are living breathing human beings, by divine rite, each one with very unique and special gifts that we are born with. We do not have to become anything. We are!

FOOD

Television makes us think that good food is something only great chefs can provide. Ordinary people are no longer capable of creating great meals or preparing simple food for their families. The food on the supermarket shelves has become too expensive for most and so the option has become junk foods that are filled with toxins to keep us dumbed down. Growing food is becoming illegal in many places which means that good food is quickly becoming a luxury item – only attainable by those slaves who play by the rules and support the system. Food should be growing naturally everywhere.

BUSINESS

We are bombarded by business reports 24/7 – subconsciously believing that we cannot exist if there was no business. Business creates the jobs that people need to survive – to earn more money – to get more entrapped in the matrix of slavery. It is nothing more than a distraction from consciousness – to keep us busy – running around doing mindless things for the "busy-ness". It is the great human distraction and creator of ego. Some of the biggest businessmen and women have the biggest egos that are held up as examples of great success by the media. The popular TV show *The Apprentice*, with Donald Trump, who is a great example of a truly sad human being, has been used extremely successfully as a tool of indoctrination. It is a brutal exhibition of dog-eat-dog, competition, lies and deceit, until only one survives. Teaching our youth all the wrong morals – basically everything that flies in the face of being human and the UBUNTU principles of unity consciousness.

NEW TECHNOLOGY

The great distraction - simply means something old that has been repackaged and covered in new shiny metal. The new car models that are released every year are the best example of the obsession by humanity to fall for this "new shiny metal" trick over and over again, keeping us more enslaved to the banksters. It is a clever distraction to waste our time and waste our lives away on meaningless activities to prevent us from contemplating our own being and consciousness. Technology is literally a trinket designed to keep us looking outward, distracting us while our inner energy is harnessed and hijacked by sinister forces that most of us will not believe in. The truly highly advanced technology used by the industrial military complex, will never be released to the people.

INVESTMENT

Fuelled by the fear factor, we are told that if we do not invest during our prime years, we will live in poverty when we get older. We will not be able to retire and go fishing. Investment is also driven by our desire to sit on a beach somewhere because our investments have allowed us to not have to do anything and simply receive money for nothing. This is what drives the capitalist machine. An ideal world where some people sit on their asses while others run around serving them. In a society that functions without money, investing makes no sense at all. Invest what? Where? Why? Once we consider these factors, it becomes obvious that this is another clever construct of capitalism and only applies to a society driven by money. Eternal bliss and happiness cannot be attained by investing. Eternal bliss is within us – now all we have to do is reach for it.

RETIREMENT

Retire from what? Retirement suggests that you are doing something you don't really want to do and at some stage you want to give it up and do something else, like following your passion and hobbies. But to achieve this you have to have money saved or invested otherwise you cannot retire and you will have to carry on slaving away till you die. If you live your life doing what your passion is, using your god-given talents while enhancing the lives of all the people in your community, what are you going to retire from? Life itself? In UBUNTU communities people do not retire, it makes no sense. People will always want to do something and the aged are those with wisdom and experience. They are the ones that will guide and lead the rest of the community with their wisdom. Older people have skills that do not necessarily require physical activity. People will always want to continue to create or do what gives them pleasure, while it enhances the lives of others. Those that are too old and fragile to do anything will automatically be looked after by the community caretakers – those who love to take care of others, which is not always financially viable in a capitalist society.

DREAM COME TRUE

Another one of those classic traps that keeps the "hope" and the "dream" alive. If we keep the dream alive means that we are just dreaming and not really living. Most "dreams-come-true" are associated with attaining, obtaining, getting, receiving, achieving, things that have a monetary value that is not affordable to those who dream of it. This feeds into the frenzy of TV competitions, lottery, gambling, and many other activities to win money, so that we can reward ourselves for being such good slaves. Why should we have to look forward to a dream come true if we can live in a world where everything is possible – because we all make it possible. In UBUNTU communities everything is available, possible, doable, achievable... because the people decide what they will do, or build, or create – not the politicians and slave masters who control the money.

STREET VENDORS

Imagine that all the street vendors who try to stay alive by selling stuff on the streets and at the traffic lights, were actually doing something positive for the community, as opposed to desperately trying to sell stuff that people don't really need or want. Imagine how much stuff we would have if these people were using their talents towards creating abundance for their community instead of peddling pieces of paper controlled by the banksters. Each one of these street vendors is a beautiful human being with a soul that yearns for freedom and justice. Each one has special talents and skills that they should be using, enriching their lives and those of others, instead of wasting their lives just to survive, and often being harassed by the police that enforce unjust laws of the corporate government and banking elite. This applies to shopkeepers and other traders. Many of these who love this kind of interaction will most likely become the providers of goods in the UBUNTU communities. A far more noble way of using their talents.

EARNING & EARNINGS
Suggests that human beings have no value and that we have to do something more than simply using our natural talents and skills. It implies that we have to work hard to earn money and respect, and do things that are alien to human nature to somehow comply with the requirements of the self appointed authorities. In the corporate world it refers to the sweat and blood exerted by millions of people to create "earnings" for the owners of the corporation or the government. The slaves create the earnings, but gain no benefits. The corporation keeps the slaves under absolute control and ensures that they continue to create earnings or fall foul of the system in which case they are punished. Each one of us is infinitely special, with inalienable rights to live in peace wherever we want. We did not agree to generate "earnings" at birth. All we have to do is to be alive and continue to create by using our god-given talents or our skills that we acquire through the application of our own human passion. Everything we create with our passion, benefits everyone around us in ways that we do not even realise. By simply being born as living breathing human beings into this world, we have "earned" the right to a life of bliss and abundance by giving expression to the most basic aspect of human nature – to create. Earnings are alien to human nature.

PRIVATE SECTOR
We marvel at the financial and economic reporters on TV as they seamlessly spew forth the activities from the various stock markets of the world. To the ignorant masses they seem like highly intelligent people who have taken years to master the complex world of finance and how it helps humanity to prosper and the world to go around. Little do the ignorant masses know, that the poor reporters have no idea what they are actually saying or how it works – because if they

did their conscience would prevent them from doing so. It becomes especially gripping when these ignorant reporters start talking about the "private sector" – as some kind of saviour of humanity. What is the private sector? These are the private multinational corporations that have taken control of our planet and are calling the shots to our governments. The private sector has taken ownership of all our natural wealth and resources – our industry, mining, agriculture, water, and especially banking – the creation of money and the control of the global media so that they can continue brainwashing the masses with meaningless economic reports while they secretly manipulate it from behind closed doors. This illusive private sector, that can also be called the "secret " sector, that so many people look up to with a sick sense of awe, has hijacked everything that gives them absolute control over living breathing human beings. The private sector needs to be dismantled with immediate effect to free the people from exploitation and slavery on every level of existence.

As you read through the list of words and expressions below, please think about each one's place in our capitalistic society and then try to imagine how it will change in a Contributionist world – will it have any effect in our lives, or will it vanish from our reality? This is a very exciting exercise as we start to lose the stranglehold of fear and allow ourselves to recognise the utopia that awaits us.

THIRD WORLD; HOPE; FINANCIAL REPORTS; BANKING; TRADING; TRADERS; BEGGARS; SHOPKEEPERS; AWARD CEREMONIES; BEAUTY CONTESTS; COMPETITIONS; GAME SHOWS; HUMAN NATURE; INDUSTRY; MANUFACTURING; ANNUAL GROWTH; ECONOMIC SLOWDOWN; FINANCE; FACTORIES; PRODUCTION LINES; CARS; FOREIGN INVESTMENT; FOREIGN SHAREHOLDING; OWNERSHIP; STATISTICS; WORLD ECONOMIC FORUM; SHELTER; HEALTH; MEDICINE; PHARMACEUTICS; LAW; POLICING; POLICE FORCE; MILITARY; ARMY; CHILDREN; WARFARE; CRIME; TALENT; AMBITION; SHOPPING; MALLS; SPORTS; HOLIDAYS; RESTAURANTS; RESORTS; CLASSIFIED DOCUMENTS; SECRETS; POLITICS; CAMPAIGNS; PROMISES; TAXES; TAX INCREASE; UNEMPLOYMENT; RISK; FRENCH TERRITORY; BRITISH COLONY; INCOME; DISPOSABLE INCOME; MATCH FIXING; BONDS; GOVERNMENT BONDS;...

Now pick up the newspaper and read the headlines – think about each one as critically as you can, and imagine how it will change in a world without money. I am confident that it will bring a smile to your face. If not the first time you try it, eventually it will, as you begin to realise how poisoned our minds have become and how indoctrinated we are by the daily news thinking that it is actually news of some kind of benefit to our lives. Then, once you have achieved this momentary realisation, put the paper down and never buy or read another newspaper again. You will feel liberated beyond belief.

FREQUENTLY ASKED QUESTIONS AND PERCEPTIONS ABOUT CONTRIBUTIONISM

These questions come up all the time like clockwork. Since 2005, I have answered these and other questions to people all over the world, thousands of times. It just shows us that we have been equally conditioned to think the same way. The education system has served the slave masters well.

It seems that fear is the main underlying motivator to defend the slave system we are in. This fear has been so firmly instilled in most of us that it leaves the majority of humanity paralysed in suspended fear – fear of stepping out of line – fear of ridicule – fear of stepping out of the box and questioning our reality. The answers to these questions are really simple and so obvious that once you get it, you will smile in amazement at how poisoned our minds have become with capitalism and consumerism and hording stuff all our lives until the day we kick the bucket.

I have to repeat this and stress it again. The system of Contributionism is so simple that we cannot mess it up. It follows the natural order of things and it is a self-correcting system. As long as we stick to the five point mantra, the answers present themselves on a platter – as long as we serve the greater good of the community above our own selfish needs.

I would like you to read these questions and think about each one for a while. Try to figure out the answers for yourself. This is the best way to get into the zone and think outside the box, by going against everything we have been conditioned to believe.

Before you look up the answers, ask yourself the following questions where applicable and see if it points you in the right direction:

- How will this situation change in a moneyless society?
- Will this benefit me only or the entire community?
- Why is this the current situation?
- Why do I want it?
- Why is this happening?
- Do I really need it?
- If everyone did this, would anyone be harmed?

Repeat the FIVE POINT MANTRA to get to the answers.
1) NO Money
2) NO Barter
3) NO Trading
4) No value attached to anything greater than anything else – because all our efforts and contributions are equally valuable.
5) Everyone contributes their natural talents or acquired skills for the greater benefit of all in their community. And therefore everything is available to everyone at all times.

It took me a long time (many years) to figure this out, shedding the deeply entrenched capitalistic conditioning to do so. I had to constantly remind myself that there is no need for hoarding; fear of loss or theft; or any of the problems facing society today. There is no more thinking about "what's in it for me", because everything is in it for 'me'. No more chasing money but simply contributing my labour of love.

But our collective consciousness has shifted a great deal since 2005 and I have seen people get the answers within minutes – answers that originally took me weeks, months, and sometimes even years to figure out.

The answers illustrate how easily we can move from the greed-driven, hoarding mentality of service to self, to a sharing mentality of service to others and our community. By serving others, we serve ourselves. There is no greater honour and satisfaction than giving – and in giving, the universe rewards us in abundance.

MOST FREQUENTLY ASKED QUESTIONS:

1) If everything is for free, can I just sit on my ass and do nothing and get people to bring me stuff – anything I want?

Answer: No – the system is called Contributionism, where everyone contributes a few hours per day of their own skills to the community. You have many skills and various passions that you have developed throughout your life. Now you can put them to productive use. The reason why everything is available to everyone all the time is because of this very simple principle. After you contribute 3 hours per day, during which you perform your "labour of love", you will still have 18 hours to sit on your ass and do nothing. In an UBUNTU community this will be highly unlikely, because you will be pursuing many other hobbies or passions – all for free, with access to all the tools you need to pursue such hobbies – just because you have chosen to stay in this community and contribute your labour of love for the benefit of everyone. If you do not contribute however, the Council of Elders will most likely ask you to leave the community. In that case you have the choice to live on your own in an isolated area – but then if you sit on your ass and do nothing – the inevitable outcome of doing nothing is death. So no matter how you see it – you will be doing something to stay alive. Just like people who beg on the streets – they had to go to the trouble of dressing and finding a hat, and finding a mug, and finding transport to the place where they plan to beg. They are not doing "nothing", they are doing something – they are begging. It is just not a very productive or dignified way to spend your day.

2) Who is going to shovel the crap?

Answer: The good news about human passion and the variety of things that interest people is, that for every budding Michelangelo or Leonardo da Vinci, there are a thousand crazy young scientists who are equally passionate about chemistry and solving the sewage situation. They know how to turn raw sewage in to compost, clean water, energy and other things we have not discovered yet because it is not financially viable. Once we let these great minds loose and allow them to play in their laboratories they will deliver many great discoveries. I mentioned EM (Effective Microorganisms) earlier, which is an example of a natural purification method that can solve many urgent problems within days. So, by the time the sewage leaves our homes, it will be converted in to many beneficial things that will beautify our gardens and improve our lives, so that nobody will have to shovel the crap. From a different perspective, shovelling the crap is our way of highlighting the hierarchy of a capitalistic society. The lower paid people are made to do the jobs that the snobs in ivory towers shy away from, like cleaning toilets, sweeping the streets, removing garbage. They pay others to do that because they have money, which is merely an expression of our ego and those who do such jobs are looked down upon by those who earn more money. In UBUNTU communities everyone is equal and there is no hierarchy created by money. Everyone in the community is required to do community work. This will include sweeping the streets and keeping public places clean among many other activities. No one will be looked down upon – it is the strength of the UBUNTU community, and not the weak link in society, which it has become today. Everyone chooses their own Labour of Love to contribute for 3 hours per day for five days of the week – and an additional 3 hours per week in any of the community projects. The rest of the time people can do what they want – following their many other passions and giving expression to their creativity. Because many people have many passions, and in a free society, people will develop many new skills and passions that they will participate in.

3) If everything is FREE, I want 10 mansions and 50 Ferraris.

Answer: There is no land ownership in UBUNTU communities. Everyone has a beautiful home of their own to live in, designed and built for them for free, by the best architects and builders, based on the size of their family or needs. Everyone is allocated land by the community and Council of Elders, based on what they do for the community. Farmers will have as much land as they need to produce whatever it is they are producing in sufficient quantity for their community. Herb farmers will use much less land than maize farmers, and so on. Material possessions do not exist because everything is available to everyone all the time. Big mansions and expensive cars like Ferraris are a side-effect of capitalism, only afforded by those with money, mostly to show off their material wealth that separates them from those who cannot afford it. They are status symbols, mere expressions of ego more than anything else, causing separation and creating envy with the rest of the problems we are trying to eradicate from our lives. Even if you had 50 Ferraris, nobody will be impressed because they can also have 50 Ferraris if they wanted to. They will have no value at all, as they have today. All they will do is take up space and collect dust. You will not be popular with your community for such behaviour. Keep in mind that transport and travel is free in UBUNTU communities. There will be new energy and amazing new discoveries in the transport, travel and automotive sector. Cars will probably no longer be made for the same reasons they are made today because they will be seen as old and inefficient. Cars will also not be allowed by the community because they pollute our environment, unless they run on new energy sources. For that reason we may see an explosion of car enthusiasts, who continue to build old cars for sentimental reasons in car clubs the way we do today. So you will have your 50 Ferraris, but they will most likely be part of the local car club, where they will belong to everyone, and everyone will have the right to drive them or join the club, where they can also build collector's cars. Such clubs will most likely spring up around many sectors that belonged in the past for nostalgic reasons. Where people appreciate the design, they love the shape of the car and recognise the intrinsic artistry of the car – not the price tag. Making cars will become an art form – not a necessity for transport. The community and Council of Elders will play a key role in this – allowing the minority principle to apply – cooperation instead of competition – to provide for the needs of all minorities as long as it does not infringe on the rights of the others or the community as a whole. In other words, everything is possible.

4) Why should I give up all the things I have worked for so hard all my life?

Answer: You will not have to give up anything, in fact you will gain everything you ever dreamed of. We gather and collect stuff all our lives. We hoard things in garages, attics and basements just in case we may need it at some time in our lives, only to throw it all out at a later stage. We decorate our homes with unnecessary furniture and create new spaces that end up looking like shop windows without ever getting used. Much of what you may have accumulated in your life will have a different meaning or value to you in a moneyless society where everything is available to everyone. You will have access to infinitely more things than you can ever imagine at this present moment. You will most likely be relieved that you can finally get rid of all the junk you have been hoarding – knowing that if you need something, you can go get it or simply order it to your exact specifications.

5) Why should I give you something if you have nothing to give me in return?

Answer: This is a response based on "what's in it for me". Remember that *everything is in it for you*. Unlike the current system where you are in it to provide energy for the system. You are the human battery that gives the program the energy to run – as was explained by Morpheus in the movie, *The Matrix*. You will not have to do anything for nothing and neither will anyone else. You will have everything you need all the time. You will choose what you want to do as your Labour of Love, from the many skills that you have developed and do that for your own satisfaction, while it also benefits the whole community. So, while you are contributing your talents and skills for everyone to enjoy and benefit from, so everyone else is allowing you to benefit from their talents and skills without restriction. And so, you will have access to a sea of talents, skills, goods, products and anything else you can conjure up in your mind. Someone somewhere will be able to do it, or make it.

6) Is this not just another form of Communism?

Answer: No – very definitely not. While communism may have started out as a noble idea to benefit the people, it was hijacked by power hungry politicians corrupted by money. Its weakness was the same weakness as every other system we've had – money. This is the critical difference between Contributionism and any other socio-political system we have ever had. Money is not part of the UBUNTU system – therefore people cannot be corrupted, bribed, paid off, or paid to do something unsavoury. In fact, there is actually very little difference between capitalism and communism in the way we have experienced it on Earth. Classic communism is just a shortcut to absolute power – while with capitalism it takes a little longer for people to realise that they are under complete control of their government and other corporations who have bought up everything else. Just like capitalism, communism is still a centralised system that requires a corporate representative called a government.

7) What about human nature – people are inherently lazy.

Answer: This is one of the most misconstrued arguments raised by many. It is impossible for us to make a value judgement on human nature while being trapped in the matrix. We have no idea what human nature is – we don't even know what it means to be human. We are so caught up in a matrix where most of us still deny that we are utterly enslaved by the system. Our perception of humanity is totally skewed by the community we grow up in. Show me a person who will not give their time and energy for something that they truly enjoy. Our values and morals are dictated to us by others with ulterior motives. Our view of the world and humanity around us is dictated by the global media and politicians who promote war and conflict above peace and unity. We are constantly told that people are inherently lazy. We are told that unless we work hard we will never amount to anything. We live with constant stress on so many levels, it is a miracle we can function at all. Most of us do work that we hate, but we have to do it just to survive. Deep down people know that they are abused, but they don't know what to do about it. Laziness is a consequence of capitalism – it is not part of human nature. Many people believe that no matter how hard they try, they will never get out of the ghetto. People are lazy because they feel defeated. It is a kind of rebellion against the invisible forces that control them. They sit around doing nothing because all their lives they have been told that they are useless and they will never amount to anything. Not everyone has the winning streak or drive to get to the top. Those are indoctrinations of capitalism that have confused us all. Maybe the so-called lazy people know instinctively that only a rat can win the rat race, and they choose not to be part of that race. Those who say that human nature is to be lazy and confrontational have become clones of the capitalist indoctrination and have forgotten what it is to be human. People are born with natural talents, gifts and passion for different things. Those talents are destroyed throughout our childhood by the education system and society at large. Eventually people forget their dreams and passions and simply take on any job just to survive. Human nature is completely contrary to these characteristics. We are all part of the great creation – our principal nature is to create, to be creative, to give expression to our God-given talents.

8) Does this mean that we are going back to the dark ages and living in caves?

Answer: If you don't know the answer to this question it means that you have not been paying attention. Be rational – how can we be going back to the dark ages when we have freed up our scientists and inventors to create free energy and new technology so advanced that we cannot begin to contemplate it in a money driven society. There is more than enough land for all the people of the world. All hurdles to progress will be lifted. We are not going back to the dark ages, we are going to the stars. Our knowledge and technology will outshine everything we have seen on Star Trek or any other sci-fi movie. Yet we will be firmly placed on terra firma, our beautiful planet Earth – living in harmony with nature – with all our needs provided for – because we understand so much more and realise that we do not need flashy cars and diamonds to impress our neighbours.

9) Is this not a free-for all and a lawless society where everyone can do what they want?

Answer: No – In the past our laws have been enforced on the people by the governments. This will no longer be the case. All existing laws will be removed because they have been created over thousands of years of control to protect the system and those who control the money. New laws and guidelines will be written by the people, for the people, based on the basic foundation of common law. Do not harm, do not steal, do not cheat. In addition to this, every community will develop its own new set of laws based on the needs of those in each community. In a society where everything is available to everyone all the time; where people follow their passion; give expression to their God-given talents without restriction; where money does not hinder progress of any kind and everyone knows everyone else, there will be very little need to enforce any draconian laws. It is a real challenge to imagine such freedom and peaceful society while still trapped in this one.

10) Who is going to make the rules?

Answer: The laws and rules will be written by the people for the people. Extreme freedom may require extreme measures to deal with those who abuse such freedom. It will be up to the will of the people, through the Council of Elders, in each community, to determine how acts of violence, crime, or other, will be dealt with. This is a living lawful society that will adapt its laws on a daily basis, if need be, to provide for the needs of the people. Remember that everyone is free to live in any community they choose, benefiting from its abundance. Those who abuse the benefits and freedoms will probably be asked to leave the community. Their actions will not be tolerated. Another way to think of it is that the rules start with you; then move out to your family; then move out to your neighbourhood, then move out to your community. Each community connects with other communities and will conduct itself in line with other communities, not to harm, but rather be beneficial to other communities. As in some sports, rules are designed for safety and general rules are applied. But the rules are considered for each situation even if the rule is technically broken. The problem we face when we stick hard and fast to rules is that we end up stagnating society (or a simple sport) and thus discretion must be applied to each situation based on the needs of society and the benefit to the people.

11) What about progress and advancement and technology – does this mean we are going to regress and go backwards?

Answer: No – most certainly not. We are going to the stars with unimaginable technology because our scientists have no restriction on their inventions. There are no secret government projects; no suppression of information and no need to keep hiding things from the people.

12) If there is no money, how are we going to buy things?

Answer: Nobody is going to have to buy things. Everything is available to everyone if they are a contributing member of the community. You can live in any community of your choice. Nobody is forced to do anything – everyone chooses their Labour of Love as their contribution to the community and in return you will have access to everything you need or want. This allows for the free sharing of everything, especially information. The bakers bake; engineers engineer; farmers farm; the drivers drive; shoemakers make shoes; artist make art, surfers teach surfing, etc. Everything is available to everyone in the community to use every day. If something is not available, the community will decide to either start producing it or get it from another town that manufactures such an item. No need to buy food for the month and budget ahead of time, or worry about the petrol price going up every month. Let me demonstrate the sharing of information with this example. I am a shoemaker and I design a pair of running shoes for one of the athletes in my town. I use the latest materials that are all available to me from those who make the materials. The shoes turn out so well that they allow the athlete to break the 400 metre world record. Suddenly every other runner also wants a pair of my special shoes. I get a call on the free Skype internet communication system from a sports coach in Paris, who had a request from his athlete for my running shoes. He gives me the name of his shoemaker and within minutes I upload the specifications for the shoe design on the internet so that it is available for everyone. My running shoes become the most used design in sports shoes in 100 years and everyone knows that I designed them. This was my gift to the people, my contribution to the world. Not my brand that only a few can afford or a patent that awaits a trade mark so that nobody else may make it while I make billions of dollars.

13) Why would I want to slave away all day for free?

Answer: You are confusing your life of slavery today where many people have to have more than one job just be able to survive, with a utopian life of bliss that we will all experience in UBUNTU Contributionist communities. Nobody will ever slave away again. Everybody does what they choose to do for their community, because they love doing it and they are good at it. Everyone follows their passion and uses their God-given talents as we were meant to. There are no jobs or careers and corporations – everyone has a Labour of Love (LOL) that they contribute to their community. The expression 'workaholic' will take on a very different meaning. You don't have to slave away any more chasing money for 12 hours a day, working in disgusting factories for some corporation exploiting you for its own profit. Everyone will only have to do their LOL for 3 hours per day, after which you have another 18 hours to do what you want – without restriction or any cost to you. Follow your hobbies, go fishing, horse riding, grow seedlings, paint or sculpt, or build a Ferrari kit-car. Nobody will ever have to slave away again. Slavery is a side-effect of capitalism. Because we will no longer chase money, all our efforts contribute to providing abundance on all levels. That is why we all only need to contribute 3 hours per day with our LOL. Otherwise there would be too much stuff. Too many bridges, too many shoes, too much crockery, too many candles and too much food that goes rotten. Nobody will ever have to feel enslaved again. The number of hours we will have to contribute daily is just a guideline and will most likely change, based on the needs of the community. It may only be a few hours per week, because there will be too much stuff available for everyone.

14) Who is going to provide the food?

Answer: The farmers grow the food, the cheese makers make cheese, the bakers bake and so on. Then there is a whole network of people doing all kinds of things along the supply chain to ensure that we get the food packed in biodegradable containers; delivered with green transport; displayed in food markets and other places that we probably cannot predict right now. There will be many people involved in the provision of food, constantly creating new ideas and trying new things that are not financially viable today. Farmers' markets and fresh food markets will probably be the most common place to get food – supplied fresh every day. Community dining halls and a myriad of restaurants run by specialist cooks and chefs will provide the community with the most delicious variety of food imaginable – at no cost to anyone. Remember, the chefs have been appointed by the Council of Elders, on behalf of the people, because of their ability to cook scrumptious food – not because they want to make money. Nobody will have to cook for themselves, unless they choose to do so, and because they love cooking. Food will be available to everyone in the community all the time, because they are accepted and respected by their community for what they contribute for the benefit of the entire community. Acceptance and respect by your community is the highest form of reward we can ever receive. No amount of money will ever match that.

15) What will happen with education?

Answer: We will have a completely fresh approach to education which has been outlined in detail under the education section. Moving away from the classroom and exam structure to a more hands-on practical way of learning true skills for life. In UBUNTU communities the children are cared for by the entire community as much as they are cared for by their biological parents. They face no danger and have freedom to roam, to play and to explore. Our day-care and learning centres will be the incubators for open minds of the future, laying the foundation of true knowledge, rather than regurgitating information from a book during an exam. Children will learn the basic life skills from the earliest age, allowing them to express their natural talents and creativity, developing their skills in as many areas as they want, without restriction. They will learn from master teachers that have been appointed by the community for their knowledge, skills and ability. The children themselves will also learn by teaching each other, just like they have been doing in martial arts schools for thousands of years. People with the highest skills who are respected to such an extent that the community will allow them to teach the children to teach themselves. To be appointed a master teacher will be one of the highest levels of honour and respect bestowed on any member of the community. Only a master teacher will be able to appoint a student under their guidance as a new master teacher. Education will start with short interactive games and workshops for young children, learning basic things about life and mother Earth, like water, soil, planting seeds, growing food, milking cows, making cheese and so on. These short workshops will increase in length as they get older and expand into more diverse areas where they learn every kind of skill imaginable. By the time children are 14 to 16 years old, the workshops will become internships of several months honing their skills in their chosen subjects. By this age every child will have a very good idea of what their natural talents are, what their passion is and what they want to do for the next phase of their life, as their contribution to the community. Their Labour of Love. Our education system will not create semi-literate young people with a piece of paper, called a certificate in their hand from some school or college, looking for a job in some office or factory. By the time a child is 16 years old, they will know how to plough the lands, grow food, make cheese, bake bread, build bridges, design tall towers, create free energy, build rockets, purify water, and spin cotton into beautiful fabrics – they would have done thousands of things hands-on and they will know more than all the professors in the world today combined. Every young adult will be a respected member of their community for what they are going to contribute with their new skills and knowledge. Anyone can decide to learn a new skill at any stage. This will be seen as part of their community service because while they are learning new skills, they will be providing valuable services in some aspect of their training. The entire education system is totally integrated into the needs of the community, creating well balanced, open minded, young adults who contribute greatly to the entire community.

16) How are we going to get electricity?

Answer: It should be noted that as much as 60% of all energy is lost in transportation from the power plant to the household. It is therefore obvious that all energy generation should be done locally by every community. They can use the wiring from the existing energy grid to provide electricity for their own town by using whatever method they can, and remain in control of their own supply. This will vary based on the location. Coastal towns may have the ocean and wind while others may have the sun, rivers and geothermal energy possibilities. We have to use whatever means we can while we look for free energy. Hydroelectricity where there is flowing water, solar, wind, gas, geothermal, wave motion and others. Our scientists and engineers will be constantly working on developing and delivering new free forms of energy – which we know already exist, but remain suppressed. It will not take long for such free energy devices to be designed as soon as the money trap has been removed. This will affect everything in our lives – how we travel, cars, trains, planes, how we build our homes, industry, manufacturing, and more. New and free energy will give rise to many new aspects of our lives that we cannot imagine while trapped in an unsustainable energy grid that is controlled by coal, oil and greed.

17) Is this not a case of taking from the rich and giving to the poor?

Answer: No – there are no rich, and there are no poor, in the Contributionism system, because there is no money to create such class separation that we have been forced into. Everyone has everything they need all the time. There is nothing that I have which you can't have. People will have what they want and need based on their taste and preference. That is why the concept of stealing does not exist – because why would I want to steal something from you if I can just get it from those who supply it to everyone? In the style, shape or colour that I want! And... if for some reason somebody does take something from someone else, in an open community where everyone knows everyone else, it will be very easy to determine who did it. The shame experienced by the perpetrator will be too much to deal with in most cases, knowing they could have obtained it from the suppliers in the first place.

18) Why don't we rather focus on improving the economy and alleviate poverty so that everyone has a job and access to sufficient food and other things?

Answer: Economy is a philosophy created under capitalism. It suggests that there is scarcity of stuff – that we have to economise and be economic in things we do. It makes some things more valuable than others and drives financial markets. Economy is a word that will not exist in UBUNTU communities. There can be no poverty because there is no money. Everyone has everything they need, everyone has a beautiful home of their own design, and everyone does what they are passionate about and good at. This makes people wake up with a smile on their face, looking forward to the day – as opposed to being grumpy while looking for every excuse not to have to go to a lousy job that they hate. A "job" is just a fancy word for doing something for money – which means slavery. We will not have to worry about improving the "economy" or "alleviating poverty" or providing food. It is all well provided for by the united community that provides abundance to all.

19) How are we going to import stuff?

Answer: We will be designing and producing a whole new range of products for our society because money is no hurdle to any kind of production. The rest of the world that still functions on capitalism, where people have to buy stuff and cannot afford things, will have very little to offer our society. As long as we have all the materials necessary, we can produce and manufacture everything ourselves, without importing inferior products from factories that make things so that they break after a few months, forcing people buy more. Our ability to design and manufacture anything will only be limited by our imagination. Even if we do not have some rare earth material, our scientists will develop an alternative material that will be infinitely more practical and eco-friendly, biodegradable and long lasting. So why on earth would we want to import anything from other mostly capitalistic countries?

20) Does this not mean a degradation of our lifestyle?

Answer: No – it means completely the opposite. It means we have everything we need or want to live a happy and fulfilled life, following our passion without restriction, creating art and participating in cultural events as we please. How could the reduction of stress and crime possibly be a degradation of our lifestyle?

21) If everything is for free, can I go to your house and take whatever I want?

Answer: No – why would you want to go to my house and take from me, when you can get whatever you want from the market, or manufacturers of the products, just as I did. This is why crime and theft of this nature will virtually disappear overnight. In a community where everyone knows everyone, knows where they live and what they do, it would be very silly to take something from someone because everyone will know about your deed immediately. Such activity will be dealt with under the laws of the community, guided by the Council of Elders. People who continuously disrupt the peace in their town will most likely be asked to leave. No other community will be too eager to accept them if they are disruptive. Why would you willingly want to disrupt the peace in your community if you have everything you need and people love you and respect you for who you are and what you do for the community? The golden question that should also be answered is: "what for?" If you can answer this to the satisfaction of the Council of Elders and/or the resident, then so be it. Maybe the resident who you took the item from will give it to you, because you need it more. But then, all you have to do is ask him.

22) What happens to the laws and police and security forces?

Answer: In UBUNTU communities there will be very little need for any kind of force. Therefore the police force, defence force and other such instruments of capitalist government corporations will dissolve and morph into valuable support groups for the community. Providing support through a variety of emergency services, in case of fire, flood, earthquake, tornados, hurricanes and other unpredictable disasters, providing critical skills in times of need to their community. The peace officers will serve the people of the community as opposed to imposing draconian laws of the government on its own people. They will have access to the most advanced tools, technology and weaponry to be able to defend the community against any unexpected provocation by outsiders. But the free sharing of technology and weaponry will prevent unnecessary provocation between communities since they know that everyone has unlimited scientific capability to defend themselves and inflict severe damage on the aggressor in the process. The absence of money in our society will be like giving warmongers a "chill pill".

23) What about those whose education and skills are higher than those of others... is their time not more valuable?

Answer: Education will change completely. People will not choose careers because they can make lots of money from it – they will follow their natural talents and hone their skills. Everyone will have access to education and training at any time to master their talents and skills. People do not get paid for their skills, they contribute them to the community for everyone to benefit from their skills and talents. In return the community honours and respects them for their contributions. There are as many diverse talents and skills as there are people, but there is no hierarchy of talents in UBUNTU communities because everyone's contribution is seen to be equally valuable as everyone else's. That is what makes the system function so smoothly and correct itself when unexpected hiccups occur. It's a self-correcting system that cannot be abused or corrupted by greed.

CONCLUSION – SHARE YOUR KNOWLEDGE WITH EVERYONE

Exponential growth is an incredible thing. When a little seed is planted we cannot imagine how many fruits and seeds it will generate in its lifetime. This is the amazing and unpredictable abundance of nature. So, now that we know what we know, we have to distribute the seeds of knowledge and information as far as we can – every single one of us. We cannot remain silent spectators in the spectacular conscious explosion taking the planet by storm. Let us participate and share our knowledge with everyone, planting the seeds of consciousness everywhere we go.

You are not alone. There are millions of people just like you, many of whom are shy and afraid of speaking out about what they know, but many are losing their fear and making themselves heard, growing stronger in confidence every day. The more they speak their truth, the more they lose their fear and the more people want to listen to them. Because deep inside each and every one of us, we all resonate with the highest truth, the universal resonance of unity consciousness from the divine creation of all. Very soon the channels of consciousness that sprout from every seed, expanding in all directions, will start to connect with others, creating a global web of consciousness that cannot be destroyed. If one out of every ten people you talk to, tell another ten people, we will manifest our utopia in no time at all.

It is now up to us to create the future we want for ourselves and all future generations. Thoughts are powerful tools – use them wisely and productively. Visualise the utopia that we all want and deserve as living breathing human beings of infinite soul. Let us manifest a NEW WORLD in our lifetime.

1) Do not be afraid.
2) Lose your fear – it has no place in an infinite universe of LOVE.
3) Start sharing your knowledge with everyone.
4) Know that you are not alone – millions like you are learning and sharing.
5) Take collective control of your community.
6) Use your collective financial strength to direct the management of your community.
7) Initiate as many community projects as possible to benefit the entire community.

8) Get your community to become self sustained in the main areas necessary to survive. Water, food, energy , housing, health, education, arts, culture, etc.

9) Use the income from these projects to create more projects that will benefit your specific community.

10) Create an interim local currency for your community to protect yourselves from exploitation by outsiders.

11) Soon, your success will spill over into all surrounding towns, because they will not be able to compete with the produce and services created by your community.

12) You will create the domino effect to start a global UBUNTU explosion.

WELCOME TO OUR BEAUTIFUL UTOPIAN WORLD OF CONSCIOUSLY EVOLVED PEOPLE – LIVING IN UNITY AND HARMONY WITH OUR PLANET AND ALL OF LIFE.

ONLY OUT OF UNITY CAN WE ATTAIN INFINITE DIVERSITY – SO BE IT.

The New Freedom Charter

Adopted by the people at the launch of the UBUNTU CONTRIBUTION SYSTEM, Waterval Boven, Mpumalanga, South Africa, on the 3rd November 2010.

"Freedom is not our right - it is our gift from the divine creator. No one has the right to take it away or enslave us in any way or manner."
Michael Tellinger 3 November 2010

- The government has betrayed the dreams of every South African, past and present, including NELSON MANDELA and other elders of integrity, who lived and died for the freedom of their people
- The government has desecrated the Freedom Charter and all our Human Rights
- They have maliciously enslaved every one of us to their corporate government and the global banking elite
- Today our people are more enslaved than ever before
- The New Freedom Charter serves the needs of the people and their inalienable Human Rights
- This is a living document that will continue to change with the times and the needs of the people, not the needs of government
- Inform yourself and learn the truth, not the propaganda
- Make it your pledge to share your knowledge with everyone you know
- This is our pledge and these are your rights

We, the People of South Africa, declare for all in our country and the world to know that:

South Africa and the land belong to all who live in it;

The government and large multinational corporations have stolen the country and our land from its people;

The people need to take it back;

Our government has been turned into an unlawful corporation with undefined shareholders, without the knowledge of the people;

No government has the right to rule the people and control their land unless it has been appointed by the people lawfully, not under false pretences or deceptions of any kind;

The government has enslaved the people to a private corporation called the REPUBLIC OF SOUTH AFRICA;

This corporation has used its courts and its judges to enforce the laws of the corporation on the people of South Africa;

The people have been turned into property and slaves in servitude to the corporation unwittingly;

The corporation called REPUBLIC OF SOUTH AFRICA has used human beings, who serve in the police and other security enforcement agencies, against their fellow human beings, not knowing that they are upholding the rights of a corporation against their own brothers, sisters, mothers and fathers, desecrating all their Human Rights and Common Law in the process;

Our Human Rights have been desecrated by the Constitution, which is not a constitution of the people but a constitution to uphold the rights of the corporation called the REPUBLIC OF SOUTH AFRICA;

The people of the land called South Africa have appointed the government to serve the people of South Africa and implement the will of the people at all time;

The people retain the right to replace the government at any time by peaceful means and public referendum, if they feel that their needs are not being taken care of;

No government, political party, corporation or individual can claim ownership of the people, the land or any part thereof;

And therefore, we, the people of South Africa, all free and equal, countrymen and brothers adopt this New Freedom Charter of the year 2010;

And we pledge ourselves to strive together, sparing neither strength nor courage, until our inalienable rights and common law have been restored to the people and our land.

The People Shall Govern!

New laws and new governing structures will be created based on the will of the people on a local and national level;

The reintroduction of African tribal structures combined with a Council of Elders will be implemented to manage and advise communities;

These new tribal councils will adopt the fundamental principles of UBUNTU Contributionism to enhance their ability to guide and advise the people;

Every man and woman shall have the right to stand as a candidate for all such councils that represent their communities and uphold the laws;

All people shall be entitled to take part in the administration of the country, town or community in accordance with the newly developed laws by the people;

Transparency will be upheld at all levels of every council, allowing everyone, at all times access to all and any information;

All decisions made will be publicised through every medium possible, to the entire community, and or country, wherever its influence falls, to ensure that everyone is aware of the decisions made on a daily basis;

The people of every community or country have the right to remove any councillor who proves to be inefficient or undesirable in the eyes of the people;

The rights of the people shall be the same, regardless of race, colour or gender;

All People and National Groups Have Equal Rights!

The principle of UNITY will be the foundation of all communities and the national governing body;

All people shall have equal right to use their own languages, and to develop their own culture and customs as long as it does not infringe on the customs of others;

The diversity and beauty of our cultures and languages will be promoted and celebrated as widely as possible;

All national groups shall be protected by law against insults to their race and national pride;

There shall be no hierarchy or levels of superiority in any aspects of society, every person's contribution will be valued as equally important as any other;

All discriminatory laws and practices shall be set aside.

The use of money and wealth as tools of separation, segregation and discrimination will be abolished;

The People Shall Share in the Country's Wealth!

The national wealth of our country, the heritage of South Africans, shall be restored to the people and new applicable laws will be created to benefit and protect the people on all fronts;

All mineral wealth above or beneath the ground will be controlled by the people and used for the benefit of all people and all communities – it will not be allowed to be monopolised by individuals, corporations or any ruling body;

All international trade shall be adapted by the people to assist the wellbeing of all the people;

All industry and manufacturing shall be supported and adapted in all possible ways to deliver abundance of all things to all people;

Tourism will be developed to include and benefit people from all walks of life to maximise the income potential to everyone in our country in our transition to UBUNTU – all national parks and other such areas will be upgraded to the best standards to attract large numbers of tourists from all over the world; this will provide thousands of opportunities for our people;

All people shall have equal rights to choose any trade, craft or professions they wish to participate in and all training and education to attain their profession will be free;

The Banking and financial system and the control of the printing of money will be eradicated until there is no more need for money in our society whatsoever; the People's Bank will provide all funding in our transitional phase to UBUNTU;

The Land Shall be Shared Among Those Who Work It!

Farmers who feed the people are the heroes of the land and will be given land, tools, seeds, implements and all assistance necessary to maximise the production of their crops and produce;

Land usage shall be adapted to benefit all the people, and made available to those who work it, to banish famine and hunger;

Since the land belongs to all the people, land ownership will be abolished and replaced by new land usage laws of the new society, which will benefit all the people, especially those who provide food;

Since money will no longer be part of the system, no land will be sold or owned by individuals, or corporations, or in any other way possible;

Existing farmers will be required to use their land for the benefit of the community, or teach other new farmers to farm the vacant land to help feed the people;

Everyone who contributes towards the community will be given as much land as is required to perform their task;

The people in each community will plan and implement the reconstruction of their community, development of public parks and recreational areas for the greatest benefit of the community;

Every community will have the right to control a specified area around its boundaries for the production of crops and other farming necessities;

These boundaries will be specified by the new legal structures to be introduced under the equal rights of Contributionism and based on the population in the community;

Each community will be encouraged to become self reliant and self-sustainable in everything they produce, and encouraged to produce three times their own needs, to help other communities in times of need;

Food will be distributed nationally between communities and to those communities that are unable to provide for themselves, and all food and other farming or agricultural produce will be available to the people for free;

All people shall have the right to settle in any community they choose and contribute to their community with their skills or talents;

All Shall be Equal Before the Law!

A new legal system of basic Common Law will be implemented as drafted by the people for the nation and the whole country, BUT each community will have the right to add new laws specific to the needs of their own unique community;

Each community will have the right to govern its town and boundaries according to the laws created by the community, as long as their laws do not encroach on the rights of others or clash with the basic Common Laws of the nation;

No-one shall be imprisoned, deported or restricted without a fair trial based on the new legal system implemented by the people under Contributionism;

The courts shall be representative of all the people;

Imprisonment shall be only for serious crimes against the people, determined by the people, guided by the Council of Elders, and shall aim at re-education, not vengeance;

The police and army and all other such groups, shall be the helpers and protectors of the people and shall be open to all to participate in on an equal basis and;

The police and the army will be restructured based on the needs of the people and the will of the people; they will be given all the tools and support necessary to perform their tasks as required by the new laws under Contributionism;

The police and the army will be regarded as peace keepers;

All Shall Enjoy Equal Human Rights!

Universal Human Rights are upheld as the supreme rights of all human beings;

No other rights shall be held higher, or imposed as superior to Human Rights;

All humans are equal in all aspects under the UBUNTU CONTRIBUTION SYSTEM;

No one has the right to undermine or erode our inalienable Human Rights in any way;

The Council of Elders will create respective laws, as agreed to by the people of every community, and on a collective national level, how to deal with those that breach the rights of others, especially the Human Rights of others;

There is no hierarchy of any kind, as it is not really possible to discriminate against groups or individuals in an UBUNTU community or a society without the class distinctions that have been created by money;

There Shall be Work and Security! (Transition period)

In a free society under the UBUNTU CONTRIBUTION SYSTEM no one shall work for money but for personal satisfaction and pride in their community – money will be removed from the system;

The expression "work" will rapidly fall away in the new society, and will be replaced with Labour of Love, since all people will follow their passion or God-given talents to enrich their own lives and the lives of others with their contribution to the community;

New laws will be set up by the people regarding the participation and contribution of members in their communities;

During the transition phase to full Contributionism, everyone who is without a job or business of their own, or an income, will be asked to participate and contribute to the national and local Public Works Projects in which all aspects of transport, health, housing, communication, energy and all other aspects of service delivery will be upgraded and made available to all;

Everyone who contributes will be paid equally and only required to contribute on average five hours per day, as part of the preparation for the transition to full Contributionism;

All who contribute shall receive free food, water, housing and electricity as part of their reward;

Every other person in every trade will be given all the tools, materials and support necessary to perform their task to the best of their ability and highest standard of their craft;

By the time we have transformed our society to full UBUNTU Contributionism, there will be no jobs, but only Labour of Love by everyone; contributing 3 hours per day of their own LOL to the community;

Furthermore, each member of the community will be required to contribute 3 hours per week towards community projects, irrespective of what other activity they are part of, or what they contribute to their community;

Each community will be unified and united in its effort to make life as easy and pleasant for everyone to enjoy life and live it to the fullest potential;

The Doors of Learning and Culture Shall be Opened!

Education and learning is the most exciting part of growing up and a fundamental part of creating a well balanced society

The aim of education shall be to teach the youth to love their people and their culture, to honour human brotherhood, liberty and peace; and to live in harmony with mother Earth;

All education on all levels will be free and children and students will choose whatever they want to learn about; daily, weekly, monthly and annually.

Adult illiteracy shall be ended by a mass community learning plan;

The current education system is completely out of line with people's needs; the entire education structure and system will be converted and all classroom based teaching will be abolished;

The concepts of 'play' and 'interactive games' as part of early learning will be introduced whereby the foundation of literacy will be established rapidly and with ease;

Classroom teaching will be replaced by an exciting and vibrant sequence of internships, where children can follow their passion and learn true skills for life, in many different areas, from masters in their fields, so that by the time they are 16 years old, their knowledge will be wide and they will have a very clear idea of what they want to do as part of their contribution to society;

Teachers will be appointed by the community and will be experts in their field; they will teach groups of children as part of their daily process in an internship capacity; the internships will grow longer in time, as the children get older and choose more specific areas of learning;

All children will first be taught the basic principles of life and survival, soil, water, Earth, plants, animals, planting and harvesting crops and farming in all aspects, to build a strong bond between all the people, and a love and respect for mother Earth; after this they can follow any path of learning they choose;

Anyone at any stage of their life can decide to change their careers and enrol in a program to learn new skills;

The discovery and development of talent from all ages, for the enhancement of our cultural life, will be promoted on all levels;

All the cultural treasures of mankind shall be open to all, by free exchange of books, ideas and regular contact with all communities and other lands;

There Shall be Houses, Security and Comfort!

All people shall have the right to live where they choose and become an integral part of the community of their choice;

Slums shall be demolished, and new suburbs built, where all people have transport, roads, lighting, playing fields, crèches and social centres, and more;

Every community will collectively plan and reconstruct their town and settlements based on the will and the needs of the people in that community;

The planning and construction will be done by trained members of the community, or outsiders who have been asked by the leaders of the community to assist in the process;

Eco-friendly designs and durable structures will replace old structures supplied by previous regimes that had no respect for the people and their communities;

All materials for all areas of building and construction will be provided to the builders by the specific industries in the closest proximity to the community; these will be mines, quarries, forestry, and any other industry which can play the role as a supplier of materials to the community;

All effort will be made and all advanced levels of technology will be used to uplift the community in areas of telecommunication and IT;

New alternative and free energy will be provided as soon as possible; water distribution will be streamlined;

All services will be free, providing free energy, free water, free housing and eventually – free food to the people in the community who contribute their services;

Parks, recreational areas, sporting and cultural facilities, will be designed and constructed according to the needs of each community and the use of all these facilities will be free to all in the community;

There shall be no rent or other charges of any kind inflicted on the people;

Hospitals and care centres for the aged will be constructed with the latest technology available in each community;

Free medical care and hospitalisation shall be provided for all, with special care for mothers and young children;

The aged, the orphans, the disabled and the sick shall be cared for by the community;

There will be no need for health or accident insurance of any kind – all medical care will be free to all;

Animal hospitals and rehabilitation centres will be constructed to the best of the ability of each community; the services will be free to all the people;

New alternative medication and treatments will be explored and applied where possible, replacing poisonous treatments by pharmaceutical companies;

Alternative healers will be given all the support they need to keep discovering natural cures for all disease;

Continued research into natural treatments and cures will be actively promoted by the central governing structures and each community, and all necessary tools and support will be provided for such research;

Fenced locations and ghettoes shall be abolished, and laws which break up families shall be repealed by the vision of the community.

Community police and security forums will establish the necessary security structures as determined by each community and its leaders;

They will have the necessary powers granted to them by the laws of each community;

All the necessary tools to implement security measures will be provided to the members of the security forums by the community;

All members of the community will participate in the security forum for a minimum number of hours as stipulated by the laws of each community;

Since money is the key driving force behind most crimes, the UBUNTU communities will be mostly crime-free and therefore imprisonment and detention will be minimal;

There Shall be FREE Transport for All

All rail and road and air transport will be free and without toll charges of any kind;

The roads and highways will be upgraded to the best possible quality;

All rail roads and railway stations will be refurbished and upgraded and new railroads will be constructed so that they link every town and community across the land, so that everyone may travel by train to every town or community they desire;

Scientists will be supported on all levels to develop new alternative GREEN and FREE-ENERGY transport alternatives;

Such FREE-ENERGY solutions have been covered up in the past by the oil and energy companies who want to keep enslaving their people – this will not be tolerated and all new discoveries will be promoted and exposed to the people everywhere;

There Shall be Peace and Friendship and Free Media!

South Africa shall be a fully independent state that respects the rights and sovereignty of all nations;

South Africa shall strive to maintain world peace and the settlement of all international disputes by negotiation - not war or conflict;

Peace and friendship amongst all our people shall be secured by upholding the equal rights, opportunities and status of all, without separation or segregation or any hierarchical structures that cause such segregation of people;

News and information will be distributed through all the normal channels freely, and anyone will have the right to contribute or distribute news and information, or start their own medium for such distribution of information;

Transmission channels for radio, television, internet and any other medium, will not be reserved for the use by an exclusive elite;

Let all people who love their people and their country now say, as we say here:

THESE FREEDOMS WE WILL STRIVE FOR, SIDE BY SIDE, THROUGHOUT OUR LIVES, UNTIL WE HAVE WON OUR LIBERTY AND RECLAIMED OUR COUNTRY AND OUR LAND FROM THE GOVERNMENT AND MULTINATIONAL CORPORATIONS WHO HAVE UNLAWFULLY STOLEN OUR LAND FROM US AND CLAIMED IT AS THEIR OWN.

UBUNTU

Under Ubuntu we can create for ourselves a new Earth.
  Where all beings are honoured for their individual worth.
Become once again a planet of equal sharing.
  With abundance for all and compassionate caring.
United we will evolve into a species at peace.
  Set free from suffering, triggering enslavement release.
No longer controlled by the vice-grip of banks.
  Without money there will be no more missiles, guns and tanks.
Treating each other with pure love and respect
  will have the enlightening, transforming effect.
Unity between nations - all races and tribes,
  will ensure that our beautiful blue planet survives.

Vanessa Bristow-Rose

Thanks to Vanessa for providing me with the perfect ending to this book.

Join the global UBUNTU movement
Become a seed of consciousness
www.ubuntuplanet.org